AS MEDIA STUDIES:
The Essential Introduction for AQA

Praise for the previous edition:

'Very useable, helpful, supportive . . . this is an excellent introduction', Pauline Turner, Head of Media and Performing Arts, Portsmouth College

'An ideal coursebook for students and an invaluable planning tool for teachers', Les Grafton, A level teacher, AQA Subject Advisory Committee

'Truly excellent! A veritable one-stop shop for those studying A Level Media Studies', Jo Wilcock, Senior Examiner AQA VCE Media and Communications

AS Media Studies: The Essential Introduction for AQA is fully revised for the 2008 specification with full colour throughout, over 100 images, new case studies and examples. The authors introduce students step-by-step to the skills of reading media texts, and address key concepts such as genre, representation, media institutions and media audiences as well as taking students through the tasks expected of them to pass the AQA AS Media Studies exam. The book is supplemented with a companion website at www.asmediastudies.co.uk featuring additional activities and resources, further new case studies such as music and sport, clear instructions on producing different media, quizzes and tests.

Areas covered include:

- an introduction to studying the media
- the key concepts across print, broadcast and e-media
- media institutions
- audiences and the media
- case studies such as *Heroes*, *Nuts*, and the *Daily Mail*
- guided textual analysis of real media on the website and within the book
- research and how to do it
- a production guide and how to respond to a brief

AS Media Studies: The Essential Introduction for AQA clearly guides students through the course and gives them the tips they need to become proficient media producers as well as media analysts.

Philip Rayner is a Senior Lecturer in Media Culture and Communications at the University of Gloucestershire.

Peter Wall is Chair of Examiners for GCE Media Studies, GCE Communication Studies, GCSE Media Studies, Applied GCSE Media and the Creative and Media Diploma.

The *Essentials* Series

This series of textbooks, resource books and revision guides covers everything you could need to know about taking exams in Media, Communication or Film Studies. Working together the series offers everything you need to move from AS level through to an undergraduate degree. Written by experts in their subjects, the series is clearly presented to aid understanding with the textbooks updated regularly to keep examples current.

Series Editor: Peter Wall

AS Communication and Culture: The Essential Introduction, Third Edition
Peter Bennett and Jerry Slater

Communication Studies: The Essential Resource
Andrew Beck, Peter Bennett and Peter Wall

AS Film Studies: The Essential Introduction, Second Edition
Sarah Casey Benyahia, Freddie Gaffney and John White

A2 Film Studies: The Essential Introduction, Second Edition
Sarah Casey Benyahia, Freddie Gaffney and John White

Film Studies: The Essential Resource
Peter Bennett, Andrew Hickman and Peter Wall

AS Media Studies: The Essential Introduction for AQA, Third Edition
Philip Rayner and Peter Wall

A2 Media Studies: The Essential Introduction for AQA, Second Edition
Peter Bennett, Jerry Slater and Peter Wall

AS Media Studies: The Essential Revision Guide for AQA
Jo Barker and Peter Wall

A2 Media Studies: The Essential Revision Guide for AQA
Jo Barker and Peter Wall

Media Studies: The Essential Resource
Philip Rayner, Peter Wall and Stephen Kruger

AS MEDIA STUDIES:
The Essential Introduction for AQA

Third edition

Philip Rayner and Peter Wall

Routledge
Taylor & Francis Group

LONDON AND NEW YORK

First published 2001 as *Media Studies: The Essential Introduction*
Reprinted 2002 (twice), 2003

Second edition published 2004 as *AS Media Studies: The Essential Introduction*
Reprinted 2005, 2006

This edition published 2008
by Routledge
2 Park Square, Milton Park, Abingdon, Oxon, OX14 4RN

Simultaneously published in the USA and Canada
by Routledge
270 Madison Ave, New York, NY 10016

Routledge is an imprint of the Taylor & Francis Group, an informa business

Typeset in Folio and Bauhaus by
Keystroke, 28 High Street, Tettenhall, Wolverhampton

Printed and bound in Great Britain by
Bell & Bain Ltd, Glasgow

British Library Cataloguing in Publication Data
A catalogue record for this book is available from the British Library

Library of Congress Cataloging-in-Publication Data
    Rayner, Philip, 1947–
    AS media studies : the essential introduction for AQA/
    Philip Rayner & Peter Wall. – 3rd ed.
        p. cm. – (The Essentials Series)
    Includes bibliographical references and index.
    1. Mass media. I. Wall, Peter. II. Title.
    P90 .M3723 2008
    302.23–dc22   2007048270

ISBN 10: 0–415–44823–9
ISBN 13: 978–0–415–44823–9

CONTENTS

PART 2: INVESTIGATING MEDIA   191

FIGURES

HOW TO USE THIS BOOK

One of the important things you will learn from reading this book is the speed with which technology is changing the way in which we, the audience, consume the media. You may perhaps find it somewhat ironic that we have chosen to communicate with you by means of the somewhat outmoded vehicle of a textbook. Certainly a great deal of what appears in this book might be better and more conveniently presented to you as a website. However, despite the advantages of a web-based approach, the web still has a number of limitations that prevent its being the most effective means of communicating with an AS Level audience. Chief among these is accessibility. Your textbook will no doubt be your constant companion over the next academic year. It should not only inform and entertain you, but also be a source of ideas and inspiration that will make your AS course an enlightened voyage of discovery and provide you with a strong foundation for working at A2. With luck it may even inspire you to become that most precious of media students – an independent enquirer after truth. Certainly we hope that the book will help give you the confidence to be critically autonomous in your engagement with media products and the issues and debates that surround them. We also hope that it will help equip you to deal with the complexity of life in a media-saturated world, where, as we suggest later in the book, our very identities are in part constructed by the media we consume.

Keen as we are as authors to ensure that students get the best value from our book, you will also find an accompanying website at www.asmediastudies.co.uk The purpose of the website is to do some of the work that a book cannot. There is a pressure on media students to use the most up-to-date texts they can find to exemplify the issues and debates that they will write about as part of their course. In consequence, this book is complemented by a website on which you will find some interesting and up-to-date examples that could not have been included in the book itself. In addition, the website will contain links to all the websites mentioned in the book. As some of these are very long and difficult to type accurately, please do visit the companion website to access these pages easily. The website will offer you detailed guidance on production work which has become an increasingly important element of your AS course, representing as it does 50 per cent of the available marks for the qualification.

This book has been written primarily for students who are studying the AQA GCE AS Media Studies course. It covers both components of the AS: Unit 1 and Unit 2. There is a considerable overlap between these units, and many of the concepts and ideas that we explore in the book will apply to both units. Although we have organised the book into self-contained chapters, you may still have to do some shuffling backwards and forwards to find material you want. For example, when you are writing your evaluation for the practical production, a lot of the material in the first part, Key Concepts, will be directly relevant to this. Looking at your own productions in relation to the Key Concepts is a very good starting point in any evaluation and this section should offer some useful guidelines. If you are not accustomed to using textbooks, then two useful tools – the contents page and the index – will help you find what you are looking for. Notice too that at the beginning of each chapter we indicate exactly what the chapter covers in a summary box.

You will notice that we have included illustrations in each chapter. These are not intended simply as decoration but are an essential part of the book. We hope you will use them to stimulate ideas and perhaps also look for your own contemporary images or clips that will serve to illustrate some of the concepts, ideas and debates with which you are engaged. Similarly, we have suggested within each chapter a number of activities that you might like to try. These activities are designed with a view to broadening and deepening your understanding. They should also serve as a useful starting point for your own independent research, which, as we have said, is essential to your success in AS Media Studies. There are also more substantial activities and worksheets available on the website.

You will also find some suggestions for further reading at the end of chapters. These suggestions have been made not only because they are relevant but also because you should find them both accessible and stimulating. While this book contains much of what you need to do well in your AS Level work, we would also encourage you to read as widely as possible around the study topics, to add both breadth and depth to your understanding.

You will also notice that there are a number of case studies in the book. These are complemented by additional studies that you will find on the website. These studies show you how to explore some of the study areas that are suggested to you by the AQA specification. Their purpose is to guide and help lead you into the topic. They are starting point only; they are not intended as a shortcut to save you doing any work. A good student will use the case studies to stimulate ideas and then go off and do their own independent research to develop some of the issues raised and to bring their own insight into the study of the topic. Following some of the suggested links should provide the type of stimulus that will enable you to explore the topic for yourself.

There is a significant emphasis in the AQA specification on adopting a cross-media approach to your study. This is an acknowledgement of the way in which contemporary media output often operates across a range of different platforms. An understanding of film, for example, will require your engagement not only with the cinematic experience of film or its DVD or television equivalent, but also the way in which the film is promoted or engaged with critically across such platforms as the web, print media and the radio. We have tried to reflect this need for a cross-media approach in the book by signalling to you ways in which you can pursue a study across these different platforms largely through web links that should point you in this direction.

Bear in mind too, that a lot of the theory that you will learn in this book originated long before newer digital and online media platforms were around. In consequence, one of the challenges facing established theories is how relevant they still are as critical tools for making sense of some of the issues and debates that surround these newer media forms. This is a new and exciting area of Media Studies and it presents you with some interesting challenges. For example, you might like to consider how effective genre theory is in your exploration of different categories of website.

One way to get the best out of the book is to use it alongside your computer so that you can get direct access to the web. It should provide an interesting experience of multi-tasking, although we have tried to facilitate this approach by offering all the web links in the book through the website. It is worth offering a word of caution at this point. It is easy to get deeply absorbed in your study. Try to ensure that you keep a record of the places you have visited so that you can both find them again and, where appropriate, offer details of the reference that you have used. Keeping organised and detailed notes that make sense when you try to retrieve them is the key to being a successful media student, so make sure you keep records and that you spend time making sure they are organised. This is sometimes less than easy when you are trying to do two things, i.e. use a book and access the web at the same time.

The section on practical production work (Chapter 13), for example, has been specifically designed to offer you some broad principles for approaching this important area of work in the book and presenting you with more detailed information specific to the media you are using through the website. In this way we hope to ensure that you get the maximum support in your production work by combining your use of the book and the website.

One of the other advantages that we get from the website is the chance to hear your feedback. We have made a great deal in the book of the way in which the mass media have become an interactive two-way process. Please let us have your feedback on what we have produced. Constructive criticism of how we might improve the book and the website is especially welcome.

Finally, we would both like to take this opportunity to thank those people who knowingly or unknowingly have contributed to this book. This includes colleagues and students past and present as well as the many thousands of exam candidates whose work we have assessed over the years. Most especially our thanks are due to Aileen Storry, our long-suffering editor at Routledge, who has brought a unique and infectious enthusiasm to the production of both the book and the website.

Our thanks also to her colleague, Anna Hines, and our copy editor, Sandra Jones, for their diligence and patience in the production and copy-editing process.

INTRODUCTION

Faster! Faster! More! More!

Although it is rather a cliché to say that the media are an important part of our lives, since the events of 11 September 2001 in New York and 7 July 2005 in London, it has become particularly apparent that media images often have a power and significance that can resonate around the world in a matter of seconds. This power and significance have been given an impetus by the development of digital media, for example, the growth of the internet, social networking sites like Facebook, MySpace and YouTube, and the growth of relatively cheap and easy-to-use portable consumer goods like mobile phones with cameras, palmtop computers, webcams etc.

At the same time, the distinction between producers and consumers of the media has become blurred and the way in which we consume media texts more complex.

The combination of the world wide web and the new electronic goods means that many people now have the opportunity to author original pieces of work and almost instantly distribute them to a worldwide audience. It also means that our knowledge of events such as the London bombings of 7 July 2005 are no longer dependent upon switching on the television or radio at 6.00 p.m. to see a news report or waiting for the next day's newspapers to read about what has happened the day before; rather we can go to websites or 24-hour rolling news television stations and see images (such as Figure i) direct from where the event is taking place and through mobile phones or web-based blogs can hear first-hand accounts of what has happened.

Figure i 7 July 2005

Figure i is an example of what is called 'user-generated content' or 'citizen media', where people recount their versions of events through images and video taken on mobile phones which are then used in mainstream media output, such as news broadcasts and/or posted on websites that are accessed throughout the world.

An ICM poll conducted for the *Guardian* newspaper in October 2005 (see http://www.guardian.co.uk/frontpage/story/0,,1587081,00html) showed that in the UK 14–21 year old internet users now spend an average of eight hours per week online and that a third of all young people online have launched their own blog or website. This is almost certainly more than the amount of time they spend in front of a television set. It is also important to remember that this rise of online media is not just limited to young people. In March 2006 Google reported that in the UK an 'average' adult spends more time online than watching television (see http://business.guardian.co.uk/story/0,,1726126,00.html).

ACTIVITY

You may wish to test these findings using your own research. Go to www.surveymonkey.com and design and undertake your own survey of people's television viewing and time spent online.

- Which is the greater?
- Why do you think this is?
- Do your own findings agree with those from Google?
- How do you account for any discrepancy?

Figure i also demonstrates how the internet and the world wide web are helping to create virtual communities. For example, this photograph has appeared on various websites and is one of over a thousand digital images that are grouped together at Flickr (http://flickr.com/groups/bomb/pool) as the London Bomb Blasts Community in remembrance of the events in London on 7 July 2005.

ACTIVITY

Figure i is also posted on the MoblogUK website (http://moblog.co.uk) which describes itself as a 'mobile weblog. A moblog. A blog for people with camera phones. A photoblog'. If you click on individual photographs you can also follow strings where people from around the world have commented on the images and the events they depict.

Consider starting your own blog or contributing to someone else's (see http://www.blogspot.com). Record the number of responses you receive to your blog. Which countries do the responses come from? What other information is available regarding the people who reply to your blog?

As media images proliferate and our ability to become producers as well as consumers of media products increases, it has become clear that we live in an increasingly 'mediated' society (see Chapter 4 on representation) in which many of our ideas about the world, our knowledge of what is happening and, perhaps most importantly, our values, come from beyond our individual daily or immediate experience. Our ideas of the world are derived largely from the modern media, which produce and 'package' versions of events and issues in their output, and which we both contribute to and consume as part of our daily lives and situations.

Figure ii

This means that the media exert a very strong influence on us both as individuals and as a society.

Figure ii is one of the most powerful images of the Twin Towers in New York burning on 11 September 2001 and has become a universally recognised symbol of the events of that day. Through the predominance of digital technology, this and other images were quickly circulated around the world, increasing the impact of those events and being used as part of a propaganda campaign to justify the 'war on terror' and the wars in Afghanistan and Iraq.

ACTIVITY

Try to remember how you received the news of the events of 11 September 2001. Compare your recollections with your peers. Did your family watch the events as they happened on television, live from New York? Think about how quickly those images were circulated around the world.

Increasingly, the term Web 2.0 is being used to describe the way in which the world wide web is developing. It refers to the idea of a second generation of web-based communities such as social networking sites, wikis, weblogs, podcasts and RSS feeds. (An RSS 'feed' allows users to get updated information from a website delivered directly to their desktop, so they don't have to continually check a website to look for updated information.) These facilitate collaboration and sharing between users and encourage peer-to-peer (P2P) activity. The growth of cheap and powerful personal computers, supported by cheap and powerful software, and the growth of social networking sites has meant that the web is no longer a static source of information or data. Rather the growth is in the *sharing* that now takes places through the web, what has been called many-to-many publishing, whether it is photographs, music, experiences, recommendations for travel etc. (see, for example, http://en.wikipedia.org/wiki/Web_2.0).

What do we mean by 'the media'?

Although the speed of change in media technology and use makes it increasingly problematic to define what we mean by 'the media', we have tried to identify certain key characteristics that seem to apply to all media products at any time in history. These basic characteristics can be summed up in the following general statements:

- The media reach a large number of people.
- The media, although centrally produced, are usually privately consumed.
- Media products are 'shared'.
- The media are controlled or 'regulated'.
- The media rely on sophisticated technology.
- The media are 'modern'.
- The media are expensive to produce.

The media reach a large number of people

What counts as a 'large' number of people will vary depending upon the historical period. *The Times* used to sell about 7,000 copies a day in the early nineteenth century. This was a high circulation when we consider that there were no other major forms of media or mass communication. In July 1985 Live Aid was seen by 1.5 billion viewers in over 160 countries. Every day the internet has a potential 'audience' of over one billion people across the world.

Most media products today are constructed to be consumed by large numbers of people although many of these audiences will 'consume' the media in many different ways. Some 'texts' will be aimed at a mass market, for example, tabloid newspapers, television soaps and major Hollywood films. Increasingly, however, audiences are becoming 'fragmented', divided up into various different groups, and media products may be aimed at small groups of people who share a common interest and perhaps read specialist magazines or access minority websites; for example, a local parish council website such as http://www.boxparish.org.uk which in 2006 had 6,530 visitors, or magazines such as *Catworld* (http://www. catworld.co.uk/ 'Where cat lovers come together') or *N16*, specifically aimed at residents of Stoke Newington, distributed in print and via the website (www. n16mag.com).

Website Activity I.1: Worksheet to determine your media consumption.

Website Activity I.2: Worksheet to determine the media consumption patterns of others.

In Chapter 7 on media audiences, we look in more detail at how the concept of the audience is changing.

The media, although centrally produced, are usually privately consumed

This may appear to be a paradox, but one of the key characteristics of the media today is that, despite large audiences, consumption is still very much a personal experience. Many millions of people will have seen a film like *Casino Royale*, yet each person's experience of the film is probably a personal and intimate one – even if we are part of an audience of 300 people all sitting together in the dark in the cinema or just with a group of friends watching a DVD.

Although we still talk of 'family viewing', increasingly we are consuming media products individually or in small groups, carrying out other tasks, either at home or perhaps in the privacy of our car – in our own 'personal space'. Nine million people may watch a particular episode of *EastEnders*, but the experience will largely be individual and private. We usually watch television in the privacy of our own home with perhaps one or two other people, or we may watch it alone in our bedroom whilst someone elsewhere in the house is also alone, watching the same programme at the same time. We may be watching a repeat of a particular episode of *EastEnders* available on a digital channel, alone and separated from everyone else who has also watched this particular episode when it was first broadcast.

We increasingly consume the media on our own; for example, we may use a computer at work, in college or at home to watch a television programme, play a CD or listen to a radio station and we may use an MP3 player almost anywhere to listen to music or the radio. The *Sun* newspaper may be read by over 10 million people each day, but for each person it is a private act, often carried out in a private and personal space (even in the lavatory!). Some commentators suggest that

Figure iii Different ways of watching – sometimes alone, even if in a public place

it is this sense of the media coming into our private worlds, our homes, and 'saturating' our daily lives, that makes them so important.

Media saturation is a term used to describe the way in which the media today 'saturate' all aspects of our lives and the extent to which our experience of the world is dominated by the media.

ACTIVITY

Take some time to look around when you are next in a public space, a town centre or on public transport and try to measure the amount of private and individualised media consumption that is taking place. How many people are texting or talking on mobile phones, listening to iPods or MP3 players, working on palm or laptop computers or looking at newspapers or reading books?

Yet we need to remember that most media products are constructed like a production line in a factory, whether it is the newspaper, the television show or the Hollywood film. The distribution is also very centralised, whether it is the transmission of a television news bulletin across the whole country at one particular point in time, the fleet of lorries that deliver the newspapers to the newsagents, or the distribution of a film over a period of time to be shown at cinemas, on subscription television and eventually on DVD.

Media products are 'shared'

The media produce texts that are both popular – hence the high audience figures – and also 'shared' in the sense that they become part of our common culture. Today we are all familiar with expressions such as 'You're fired!' or 'Phone a friend'. Even those who do not regularly watch or have never seen the television shows *The Apprentice* or *Who Wants to Be a Millionaire?* will know the phrases, their

Figure iv The slogan from this T-shirt is instantly recognisable to many readers

origins and what they signify. These phrases have become part of our daily vocabulary in the way that 'Good morning, have you used Pears Soap?' was in the late nineteenth century. Although the level of our particular knowledge may vary, almost everyone is familiar with the stories of the *EastEnders* characters Phil Mitchell or Dot Cotton. Media images become a common 'language' – across the world millions of people know about Luke Skywalker or Harry Potter or what MTV stands for. Although many commentators suggest that this 'colonisation' of the world's media by predominantly American companies and artefacts is damaging, it is again a sign of the media's power and the universality of its images.

Today we are all very 'media literate' and share a sophisticated understanding of the 'language' of media images that are constantly being shown, repeated and referred to (see the subsection on semiotics, p. 33).

The media are controlled or 'regulated'

Perhaps because of the large audiences they attract, and the power, reach and popularity of the media, another key characteristic of the media is the way in which they are seen to be in need of control or regulation. Even in cases of media forms like the internet, where there is some difficulty in deciding how to control and regulate it, there is nevertheless the desire to make rules about who has access and what is available. It is not uncommon to hear of workers being sacked because they have been writing 'inappropriate' or 'libellous' blogs (see, for example, http://news.bbc.co.uk/1/hi/world/europe/5196228.stm). (See also the section on the regulation of the media, p. 171).

Consider, for example, the number of authoritarian countries like China, Burma or Ethiopia in which the media are still largely restricted by the government as a means of 'controlling' the circulation of ideas and criticisms. Often one of the first things that happens in a revolution is that the national media and communications centres are taken over, so that the new leaders can 'control' the messages that are transmitted. In this way they use the media to win the 'hearts and minds' of the people.

In Britain there are continuing debates surrounding the media, for example, about the dangers of the internet or the right of privacy for celebrities and members of the Royal Family such as the Princes Harry and William. In 2007 the British Board of Film Classification banned the Scottish video-game *Manhunt 2* because of 'its unremitting bleakness and callousness of tone in an overall game context which constantly encourages visceral killing with exceptionally little alleviation or distancing' (see http://living.scotsman.com/computergames/Ban-halts-play-as-firm-3298211.jp and figure vi).

Figure v Protesters in Burma

Figure vi *Manhunt 2*

In 2007 the BBC show *Blue Peter* was fined for fabricating competition winners and several television shows were criticised for their use of premium rate telephone calls.

The media rely on sophisticated technology

The media depend on sophisticated technology to produce and transmit the texts they create. Even in today's world, in which media hardware is seemingly becoming smaller and more personalised (for example, MP3 players, mobile phones with digital or video cameras, or wristwatches with television receivers inside them), the media are still very dependent upon a highly sophisticated technology. We may perhaps take this level of technological sophistication for granted. However, it is important to consider the technology required to make the television programmes that may be seen on a wristwatch, or to download music from the internet, or to produce 'blockbuster' films or glossy magazines. When studying the media, we need to consider how this technology has developed, been mass-produced, marketed, bought and used.

In the recent conflicts in Afghanistan and Iraq, the television news reporters' increasing use of video satellite phones has meant that we, the viewers at home, can receive live, up-to-the-minute news reports from remote parts of the world which a few years ago would have taken several days to reach Britain.

Increasingly, media producers are encouraging us, the consumer, to use this new technology ourselves to participate in the creation of media texts, what is called 'user-generated content', through the use of eye witness material such as that in Figure i.

The internet and the world wide web are giving people the opportunity to become directors in their own right as well as the ability to circulate these images around the world and to rapidly share what they say with others.

ACTIVITY

Go to http://www.youtube.com/watch?v=A4uyN5rQbbU. Think about what technology is required for this video clip to be made, posted to YouTube and then accessed by people like yourself. Think also about the clip's content and the reasons for the making of the clip. How many people will have access to this clip? What do you think are the reasons this clip was made and posted onto YouTube?

The media are 'modern'

The media are seen as being 'up to date' or 'modern' – or even 'postmodern' (see p. 21). Although we can trace newspapers back to the early 1700s when the *Daily Courant* (the first daily newspaper) was first printed, the media (as we understand the term today) are a very modern phenomenon. Increasingly, it is part of any definition of the media that they respond to, and quickly incorporate, the most up-to-date innovations and trends such as the 'convergence' of communications, computing and telephone technologies. This means that we often take for granted the range of media services available to us today, for example, MP3 players, digital phones that can double as still or video cameras with internet access, broadband access that allows us to download films or television programmes 'on demand', over 300 digital television channels (many of them interactive) and a range of digital radio stations.

One characteristic of this modernity is the assumed death of the older, previous technology. For example, when television was introduced, people assumed that the cinema and newspapers would disappear. The death of newspapers has also been predicted as a result of the internet, but what seems to be happening is that newspapers are evolving, offering more lifestyle supplements and becoming less reliant on covering the latest hard news. *The Encyclopaedia Britannica* is an interesting example of the way in which media products adapt. Some years ago people bought the *Encyclopaedia Britannica* as a series of 32 books, then with the growth of CD-ROMs the *Encyclopaedia Britannica* became available, at a cost, as a series of CDs. Today much of the *Encyclopaedia Britannica* is available free from its website and it is possible to subscribe and get daily updates via email, telephone texts or as an RSS 'feed'. We also need to remember that one of the most popularity media artefacts in 2007 was the book *Harry Potter and the Deathly Hallows*.

ACTIVITY

Take some time to go around your home noting all the media hardware that there is. For example:

- How many television sets are there?
- How many CD and DVD players and recorders?
- How many radio receivers (including MP3 players, computers, car radios, etc.)?
- How many mobile phones and telephone points with broadband access?

In Britain, according to Audpro Radio Marketing (http://www.audpro-radio.com/index.php), there are six distribution systems (radio sets) in every household. Does your research support this claim?

Think about your home's 'old' technology, for example, do you still use a video recorder, a cassette player or a CRT-television? How recently or frequently is your home's media hardware changed/updated? What does this tell you about the way the media is changing and the role that it plays in our everyday lives? You could then work out how many telephones, television sets, computers and other media equipment there are per person in your household. Compare your results with those of your peers.

Website Activity I.3: Charting changes in consuming popular music.

The media are expensive to produce

The media, partly because of the technology required to produce and distribute texts, are expensive and so tend to be owned either by large commercial companies, often multinationals (and, increasingly, American ones), or by state-owned or government organisations. This means that the media tend to be highly centralised and a few companies have a lot of power and control in particular industries. (See Chapter 8 on media institutions.) It is interesting to watch how internet and dot.com companies, such as MySpace (bought by News Corporation), Facebook (bought into by Microsoft) and Last.fm (bought by CBS) are being increasingly taken over by established companies that have already been financially successful in other areas of the media. Some websites are subverted, for example, by PR companies using sites like Facebook as a way of promoting their products or clients. You might look up big stars and see how many have their own pages (for example, http://www.neonbubble.com/videos/stephen-fry-facebook-message-generator). Do you think they keep them updated themselves?

ACTIVITY

These 'key characteristics' are our own suggestions, and you may disagree with them. You can 'measure' different types of media, for example, the media that you use, against this list of key characteristics to test how accurate it is. Can you suggest any other key characteristics that could be applied to all media?

Why are the media important?

The way in which the media are changing also presents difficulties when trying to study, analyse and understand the role and influence the media have in society in general and in our lives in particular. Although the question of why the media are important is a complicated one, below we suggest some possible answers:

- The media tell us what is going on in the world.
- The media are a central part of our lives.
- The media are influential.
- Domestic media hardware has become an intrinsic part of our homes and our lives.
- The media are very profitable.

The media tell us what is going on in the world

The media are important because they tell us what is going on both in the world at large (for example, natural disasters, wars) and at home (for example, political and sporting events, star 'gossip'). Try to imagine what life would have been like before broadcasting. Think about what we would know (or not know) of the world without television, radio, newspapers or the internet.

The media are a central part of our lives

We turn to the media for entertainment, to relax after a hard day's work. We use the media for information, whether it is to find out the latest cricket results, the weather tomorrow, or what is happening in the rest of the world. Perhaps less willingly, we accept the media as a source of persuasion, most noticeably through advertising but also through campaigns like the 'drink/drive' ones at Christmas or political campaigns during an election.

The media are influential

Because the media are so much a central part of our daily lives, they obviously wield influence; however, it is not always clear what that influence is and whether it is good or bad (it is most probably a mixture of both). Often the media are blamed for many of the problems in today's society: violent films encouraging crime (see section on the 'effects' debate, p. 135), sexual advice in teen magazines encouraging promiscuity (see p. 234), the internet being used by paedophiles to 'groom' victims, pin-ups in 'lads' magazines encouraging sexist attitudes, or tabloid newspapers running 'name and shame' campaigns.

We need to recognise that, despite the prevalence of the media in our lives, there are other influences that are as strong or even stronger. Family, education, religion, peer groups and ethnicity all help to shape our ideas, values, beliefs and behaviour, and it is very difficult to isolate one factor and say that the media caused that to happen.

ACTIVITY

Draw up a list of your own examples to show the influence of the media. Separate your list into negative and positive influences; positive influences could include encouraging healthier lifestyles, anti-drink/drive campaigns, charity promotions, supporting national sporting events. Compare your lists with a colleague's.

Figure vii

Domestic media hardware has become an intrinsic part of our homes and our lives

One of the ways to understand the importance of the media in our everyday world is to think about the hardware we have in our homes for receiving the media's products. In Britain 99 per cent of all homes have at least one television set – although many homes nowadays have several, perhaps one in each bedroom as well as a communal one. Over 32 million people in the UK, or over 60 per cent of the population, is described as being 'online', having access to the internet through work, home or study (for comparative figures for other countries go to http://www.internetworldstats.com/stats4.htm). In 2007, 13.9 million households in the UK (57 per cent) could access the internet from home, 65 per cent of households had a PC and 79 per cent had a mobile phone (see http://www.statistics.gov.uk). For many people today it is difficult to imagine how they kept in touch with each other before the arrival of email or telephone texting.

Website Activity I.4: Testing BARB's lifestyle survey.

ACTIVITY

Watch the advert for Vodafone at http://www.utalkmarketing.com/Article.aspx?id=2007. To what extent do you think the advert succeeds in being 'more emotionally engaged with the customer'? What are the assumptions and implications of the tag line 'Make the most of now'? Why would we want mobile access to the internet? Who would most benefit from this?

Figure viii

The media are very profitable

Companies and organisations such as News International, Time-Warner/AOL and Disney exist to make a profit. They do not make films or produce newspapers because they are nice people who want to help us be entertained and/or better informed; they make films like the Harry Potter films or print newspapers like the *News of the World* because they know that they will make large amounts of money. (See, for example, Chapter 11 on lifestyle magazines and television.) However, it is also important to realise that media organisations can often make mistakes and actually lose large amounts of money, for example, the merger between radio stations GWR (owners of Xfm and Classic FM as well as many local and regional stations) and Capital in London to form the company GCap has resulted in Capital Radio losing its position as London's number one station, a sharp reduction in advertising revenue and decline in its share price.

ACTIVITY

Look through the financial pages of newspapers to see what information is available about media companies. Access the websites of media companies to try to find out about their financial details or the amount of profit (or loss) that they make.

Postmodernism

This is a term that is used a lot, although there is still some debate and uncertainty about what exactly 'postmodern' means, the value of the term and the extent to which we are living in a postmodern society (see, for instance, the essay 'Postmodernism and popular culture' in Strinati, 2004).

According to most art historians, 'modernism' was a movement that started in the late nineteenth century and ended around the 1960s. So 'postmodernism' is a term that is used to characterise the type of society and culture that has developed in Western societies since the 1970s and into the beginning of the twenty-first century.

The idea of postmodernism is partly based on a particular view of contemporary life – a high-tech, post-industrial society dominated by the 'flow' of media images and information around the world. It is claimed that we are increasingly living in a 'world time' in which news, financial trading or sporting events are all transmitted 'live' around the world. It is possible to be at home in Birmingham on a Sunday morning and watch 'live' a Formula 1 car race as it takes place in Malaysia. We can trade money and shares around the world 24 hours a day. Enormous amounts of information and imagery can be distributed around the globe almost instantaneously and accessed by large numbers of people in a way that would not have been possible 20 years ago. More and more we 'borrow' from other cultures for our music, furnishings, food, clothes and so on. What Marshall McLuhan (1964) called the 'global village' is increasingly becoming a reality.

Postmodernism is said to reflect modern society's insecurities and uncertainties about identity, history, progress and truth, and the break-up of those traditional agencies, such as religion, the family or, perhaps to a lesser extent, class, which help identify and shape who we are and our place in the world. Artists like Madonna, Michael Jackson and David Bowie are all cited as examples of postmodernism in the ways in which they have created or re-created different identities for themselves.

Figure ix is an example of how identity can become confused and manipulated. Borat Sagdiyev (http://www.boratonline.co.uk/) is a character created by Sacha Baron Cohen, also creator of the Ali G and Bruno characters. These fictional characters have been confused by people as real people (see http://www.youtube.com/watch?v=g0b_ITEgICw) and this confusion has been used by Sacha Baron Cohen as a source of both comedy and humiliation.

According to some theorists, we are made up of several shifting and fragmented identities and increasingly our identity is now defined by our lifestyle and what we consume rather than by what we produce or by our background. The growth of social networking websites like Facebook, Bebo and MySpace and virtual worlds like Second Life are increasingly enabling us to create identities that may or may not be real, and to share them with other, real or not, identities across the world. These websites give us an opportunity to experiment with different identities, to change our physical appearance (even our gender), reveal secrets or make up

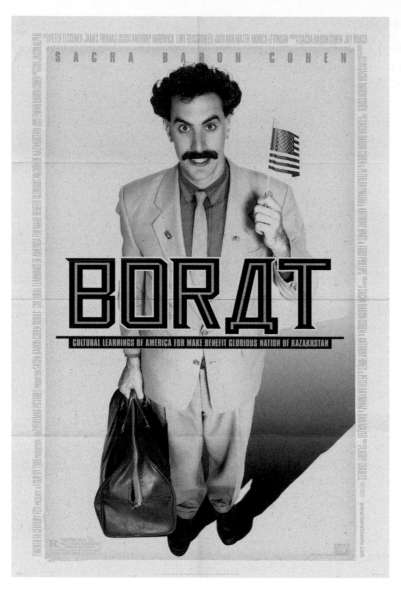

Figure ix *Borat: Cultural Learnings of America for Make Benefit Glorious Nation of Kazakhstan* (2006)

stories about ourselves and discuss problems that we may have not felt able to discuss face-to-face with friends and family.

Jean-François Lyotard in *The Postmodern Condition* (1979) suggests that what he called 'meta-narratives' or grand theories, such as religion, Marxism, capitalism or science, no longer have the same importance in our lives. The concept of progress – the certainty that the developments of the arts, technology, medicine and knowledge would be moving inevitably towards a 'greater good' – is now seen

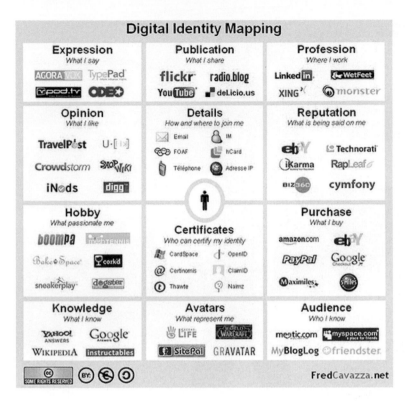

Figure x

to be questionable. Progress is seen by some as a way of controlling people and, using examples like CCTV or the government's reading of private emails, as 'spying' on ordinary citizens.

One of the films often cited as 'postmodern' is Ridley Scott's *Blade Runner* (1982), in which science, technology and progress are all questioned and shown in some way to have 'failed'. The world in *Blade Runner* is polluted by industry and over-crowding; only the rich escape to the 'off-worlds'. One of the key themes of the film is the 'blurring' of the differences between the real and the artificial, between the humans and the replicants. Increasingly, it is no longer possible to be clear about what it means to be 'human'.

Another media text described as postmodern is David Lynch's television pro-gramme *Twin Peaks* (1990). A characteristic of postmodernism is the way in which 'high' art and popular culture are mixed together, and in *Twin Peaks* we can see an example of popular culture (the television 'whodunnit'/soap opera) mixed with 'high art' (the work of film director David Lynch, which includes films such as *Eraserhead* (1977), *The Elephant Man* (1980) and *Blue Velvet* (1986)). *Twin Peaks* also 'blurs' the distinction between various genres of television programme by being part cop-show, part comedy and part Gothic horror, amongst others.

Figure xi *Second Life* avatar

ACTIVITY

It is perhaps a little ironic that all of these examples of 'postmodernism' are now rather dated. Can you think of more recent examples of postmodern products, either films or television programmes? In what ways are your examples 'postmodern'?

Another key idea of postmodernism is that of 'simulacra', a term introduced by Jean Baudrillard to explain the way in which simulations or copies are replacing the 'real' artefacts. According to Baudrillard, simulacra are simulations or copies that are replacing the 'real' artefacts so that increasingly reality becomes redundant and we can no longer distinguish between the real and the representation of the real. Examples might include theme parks, 'fake' Irish or Australian pubs, or American-style coffee-houses where the 'pretend' version seems as real as, if not more real than, the actual thing it is copying. This idea can be extended to include much of television's output, programmes such as *Tribe*, where we, as 'armchair travellers', can visit countries all over the world, see exotic sights and perhaps feel that we have 'experienced' or understood these different places. 'Confessional' shows like *Jeremy Kyle* can also be seen as false copies that 'pretend' to offer solutions to personal problems but are actually only there to entertain the viewer. In the postmodern world, style is 'celebrated' at the expense of substance and content, while the fake and the artificial increasingly replace the real.

Another useful term associated with postmodernism is 'bricolage' (see Chapter 5 on media intertextuality). The term was used to describe the punk movement and the way in which punks took a variety of different objects (such as dustbin liners, safety-pins, Mohican haircuts and bondage trousers) and by combining

Figure xii A 'fake' Japanese pagoda – how do you know if it's real or not?

a sequence of shots in a film or television programme is a syntagm put together to communicate a meaning.

Just as there is a great variety in the forms and style of media texts, so the codes used to construct meanings are varied and frequently depend upon the form of the media text. In most cases the text will use a variety of codes – visual, audio and written – that 'fit' together in a certain way, or syntagm, to create a particular meaning.

Look at the Diesel advertisement (Figure 1.1). We see that this is a text that is print-based but contains visual and written codes. Its exact meaning may be quite difficult to 'fix', except to say that it is an advertisement and is trying to 'sell' a product, a particular brand of clothing. In this advertisement additional meaning is given through the use of colour codes and a few written words at the top and bottom of the advert.

Some adverts do not even seem to be trying to sell a specific product but are, presumably, just trying to make us aware of a particular company or name, for example, the United Colors of Benetton campaign (see p. 175).

Figure 1.1

Most of us living in Western society at the beginning of the twenty-first century are sophisticated media consumers and will be able to 'read' the Diesel advertisement fairly quickly. We would probably normally only glance at it as we skim through a magazine. However, as media students, we now have to distance ourselves from our daily and often unreflective consumption of media texts like this illustration. Our task is to break down or 'deconstruct' the illustration into its component parts and fully to 'reveal' and understand how the advertisers have used the various signs and codes in their attempt to create a particular meaning or set of meanings.

One of the key theoretical tools to assist us in this process of deconstruction is semiology, or, as it is often called, semiotics.

Semiotics

The word 'semiology' is derived from the Greek word *semeion*, which means sign. Semiology is an attempt to create a science of the study of sign systems and their role in the construction and reconstruction of meaning in media texts. Semiology concentrates primarily on the text itself and the signs and codes that are contained within it.

One of the most influential theorists of the way visual images transmit meanings was Roland Barthes (1913–80). Barthes was influenced by the structuralist work of the Swiss linguist Ferdinand de Saussure (1857–1913), who first promoted the idea of semiology in his book *Course in General Linguistics* (1983 [1916]).

Saussure saw language as a cultural creation rather than something innate, and as a social system that was ordered, coherent and governed by sets of rules. The American Charles Peirce (1839–1914) took Saussure's ideas and expanded them to include not just language but other 'social constructs' in society, such as the way society itself is ordered, labelled and governed by sets of rules. Peirce introduced the term 'semiotics'.

Roland Barthes took these ideas still further and in *Mythologies* (1993 [1957]) applied them to areas of daily life and popular culture such as the face of the actress Greta Garbo and soap detergent advertising.

What semiotics allows us to do is to look at some of the underlying structures that determine how media texts are constructed. It allows us to explore sign systems that are used within texts and to discover how these make meanings for the audience. Semiotics is part of a broader area of cultural study called structuralism. One of the functions of structuralism is to reveal some of the underlying structures which underpin cultures, for example, to investigate the common elements that different languages have with one another.

For students of the media, semiotic analysis is a useful tool in the analysis of texts as it helps to reveal the underlying meanings that are 'suspended' within a text. You can then take this analysis further and consider the ideologies, or belief systems, that underpin texts and their construction.

It is important to be aware that most sign systems, like the Diesel advertisement, do not necessarily have one particular 'fixed' meaning. Part of the meaning of the sign is dependent upon the social and cultural background of the 'reader' of the particular sign system.

As part of the process of semiotic analysis, we, the audience, are called 'readers' because this helps to suggest a greater degree of creativity and involvement in the construction of the text's meaning. 'Reading' is something we learn to do and is influenced to a large extent by our social and cultural background. As the reader of a text, we will bring something of our own cultural and personal experiences to a text. For example, a person who has had bad experiences at the hands of the police will read an episode of *The Bill* in a very different way to a person who has had positive experiences in dealing with them.

Signs

The Diesel advertisement is a sign. It consists of a signifier, the printed magazine advert itself, and something that is signified, the 'idea' or 'meaning' behind the set of images used in the advertisement.

Fiske and Hartley in *Reading Television* (1978) describe the sign as being made up of two components: the signifier and the signified

signifier [+] signified [=] sign

The signifier is a physical object, for example, a sound, printed word, advertisement. The signified is a mental concept or meaning conveyed by the signifier.

Peirce differentiated between three different types of signs: symbolic (or arbitrary); iconic; indexical. A symbol is a sign that represents an object or concept solely by the agreement of the people who use it.

Symbolic signs have no obvious connection between the sign and the object. For example, the word CAT has no obvious link with a small furry animal usually domesticated as a pet. It only works because we understand the rules that say the letters C-A-T, when put into a certain order, mean or 'signify' that small furry animal. If it was a different 'we', for example, a group of French speakers, then the 'rules' would be different and we would use the letters C-H-A-T to signify that small furry animal.

These types of signs Peirce also called 'arbitrary' as their 'meaning' is the result of agreement amongst their users. These types of signs do not have any direct or intrinsic connection with what is being 'signified'. This means that some arbitrary signs can have several meanings that are 'contested', or about which people might not agree. The Union Jack has a variety of meanings depending upon who is using it – the British monarchy at a national ceremony, the Unionists in Ulster or a Sex pistols' T-shirt (see http://www.ebtm.com/p-1822-sex-pistols-t-shirt-god-save.aspx).

Figure 1.2

Iconic signs are like the religious paintings, statues and stained-glass windows found in churches. Photographs are a good example of an iconic sign. They have a physical similarity to the objects that they 'signify'. We are familiar with iconic signs in our everyday lives, for example, the use of a wheelchair to signify facilities for disabled people. Wherever we are in the world, we can usually find the men's and women's toilets by looking for the iconic signs on the doors.

Indexical signs are the signs that have some kind of direct connection with what is being 'signified'. Smoke is often used as an indexical sign for fire, and a tear running down someone's cheek can be an indexical sign for sorrow.

So why is it useful to know about these signs in order to study media texts? Let us look at some of the reasons. Media texts are usually complex messages. Most texts are composed using all of the types of sign that we have indicated. Both printed words and a spoken commentary employ arbitrary signs to communicate with an audience. Photographs in magazines or moving images in film or on television are iconic signs, which work because of their similarity to the thing they represent. We may also see or hear indexical signs; someone sweating profusely may be an index of either extreme temperature or high levels of stress. Similarly, tears or the sounds of sobbing provide an index of grief.

An audience consuming the media by watching television, for example, is creating meaning from a complex system of signs that they have become used to 'reading'. By understanding the nature of signs and how they work, we can gain some insight into the process by which media messages are interpreted.

As you may have realised, iconic signs are especially significant in our study of the visual image, in photography, film and television. It is because iconic signs so closely resemble the object they represent that they seem so natural. In the process it is easy to forget that we are looking at a sign and confuse the sign with reality itself. As we will see in Chapter 4 on representation, this has important implications for the way in which we read the representation of reality in the media.

A recent example of the complex way in which signifiers work can be seen by looking at your mobile phone. Even a basic mobile phone will use a complex set of signs which consists of numbers, letters and other symbols, many of which are quite arbitrary in the way in which they signify. Also on the screen of the mobile phone you will find a combination of signs, some of which are iconic and other indexical. Iconic signs might include a picture of a camera or a radio (see Figure 1.3). Indexical signs are likely to include a calendar or a bell to represent a diary or alarm function. There might also be the logo of the network to which the phone is connected which may be represented by a series of letters in a symbolic way.

Look at the illustration of the Nokia phone below.

Figure 1.3

Identify those symbols that are: (a) iconic, (b) indexical and (c) abstract.

- Why do you think Nokia have chosen to use the symbols that they have?
- Do some work better than others because they are more readily understood?
- How similar are the symbols used on this phone to other phones you might have used?
- Are they better?

The photograph used in the Dolce & Gabbana advertisement (Figure 1.4) could have many different readings and can be considered, therefore, to be polysemic. As we have seen, individuals can read messages in different ways and are capable of taking quite different meanings from one image. Advertisers may well deliberately exploit the ambiguity of an image such as this advertisement to create an impact in different ways on different people. Consider, for example, whether

Figure 1.4

KEY CONCEPTS

people of different genders and age groups are likely to read the image differently. We are directed, however, towards a particular or preferred reading by the inclusion of the name of a well-known fashion company and the fact that this text would probably have appeared in lifestyle magazines such as *Company*, *FHM* or *Elle*.

Anchorage is the fixing or limiting of a particular set of meanings to an image.

One of the most common forms of anchorage is the caption underneath a photograph. It is the name Dolce & Gabbana that provides the anchorage for this text, in the same way that the wording at the top of the Diesel advertisement, along with the picture of the product itself, directs us towards its preferred reading.

ACTIVITY

Without the wording, the Dolce & Gabbana photograph could be very ambiguous and difficult to put into context. Try putting different captions of your own to the photograph to illustrate some of its possible meanings and suggest where else the photograph might appear. Compare your responses with your peers.

Codes

Signs often work through a series of codes that are, like signs, usually socially constructed and, therefore, agreed upon by society as a whole. There are many different types of code at work in media texts; some of the most common are: dress codes, colour codes, non-verbal codes, technical codes.

Dress codes relate to what people wear in particular situations. If we see people in evening dress we usually make the association of glamour, wealth or sophistication.

Colour codes in particular vary within different cultures. Black, for instance, is usually the colour of mourning in most Western countries, but in some Asian countries mourners will often dress in white. Red is a particularly strong colour in terms of what it signifies: depending upon the context it can mean danger, stop (as in traffic lights) or socialism. It can also mean excitement and glamour if it is included in a fashion picture of a woman, perhaps with red glossy lipstick, painted fingernails or a red dress.

Non-verbal codes are to do with gesture and body language, and again these vary from culture to culture. In some countries it is normal to shake hands every time you meet someone, whereas in other societies you may kiss on the cheek. In some Muslim countries, on the other hand, such open gestures of intimacy between couples would be frowned upon.

In a media text such as the Diesel advertisement, non-verbal codes would include facial expressions and different postures or gestures. In an illustration such as the Dolce & Gabbana ad, where two or more people are featured, proxemics (the way in which the people appear close together or keep their distance) is an important issue. The closeness of these two figures suggests to us the intimacy of their relationship. Only people who are emotionally close would be expected to get so close to each other physically.

Technical codes relate to the way in which particular texts are reproduced and the media used. This may be a photograph or a film (such as *Schindler's List*) that is shot almost entirely in black and white to convey an idea of documentary 'realism'. It may be the use of a close-up in a film or television programme to convey a character's strong emotions. (See Chapter 13 on production for further discussion.)

Andrew Crisell in *Understanding Radio* (1994) identifies silence as an important code used in radio texts alongside more obvious codes such as words, sounds and music.

As particular media have their own sets of codes and sign systems, we can see that the Diesel illustration 'works' in the context of a fashion magazine. It is read by (predominantly) women readers who are familiar with the signs and conventions of this type of illustration. The advertisement would work less well in a newspaper like the *Big Issue* because its 'glossy' image would not work on the recycled newsprint the *Big Issue* uses and readers would possibly not respond to the advert in the way that the advertisers planned.

Part of the 'meaning' generated by the Diesel advertisement is dependent upon (a) where it is placed and (b) who 'reads' it.

Denotation and connotation

According to Roland Barthes we, the 'reader', go through various stages when we deconstruct the meaning of a sign.

The first stage he called denotation, what an image actually shows and what is immediately apparent, rather than the assumptions an individual reader may make about it. In the case of the Diesel advertisement, the denotation consists of a young woman in a speedboat sailing down a river. We may say that the woman is fashionably dressed and is at the wheel of a speedboat which is cutting through the water. We should also notice that at the bottom of the page is the slogan 'global warming ready' inside a rectangular box.

The next stage that Barthes identified, connotation, is the meaning of a sign that is arrived at through the cultural experiences a reader brings to it, where we, the 'reader', add our own pieces of information. We fill in what is missing from the denotation stage and attempt to identify what the sign is signifying. In the case of the Diesel advert, this will probably mean that we 'add' the information that this is an illustration of an independent and attractive young woman, who has been shopping, presumably for Diesel clothing, and has decided to use a speedboat to drive home down the River Thames rather than risk the congestion of London traffic.

We should be able to identify the various codes that are at work in this sign, particularly those to do with the clothes that the young woman is wearing, her body language, the London skyline and the Union Jack flag.

ACTIVITY

Look carefully at the facial expression of the woman in the Diesel advertisement. Now conduct a piece of research by asking people what they think her expression communicates about her emotional state.

- Do their responses vary? If so, why?
- Why do you think the advertisers used this image?
- Can you think of other ways in which the same meaning could have been created?

We may wish to add other connotations that say that this young woman seems to be rather affluent, that she is not working but appears to have the time to enjoy herself. She has the money required to go shopping and own a speedboat illustrated in the advertisement.

The idea of alternative ways of presenting an image is also important in the analysis of moving images. For example, a director may choose to shoot someone's face in close-up. All the other possible sizes of shot, for example, mid-shot or long shot, have been rejected in favour of the close-up. It can be argued that at some level we are aware of all the shots that have been rejected in order to include the one that has been selected.

There may be different connotations that other 'readers' add. It is sometimes helpful to ask what has been excluded from the image or how it might have been presented differently. For instance, the setting although dramatic seems quite unrealistic. The Thames looks more like the open sea than a river running through a major city. Why do you think a few buildings have been included and what difference might it make if these were old warehouses rather than Big Ben and Tower Bridge? What if a different type of boat were used, for example, if she were rowing?

We also need to consider the connotations associated with the written slogan. We need to look at the words 'global warming ready' and the typeface that is used. We may identify connotations that suggest a clever play on words bringing together ideas of ecology, and care for the environment, with those of warm but fashionable clothing and those of a global fashion brand.

We have, through our reading of the connotations of the Diesel advertisement, added 'extra' layers of meaning beyond that denoted by the images themselves. In so doing, we also become part of a shared experience with the producer of the advertisement because we have understood the cleverness of the construction of the message.

ACTIVITY

Collect a selection of advertisements from various magazines and then, using the worksheet on p. 46, describe what you can see in terms of the denotative content of the advertisements. Remember that denotation only means what is there and you must be very disciplined in not adding information or assuming more than is shown. This can be quite a difficult exercise as most of us have become very sophisticated in reading in the additional information that advertisers intend us to supply ourselves.

One way of noting everything that is contained in the illustrations is to cover each advertisement and slowly reveal it bit by bit. This will help you to identify some of the smaller details that are often overlooked when we glance or skim through printed material.

Using the same set of advertisements, now describe what the connotations are. Again try to look at all the aspects of the illustrations and try to say why the advertisers put them in.

Compare your interpretation of the same advertisement with a colleague's. This can be a useful means of illustrating how meaning is now 'fixed' but is partly dependent upon the individual reading.

Semiotics is a valuable tool for the analysis of print and moving image texts. Of course, since semiotics was first introduced into the Media Studies toolkit, technologies for delivering media products to audiences have undergone significant development. One type of media text that you will need to look at in an analytical way is the website. As you are probably aware, websites come in a range of different types, from simple single-page static sites to a complex multi-layered site like the BBC. A complex website will feature and combine a broad range of sign systems such as still images, moving images, sounds, spoken and written words, and animations. The tools of semiotic analysis are still valuable despite the complexity of the sign systems at play. Once you have looked at the constituent parts of the site, you need then to explore the ways in which these elements combine to create the whole.

A good place to start when looking at website analysis is to get a sense of the codes and conventions of website design. As a relatively new media form, these are to some degree still developing. There are, however, sufficient established conventions to support an analysis. You should especially consider home pages. Give some thought to the way in which a home page is the landing place for visitors directed to the site from a search engine. Consider how its function is both to hold the browser's attention and to direct them to other pages on the website. An analysis needs to look at both how this is done and how effective it is. Particularly relevant to this exercise is to consider the way in which hyperlinks and menus are used as a conduit to signpost visitors through the site.

Look carefully at the 'Liquid Space Experience' page of the Diesel website (http://store.diesel.com/home.asp?stl=1&tskay=3FD17CD7). The page relies heavily for its impact on the illusion of an underwater world in some ways reminiscent of an aquatic screensaver. The predominantly black colour of the screen creates a cool and neutral underwater space apart from time and space. Notice how this undersea world seems populated by indistinct but vaguely recognisable life forms until the female model is thrown forward in an acrobatic way to the centre foreground of the screen.

Look too at the organisation of the page. The centre of the screen to which we give visual priority is the focus of the moving image. The static material print information occupies the periphery of the screen but serves the important function of anchoring the meaning of the visual image by telling us what the model is wearing, a chunky hand-knitted oversized gilet, and how it can be purchased online.

Now look carefully at the site yourself. Consider for example, how the model moves within the screen space. What is the impact on the viewer of the illusion of the underwater spade in which even the cursor swims in a fishlike manner? Think about the other information that we are offered on the page and the way in which we are invited to navigate into other areas of the site. Do you think that the page is 'user-friendly' in that it helps the visitor to find their way around?

Now look at the worksheet at the end of this section (p. 46) and try answering the questions in relation to this website.

The process model of communication

Semiotics, with its emphasis on the text and its codes and signs, can be seen as a move away from earlier analyses that saw the media as a 'process' model of communication. The model suggested that the medium used was perhaps more important than the message itself (see Chapter 7 on media audiences).

The process model considered the audience's interaction with the media as part of a linear process – SENDER-CHANNEL-MESSAGE-RECEIVER – in which the meaning of a text was thought to be 'fixed' by the producer.

In the Diesel example, the sender is the producer of the advertisement, in other words is the agency that created it on behalf of the clothing manufacturer. The channel is that of magazine advertising. Other channels such as television and billboard advertising are also likely to have been used. The message is basically 'buy Diesel and you will be like this woman'. The receiver is the reader of the magazine. The process model assumes that the message created by the sender and the message received are likely to be the same. The meaning of the message is thought to be set by the producer.

You can see that semiotics offers a much more sophisticated view of how media texts communicate meaning and are interpreted by audiences. However, just as the process model has been criticised for being too simplistic, so the semiotic approach has itself been criticised.

Criticisms of semiotics

Critics have suggested that semiotics is not really a 'science' in the way that Barthes claimed, and that because all signs can have different meanings depending upon the individual reader's interpretation, there is some difficulty in judging which interpretations are the most 'valid'.

You might like to consider how far the meanings that we can take from a text were actually intended when the text was produced and how far they are created just for the purposes of analysis. It is easy to get carried away with the notion that there are hidden meanings within all media texts and it is our job as media students to reveal these.

Some theorists prefer to talk about the way in which audiences and individuals respond to media products. This emphasises the way in which texts often work on an emotional rather than an intellectual level. We may go to see a really poor romantic comedy and we may walk out laughing at how awful it was or we may walk out crying caught on the tide of emotion that the film created within the audience. Consider for example, the different responses that might be made by different individuals confronted with a copy of *Nuts* magazine (Figure 11.4).

Another weakness of semiotics is that it can sometimes be difficult to measure the effect or influence of the audience or reader in creating signs. For instance, the flowers left outside the various royal palaces after the death of Diana, Princess of Wales, could be seen as 'signifying' national mourning – but only after the event had started and had become widely publicised in the media. This seemed to create a snowball effect, whereby many people decided to join in. In this case it is difficult to say whether this 'signification' originated with people expressing their sorrow or through media manipulation of that sorrow.

Figure 1.5

Critics have also suggested that the denotation stage is not very useful because it is so artificial and all readers automatically 'add' connotations.

ACTIVITY

Consider some of these criticisms and suggest ways in which they may be answered. Suggest reasons why you think semiotics may be a useful tool for analysing media texts.

WORKSHEET

Use the worksheet overleaf to help you with the analysis of an advertisement of your own choice. Consider each of the following aspects:

Portrayal of people in the advertisement:

- How old are they?
- What gender are they?
- What racial group do they come from?
- Which social classes are represented? How do you know?
- What do the clothing codes tell you?
- What are their facial expressions? Why?
- What is their posture? Why?
- What roles and stereotypes are being represented?
- How would you describe the relationship between the people?
- What other people could have been included? Why have they been excluded?

Technical codes:

- Is the illustration in colour or black and white? Why?
- How have the images been framed and cropped?
- Are all the elements of the image in focus? If not, why?
- Has anything been left out of the illustration? Why?
- How has it been lit and what is the camera angle? Are these important?

Text included in the advertisement:

- How does the slogan relate to the images?
- What other information are we given to help explain the images?
- Who is being addressed?
- What typeface has been used? Why?

Objects that are included:

- Where is the advert set? How do we know?
- What objects are included in the advert? Why?
- Does the product appear in the advert? If not, why not?
- What else could have been included but has not been? Why?
- What do the background colours and textures signify?
- What colour codes are at work?

The function of the advertisement as a whole:

- What kind of advertisement is this? Does it refer to any other advertisements or media texts?
- What is the narrative and how do we make sense of it?
- Who are we supposed to identify with?
- What is being promised by this advertisement?
- What are the values that underpin it?
- Who is in control in this image and where does the power come from?

The audience for the advertisement:

- Who is the advertisement aimed at? How do we know?
- Is any prior knowledge required to understand the advertisement? If yes, what?
- In what publications might the advertisement appear? Why?
- Whereabouts in the publication might the advertisement appear?
- Is the advertisement part of a larger campaign? If so, what are the other components of the campaign?

further reading

Berger, J. (1972) *Ways of Seeing*, Penguin.

Davies, S. (2002) 'A Semiotic Analysis of Teenage Magazine Covers' http://www.aber.ac.uk/media/Students/sid9901.html.

Dyer, G. (1982) *Advertising as Communication*, Methuen.

Monaco, J. (1981) *How to Read a Film*, Oxford University Press.

2 NARRATIVE

In this chapter we:

- consider the significance of narrative in both fiction and non-fiction texts
- look at narrative construction and mode of address
- examine the relationship between narrative and genre.

Narrative construction

Narrative is the way in which a story is told in both fictional and non-fictional media texts. From our earliest days, narrative is an important part of our lives. For many people, their earliest recollections relate to bedtime stories or stories told by their teacher in primary school. Another reason why narrative is so important to us is that it acts as an organising principle that helps us make sense of the world. To a child the world is a mass of unconnected and incomprehensible events, some pleasurable, some frightening, none of which makes a great deal of sense. Narrative, or storytelling, performs the important function of interpreting the world and shaping it into a comprehensible and comfortable form that allows us to see the forces of light and dark, and good and evil, battle against each other. Usually we are rewarded with the comforting outcome of the triumph of good and the reassurance of an equilibrium in which all will live 'happily ever after'.

As we grow up, narrative remains an important source of reassurance in a hostile universe, in much the same way as it did when we were children. Indeed, satisfying our need for narrative can in itself become associated with reward or punishment. Bad behaviour at school or at home may be punished with the denial of an end-of-day or bedtime story. Good behaviour, on the other hand, is rewarded with a narrative.

Narrative, therefore, plays an important role in our growing up and consequently in forming our social values.

> **Indeed so commonplace and natural does story-telling appear that it may seem invisible to study. Yet story-telling is a complex process with important implications.**
>
> (Tilley 1991)

ACTIVITY

Watch on television a children's programme that involves some element of storytelling such as *Shaun the Sheep*. Paying particular attention to the narrative, consider how conflict within the narrative is developed. What devices are used to indicate to the audience where their sympathies are expected to lie between the characters?

Figure 2.1 *Shaun the Sheep*

Clearly narrative is a powerful force not only to help us make sense of our world, but also with the potential to influence our behaviour. Similarly, for the media producers, narrative is an important tool for organising seemingly random and incoherent events into a coherent and logical form that an audience can assimilate. Consider, for example, a news story that has occurred in some remote part of the world. It may be a disaster, such as an earthquake or a famine that has damaged the lives of many thousands of people in a terrifying way. A journalist writing a newspaper story has to explain what has happened in a few hundred words and, perhaps, a couple of photographs. Often the journalist will do this by focusing on specific detail about the impact of the disaster on the lives of individual people or families. In this way the audience has a clear point of reference with which to make a comparison with themselves or their own families. The scale of the disaster, too vast to comprehend, is understood in terms of the individual human being, with whom we, the audience, can empathise.

Narrative can be used as a potent means of influencing the responses of an audience to a particular event. This is often determined by the way in which the information is presented. Certainly when we are being told about a conflict, in a western or gangster movie for example, the narrative often unfolds in such a way as to make us 'take sides' in support of one party or the other. The narrative can thus be used to position an audience in such a way as to limit the range of readings available to them from the text.

It is important to note that although the term 'narrative' is associated, through its literary origins, with fictional texts such as films and novels, it also plays an important part in non-fiction texts such as newspaper stories. Consider how the news photograph (Figure 2.2) exploits the moment of conflict between the police and the protesters to achieve its effect.

So we have seen that narrative is a means by which media producers shape and control the flow of information to an audience. At a basic level, narrative can be seen as the sequencing of information about events into a logical and cohesive structure in time and space. Indeed, it has been argued that the underlying structure of all narratives is basically the same, with variation only taking place in terms of character and setting. The Bulgarian theorist Tzvetan Todorov reduced the concept of narrative to a simple recurring formula:

equilibrium → disequilibrium → new equilibrium

A narrative starts with a state of equilibrium or harmony, for example, a peaceful community getting on with and enjoying life. A firm sense of social order is established. Into this world of stability comes a force of disequilibrium or disruption, an evil outsider, intent on destroying the sense of well-being. By some mechanism such as the intervention of another outside agency, such as a lone gunfighter, the force of evil is overcome and order and harmony, in the form of a new equilibrium, are restored.

Figure 2.2 Protesters and police in Burma. A photograph can be read as a frozen moment in an ongoing narrative. What do you think were the events leading up to the moment in this photograph? What do you think happened afterwards?

You will see the plot of many Hollywood movie genres, for example, western, sci-fi or even musical, fitting into this structure. Less obviously, the plot of the television news follows a similar pattern. The opening shot introduces us to the harmony of the studio as the news programme opens. The tragic events of the world news, reports of wars, famines, social unrest and political intrigue, invade our living space and disrupt the harmony. Finally we are offered a light and comic story to provide relief from this narrative of world disorder and disaster before we are returned to the newsreader shuffling papers and calmly saying good night. The equilibrium of the familiar world – our living room – is re-established, disrupted only briefly by the tragic events of the world at large. Similarly, in a programme such as *Crimewatch*, despite depicting the nightmare deeds of the criminal community, the narrative closes in the security of the studio with a familiar and friendly presenter reassuring us that we are unlikely to become victims ourselves. We may have experienced the dangers of the world, but are told that we can still sleep soundly in our beds.

In their book *Film Art: An Introduction* (2006), Bordwell and Thompson offer a technique for looking at film narrative in segments or sequences. These are called scenes, or distinct phases of the action occurring within relatively unified space and time. The segmentation allows us to see major divisions within the plot and

Figure 2.3 *Shaun of the Dead* (2004). The horror movie is another example of a film genre in which external forces disturb the equilibrium of a community.

how scenes are organised within them. This is a useful device that can be applied to a number of different narratives in order to reveal the way in which they are constructed. Few films or broadcast texts are likely to break down into the complex narrative structure of *Citizen Kane*, however (see Figure 2.4).

As you can see, this film relies heavily on flashback as an organising principle for the narrative. Instead of presenting a chronological life of Kane, common in biopics, the structure employs elements of the detective story as each flashback signals a different phase in the investigation of Kane's life and the meaning of his enigmatic dying word, 'Rosebud'.

ACTIVITY

Using Figure 2.4 as a guide, produce your own narrative segmentation of a film or fictional television programme you have watched recently. A comedy film or situation comedy might make an interesting example. You should try to identify, for example, the way in which different strands

continued

CITIZEN KANE: PLOT SEGMENTATION

C. Credit title
1. Xanadu: Kane dies
2. Projection room:
   - a. "News on the March"
   - b. Reporters discuss "Rosebud"
3. El Rancho nightclub: Thompson tries to interview Susan
4. Thatcher library:

   First flashback
   - a. Thompson enters and reads Thatcher's manuscript
   - b. Kane's mother sends the boy off with Thatcher
   - c. Kane grows up and buys the *Inquirer*
   - d. Kane launches the *Inquirer*'s attack on big business
   - e. The Depression: Kane sells Thatcher his newspaper chain
   - f. Thompson leaves library

5. Bernstein's office:

   Second flashback
   - a. Thompson visits Bernstein
   - b. Kane takes over the *Inquirer*
   - c. Montage: the *Inquirer*'s growth
   - d. Party: the *Inquirer* celebrates getting the *Chronicle* staff
   - e. Leland and Bernstein discuss Kane's trip abroad
   - f. Kane returns with his fiancée Emily
   - g. Bernstein concludes his reminiscence

6. Nursing home:

   Third flashback
   - a. Thompson talks with Leland
   - b. Breakfast table montage: Kane's marriage deteriorates
   - c. Leland continues his recollections

   Third flashback (cont.)
   - d. Kane meets Susan and goes to her room
   - e. Kane's political campaign culminates in his speech
   - f. Kane confronts Gettys, Emily, and Susan
   - g. Kane loses election and Leland asks to be transferred
   - h. Kane marries Susan
   - i. Susan's opera premiere
   - j. Because Leland is drunk, Kane finishes Leland's review
   - k. Leland concludes his reminiscence

7. El Rancho nightclub:

   Fourth flashback
   - a. Thompson talks with Susan
   - b. Susan rehearses her singing
   - c. Susan's opera premiere
   - d. Kane insists that Susan go on singing
   - e. Montage: Susan's opera career
   - f. Susan attempts suicide and Kane promises she can quit singing
   - g. Xanadu: Susan bored
   - h. Montage: Susan plays with jigsaw puzzles
   - i. Xanadu: Kane proposes a picnic
   - j. Picnic: Kane slaps Susan
   - k. Xanadu: Susan leaves Kane
   - l. Susan concludes her reminiscence

8. Xanadu:

   Fifth flashback
   - a. Thompson talks with Raymond
   - b. Kane destroys Susan's room and picks up paperweight, murmuring "Rosebud"
   - c. Raymond concludes his reminiscence; Thompson talks with the other reporters; all leave
   - d. Survey of Kane's possessions leads to a revelation of Rosebud; exterior of gate and of castle; the end

E. End credits

Figure 2.4

ACTIVITY

As we have indicated, narrative is an important concept in non-fiction as well as in fictional texts. Consider how conflict is used as a basis for telling stories in either of the following non-fiction texts:

■ **Newspaper articles** – Consider how a range of different types of stories are presented. You should look at political stories, sports stories as well as foreign news and celebrity stories. Identify the two sides represented in the conflict and see if you think there is a bias in the story towards one side or the other.
■ **Factual television programmes** – You should include current affairs programmes and documentaries in your survey. One useful means of exploring conflict is through wildlife programmes, especially those that feature predatory animals. The heroes and villains of these programmes are likely to change according to which ones have 'star billing'.

Mode of address

Mode of address is the way in which a particular text will address or speak to its audience and is an important concept in narrative study. It refers to the way in which a media text can be said to 'talk to' its audience. As such, it also has important implications for the way in which the audience responds to the text. For example, the use of a voice-over, an off-screen narrator who talks directly to the audience, is often seen as an authoritative mode of address, providing the audience with information that is incontrovertible. The authority of this voice is often further reinforced by the use of a well-known actor with a particularly distinctive voice.

The use of voice-over is a feature of news, current affairs programmes and some documentaries, in which this commentary holds the narrative together and develops it. Similarly, voice-over is used as a narrative device in cinema. It is a distinctive feature of the genre *film noir*, for example, in Josh Hartnett's commentary on the action in Brian de Palma's *Black Dahlia* (2006) where the film begins with Officer Dwight 'Bucky' Bleichert's voice-over:

> 'Mr. Fire versus Mr. Ice. For everything people were making it out to be, you'd think it was our first fight. It wasn't. And it wouldn't be our last.'

Such a voice-over is an off-screen (asynchronous) voice that directly addresses and confides in the audience. One effect of using this device is to make the audience a party to information that may not be shared by the rest of the characters on screen. It therefore offers us, the audience, privileged information about what is going on. We are positioned to accept, often without question, the information being communicated by this off-screen voice. In this instance it also sets up both an enigma and a conflict – who are these people and why are they fighting? What will be the outcome of their fight? On occasion, the off-screen voice may also make us wary of trusting the character, for example, in the opening scene of *Taxi Driver* (1976), in which Travis Bickle, played by Robert De Niro, reveals his conflicted personality in a tirade against humanity.

ACTIVITY

Make a recording of a documentary that deals with complex medical or scientific issues about which you are likely to know very little.

- What methods does the commentary use to help the audience understand the complex information being conveyed?
- Is there a sense of conflict engendered in the programme?
- If so, how is this set up/resolved?

In what different ways could an image like the one overleaf (Figure 2.5) be read if the voice-over gave different information about the scene. Try adding your own voice-over to a film with a definite ideological slant and see how the words change the way the scene is read by the audience. To what extent are the audience guided in their understanding through your voice-over? In what ways do they resist the reading your voice-over presents?

The issue of audience positioning is a complex one and is dealt with more fully in Chapter 7 on Media Audiences. An important effect of narrative, however, is the way in which it can be used to place or position an audience in relation to the text. In the example of *Taxi Driver*, the device is used to provide the audience with the opportunity to be party to information not shared by other characters in the film. This was an important device used in *film noir*. Not only does it provide the audience with information that assists the development of the narrative, it also gives access to the innermost thoughts of the main character, thus providing the audience with an insight into motivation and psychological make-up.

Roland Barthes explored the concept of narrative as part of his work on structuralism. He argued that narrative works through a series of codes that are used to control the way in which information is given to the audience. Two of these

Figure 2.5 *Bowling for Columbine* (2002)

codes are particularly important for our understanding of how narrative functions in media texts. The first is called the *enigma code*. An enigma is a riddle or puzzle, and some types of narrative make extensive use of this code. An obvious example is a detective story, in which we, the audience, are invited to solve the puzzle of 'whodunnit' by interpreting the clues and pitting our wits against those of the fictional detective whose job it is to find the perpetrator of the crime.

This is an obvious use of enigma as a narrative device. However, there are many other, less obvious, ways in which these enigmas are used. One example is the use of trailers for programmes to be broadcast later on television or radio. These often rely on teasing the audience with information that can only be fully understood by tuning in to the programme itself. Similarly, a non-fiction text such as the news begins with headlines, which provide cryptic details of the stories that are to follow, ensuring that the audience stays with the programme to find out the full story behind the headlines. Print media use similar devices, with newspaper headlines or magazine front covers offering brief information to invite the reader to purchase the product and consume the larger narrative within (for example, 'POP STAR IN DRUGS TRAGEDY'). Similarly, advertisers often use billboards to tease us with little clues about a product, such as a feature film, to be launched on to the market.

One of the pleasures that an audience receives from consuming a media text is that of predicting the outcome to a particular narrative. Clearly this is much of the appeal of crime-based texts, in which the audience is positioned alongside the detective in trying to solve the crime or mystery.

Another code that Barthes writes about is the *action code*. This is a narrative device by which a resolution is produced through action, for example, a shoot-out.

Figure 2.6 *Crank* (2006). Barthes argues that the action code sees problems resolved through action such as violence or gun play, as in this shot. Can you suggest other similar examples?

This code suggests how narratives can be resolved through action, often on the part of the protagonist or hero. Typically a resolution is achieved through an act of violence, such as a gun battle. The action code is, therefore, often considered to be a male genre, with problems being resolved through action such as physical violence or a car chase.

Relationship between narrative and genre

A study of different genres in film and television will suggest that the formula requires the narrative to be closed in a different way for each different genre. For example, a soap opera will usually end with a cliffhanger, a narrative device designed to create suspense for the audience and ensure that they tune in to the next episode.

Narrative is also often recognised for the different devices it employs to engage the audience with the text. Alfred Hitchcock spoke of a device that he called 'the bomb under the table'. Here suspense is built for the audience by making them party to information not shared by the characters on screen – in this case, a bomb under the table ready to explode but about which the on-screen characters are wholly unaware.

Most narratives will move in a straight line, following the basic chronology of a story unfolding. This is often called a linear narrative because it involves a plot that moves forward in a straight line without flashbacks or digressions. However, in controlling the flow of information, a number of devices can be employed to realign the narrative.

One obvious example is flashback, whereby the narrative allows a character to remember events that have happened in the past, usually to shed light on events 'currently' taking place within the narrative. Similarly, a complex narrative may allow events taking place in two different locations at the same time to be shown alongside each other. This is called parallel action in which two scenes are observed as happening at the same time by cutting between them and provides the audience with a privileged view. An extreme form of this is the use of split-screen techniques, whereby two narratives can literally be shown simultaneously on screen.

Some media texts play on the need of the audience to find logical sequencing in narratives by denying this. For example, if we are watching a film and a character we know to have been killed suddenly but who inexplicably reappears, we find it hard to make sense of. Indeed the contract that we, the audience, agreed to whereby we suspend our disbelief is clearly threatened by this. *Pulp Fiction* is an example of a film that uses this device, confounding the audience by the reappearance of a character whose death we had witnessed earlier.

This method of deliberately disrupting narrative flow in order to achieve a particular effect, such as the repetition of images or the disruption of a chronological sequence of events is called anti-narrative because it works in contrast to the accepted chronological cause and effect patterns of a narrative. One reason that film-makers and producers of televison programmes are able to do this is because audiences have become extremely sophisticated in the way in which they read complex moving image texts. Read through Chapter 9 on *Heroes* and consider how this programme uses a complex narrative pattern which plays with established notions of time and space to engage the audience.

Narrative and new media platforms

As you will have seen, narrative is a particularly useful tool for exploring the way in which media texts are constructed and the ways in which they can be consumed or read by audiences. As one of the prime concerns of narrative study is to explore the way in which the flow of information is controlled within a text, it also has useful applications for looking at more recent media forms. If you consider the structure and organisation of a website, you should be able to see how narrative is a key element in the way in which an audience will engage with such a text.

Websites are generally constructed to have a home page or landing page which is the first page to be accessed either via a search engine or from a list of bookmarks. The home page fulfils a similar function to a newspaper front page or magazine cover in that it both reassures the reader that they have arrived at the right place and ensures that what they see grabs their attention sufficiently to keep them viewing.

The home page is also the link or conduit through which the rest of the website can be accessed. A good home page will not only engage in its own right but also offer a pathway to other areas of the site. The use of hyperlinks and menus are critical in this process of signposting the way to further information and detail within the site. Notice how a good website will always provide a link from whatever pages you are on back to the home page so that if you become lost in the narrative, there is a readily available escape route back to where you started.

Of course, the paths through the web can be labyrinthine simply because of the temptation that afflicts all surfers to click on links either in the hope of finding what they are looking for or more likely for the sheer pleasure of doing so. Web browsers are, however, designed with this random surfing in mind. Such functions as the back button, the bookmark facility and the history menu provide ways of signposting the narrative so that it is always possible to pick up the trail and set off in a more productive direction.

What is especially interesting about the narratives of the web is the extent to which we, the audience, are empowered to drive the narrative forward. In a traditionally constructed text, it is the producer who determines how the information flows. To a large extent we have little control over what information we receive and the order in which we receive it. Web narratives are quite different. They permit us to link together many separate elements of the web in the order that we choose, be it logical or not. In this way narrativity on the web has become highly participative. The individual surfer is able to create a unique narrative through the association of the sites they visit in the order in which they have chosen to visit them. In effect they link together disparate elements from the web and create their own personal narrative by the associations they create between sites. Part of the pleasure of these narratives is their random nature. Hence the 'I feel Lucky' option in the Google Search Engine.

ACTIVITY

Other media forms such as the blog and the podcast clearly have narratives. Some of these relate closely to the narratives of established media forms. For example, the podcast shares many narrative conventions with a traditional radio broadcast.

Look at a couple of sites that offer blogs and podcasts and identify how the narrative devices they use are similar to and different from more established media forms. You might like to consider for example, that in a blog, the chronology means that the most recent entry is generally the first one to be accessed.

If you get stuck, try looking at the following:

http://www.stephenfry.com/blog/
http://www.britblog.com/
http://dilbertblog.typepad.com/
http://podcast.com/
http://www.bbc.co.uk/radio/podcasts/directory/

further reading

Bordwell, D. and Thompson, K. (2006) 'Narrative as a Formal System' in *Film Art: An Introduction*, 6th edn, McGraw-Hill.
Branigan, E. (1992) *Narrative, Comprehension and Film*, Routledge.
Eco, U. (1981) *The Role of the Reader: Explorations in the Semiotics of Texts*, London: Hutchinson.
Tilley, A. (1991) 'Narrative' in Lusted, D. (ed.) *The Media Studies Book: A Guide for Teachers*, Routledge.

3 GENRE

In this chapter we:

- consider and explain the concept of genre
- look at the function of genre in relation to audiences and producers of media texts
- consider the role of genre as a critical tool in the analysis of media texts.

Figure 3.1 *Goodfellas* (1990). What clues are present in this still as to the genre of the film? Try the activity overleaf to help you

Look at the image in Figure 3.1. Try to identify the type of film this image is taken from.

- Can you work out what sort of storyline the film is likely to have?
- Can you determine who the villains may be?
- Can you make any suggestions as to the actors or directors that might appear in this type of film?
- What else can you deduce about the film?

The function of genre

In working out the answers to the questions above, you will have used your knowledge of genre. Genre is the term used for classification of media texts into groups with similar characteristics. The concept of genre is useful in looking at the ways in which media texts are organised, categorised and consumed. It is applied to television, print and radio texts as well as to film. The concept of genre suggests that there are certain types of media material, often story types, that are recognised through common elements, such as style, narrative and structure; these are used again and again to make up that particular type of media genre.

Genre is a formula that, if successful, is often repeated and can be used over a long period of time. For instance in a gangster film, like the one in Figure 3.1 (*Goodfellas*, 1990), we expect to see some, or all, of the following elements, which would also probably have been in a gangster film from the 1930s:

- car chases
- urban settings
- guns
- mafia
- heroes
- corrupt police/politicians
- villains
- beautiful women
- violence
- Italians

Iconography

An important element in identifying a genre is the look or iconography of the text. Iconography refers to the signs that we associate with particular genres, such as physical attributes and dress of the actors, the settings and the 'tools of the trade' (for example, cars, guns). Iconography constitutes a pattern of visual imagery that remains common to a genre over a period of time. In the above example of gangster movies, the urban settings, guns, car chases and perhaps a plate of spaghetti with meatballs, all contribute to the iconography which signifies to the audience the genre of film they are viewing.

There are also certain actors that we may associate with this genre of films (James Cagney in the 1930s and more recently Robert De Niro) as well as certain directors (Martin Scorsese and Guy Ritchie).

ACTIVITY

Look at a selection of films that are currently being shown in your area and try to categorise them into different genres.

- What types of stories do the films tell?
- Where are the films set?
- What type of characters appear in the films?
- What particular actors and/or directors are associated with the films? Have they been involved with similar types of films before?
- What is the 'look' or iconography of the film?
- What music is used?
- Suggest reasons why the particular genres you have identified might be popular.

ACTIVITY

Take two examples of films of the same genre from different eras that interest you, for instance *War of the Worlds* (1953) and *Independence Day* (1996), or *Shaun of the Dead* (2004) and *The Plague of the Zombies* (1966), and identify their similarities and differences. Suggest reasons for these similarities and differences.

cliffhanger at the end of each episode deliberately seeks to withhold the narrative outcome to ensure the audience returns for the next episode.

David Morley in *Family Television* (1986) found that men often disapproved of watching fiction on the grounds that it was not 'real life' or sufficiently serious. He also found that men tended to define their own preferences (sport, current affairs) as more important and more 'serious'. Morley suggests that men do in fact enjoy more 'feminine' genres but are perhaps not prepared to admit it.

ACTIVITY

How far do you think Morley's are assertions about gendered consumption? Here is an activity you can have a go at to test it out.

First, identify two groups: one of males and another of females from a range of different age groups.

Now design a brief questionnaire for them to complete. Remember that you need to get some details of their age and background as well as their gender. Use the questionnaire to explore their likes and dislikes in terms of particular genres across any medium. Try to get a reasonable size sample of say 10 to 20 from each group.

Once you have got the questionnaires completed, do some analysis of the results. It is a good idea to try to represent your findings graphically, for example, in the form of a Pi chart. Now consider your results and try to establish whether consumption of genre in the media is gender-specific.

ACTIVITY

Look at the promotional material that is used to market either a new radio, television or cinema product.

■ Identify those elements that are recognisable as belonging to a particular genre by the audience.
■ Are there any elements that distinguish it from other established products of the same genre?

Often the promotion and marketing for new texts invite the audience to identify similarities between a text and predecessors in the same genre. The audience can then take comfort in the fact that what they are being offered is something that they have previously enjoyed and the producers hope they will enjoy again.

It has been suggested that proficiency in reading texts within a genre can also lead to the audience's pleasure being heightened as they recognise particular character types or storylines.

On a more sophisticated level, audiences can also find pleasure in the way in which genre conventions are subverted. A comedy series like *The Office* delights in subverting the conventions of the fly-on-the-wall documentary. A director like Quentin Tarantino plays with the notion of genre in many of films by juxtaposing different genres within a single movie.

ACTIVITY

Select a magazine or newspaper that you read regularly and consider how you consume it:

- Make a list of the features that you most look forward to reading. In which order do you read them? Why?
- Do you read a range of magazines or newspapers from the same genre? If so, what are the similarities/differences between them?
- Do similar stories/features appear in similar places in different publications? If so, why?
- Are similar products advertised in these magazines or newspapers? If so, why?

Genre and producers

Producers are said to like the concept of genre because they can exploit a winning formula and minimise taking risks. The concept of genre also helps institutions budget and plan their finances more accurately and helps them to promote new products.

One of the main functions of most of the mainstream media is to make a profit. Just as a high-street retailer has to sell goods that the customers will want to buy, so a media producer has to create texts that audiences will want to consume.

One way to do this is to find what audiences already enjoy and offer something similar. Genre is an easy way of doing this. Where a formula has been proved popular with audiences, it makes sense for the producer to use that formula again and to create a new product that contains similar recognisable features that, it is hoped, will have an immediate appeal to an established audience.

ACTIVITY

How might the use of a proven formula apply to the popular music industry? Is this also the case when listening to radio music stations? Give examples.

It is for this reason that certain genres seem to be continually popular, such as hospital dramas on television. Some genres, like wildlife programmes, although popular for many years, have changed over time as technology has changed, although the codes and conventions or the presenter may have stayed the same. Indeed, genre is such a useful tool that it is now the case that small niche audiences are targeted by themed cable and satellite channels carrying programmes of just one genre. These niche audiences are groups of people with specific media interests, such as holiday, history or 'adult' programmes. This has the very real advantage of delivering a ready-made audience to advertisers marketing specific products. For example, a channel dedicated to travel programmes will clearly attract an audience who are in the market to buy holidays. For example, recent popular genres include moving house such as *Location, Location, Location* or 'around Britain' programmes such as *Best and Worst Places to Live in the UK*.

ACTIVITY

Look at programmes in these genres and try to identify similarities or differences between them. Consider who the target audience is and why the programme is popular.

Other changes in genres over a period of time may be the result of changes in society itself. Consider, for example, the police series on television. The representation of police officers in programmes like *Dixon of Dock Green* (Figure 3.4), broadcast in the early 1950s, is quite a long way removed from the way they are represented in some more contemporary programmes like *CSI: Crime Scene Investigation* or *NYPD Blue*, although some might argue that there are still many similarities between *Dixon of Dock Green* and *The Bill* (Figures 3.4 and 3.5).

Figures 3.4 and 3.5 Genres change over time. Consider, for example, the representation of the police in the series *Dixon of Dock Green* (top) and its contemporary counterpart, *The Bill* (bottom left and right).

The dominance of genre, coupled with the caution of many media producers, can mean that some new texts are marginalised because they do not fit into the generic conventions that audiences recognise and accept. However, there are always new combinations of programmes being produced that can be difficult to fit into a particular genre but yet prove successful. For instance, where do series such as *Heroes* and *24* fit?

New genres or new takes on existing genres are often created by taking the conventions of existing genres and mixing these together to create a new 'hybrid'. This process is called hybridisation. It is often difficult to tell whether *The Bill* is a crime series programme or an example of a soap opera set in a police station. This ability of genres to transmute into other forms obviously can in the eyes of many theorists limit the value of genre as a tool in analysing texts. You might like to consider, for example, the way in which the horror movie has developed the capacity for self-reference to the point that some texts have deliberate comic elements about them. It is hard to argue the value of genre as an organising principle of the construction and consumption of texts when they can shift their shape in this way.

Indeed, some would argue that the most successful of media texts are those that do not readily fit into established genres. However, a counter argument might rest on the vast majority of media output conforming reasonably well to established genre conventions. For example, programmes like *Casualty*, *Holby City* and *The Royal* all fit reasonably comfortably into the genre 'medical dramas'.

ACTIVITY

Look at the stills from television cop shows broadcast around 50 years apart (Figures 3.4 and 3.5). What can you tell by looking at these stills about the way in which the genre has changed over that period of time?

Genre as a critical tool

The idea of genre has been used for a long time. For example, Literary Studies categorises texts into such genres as sonnets, tragedies and picaresque novels. It was the film theorists of the 1960s and 1970s who recognised the importance of genre to Film and Media Studies. They saw genre as important because media texts are the product of an industrial process, rather than the creation of an individual, as typified by the Hollywood studio system or indeed Bollywood today.

Much of the early work of theorists such as Steve Neale and Tom Ryall was concerned with defining the nature of genre and considering how the concept of genre influenced both the way in which texts were created and the ways in which audiences consumed them. This relationship is often depicted as a triangle in which the dynamic between audience producer and text each occupy the three points of the triangle (see Figure 3.6).

Grouping texts according to type makes studying them more convenient, recognises the industrial constraints upon producers of media texts, and also allows these texts to be looked at in terms of trends within popular culture (for example, the western or sci-fi in 1950s and 1960s). Genre theory acknowledges that while an individual text may not be worthy of detailed study, a group of texts of the same genre can reveal a good deal, especially in terms of audience appeal (for example, Hammer films).

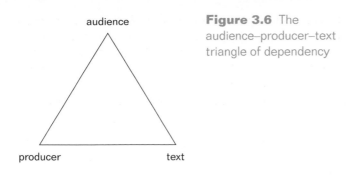

Figure 3.6 The audience–producer–text triangle of dependency

audience

producer   text

This grouping can, however, seem at times quite arbitrary. Often texts are grouped into a genre because of the themes that they deal with. Situation comedy has for its theme humorous events that take place within situations such as family life. There are of course other characteristics that might be used to link them together. For example, geography might be considered a common factor in linking together different texts. Those that deal with or are set in London, it could be argued, should share generic conventions. In this case, *The Bill*, *EastEnders* and *Only Fools and Horses* might form a genre category of their own rather than being crime series, soap opera and sitcom. You might like to consider the way in which a social networking site creates genres by hyperlinking similar content to the specific content you are viewing. In the same way, online retail sites such as Amazon offer links to DVDs or CDs of a similar genre when you search for a specific title.

ACTIVITY

- Select a range of texts from different media platforms, including the web, that are focused on London.
- Identify which genres these texts would normally be associated with.
- Consider if there were to be a genre called 'texts about London', how well these texts might form a group together.

Limitations of genre

As you will see from the above activity, although genre is a useful means of grouping together texts so that we can consider them as a unit, the assumptions that we make about how best to group them are at times quite arbitrary and even flawed.

1 The concept of genre clearly can have limitations when applied to a range of media texts because of the variety and the need for constant updating of texts that are being produced. Many texts may look similar but are too different to be grouped together.

2 Sometimes the category becomes too generalised to be helpful. For instance, soap opera could be described as a genre because there are many common characteristics (domestic settings, continuing storylines, cliffhanger endings, familiar characters, and so on) but how helpful is it to say that *Doctors* and *EastEnders* belong to the same genre? We need to be able to distinguish between subgenres within a genre, for example, American 'fantasy' soap operas and British 'realism' soap operas. How would you describe Australian soap operas such as *Neighbours* or *Home and Away*?

3 Although we have used the concept of genre for all types of media text, it has been argued that genre is most useful for film and television and is of limited use when applied to newspapers, magazines or radio.

4 The value concept of genre is further tested by the ways in which technology has presented us with both new ways of consuming media texts and the platforms used for their consumption and delivery. While it is possible, for example, to group websites into 'genres' according to their themes, such as news websites or even pornographic websites, it may be difficult to see the precise value of doing this. News is probably better analysed in its cross-platform role by considering how the technologies of print, moving image, sound and the web shape the nature of the product which we call 'news'.

ACTIVITY

Carry out a survey of the television schedules and try to categorise the main genres that appear. Also look at satellite, cable and digital channels.

- What are the most common genres that occur on the main terrestrial and Freeview channels? How many of them are established genres and how many are more recent or hybrid genres? How would you account for the popularity of two or three of the most popular genres in the schedules?
- Do you think that certain genres are especially appealing to different audiences? Consider, for example, when specific programmes are scheduled and what sort of audience is likely to view at that time.

- Do you think genre plays an important role in determining the way in which schedules are created?
- Consider how the concept of genre is used by digital and satellite channels. Look, for example, at the way in which Sky Movies is segmented into different channels. How do these channels use genre as a way of organising the scheduling of films? Are other channels themed in this way? Look, for example, at the way in which factual programmes are scheduled.

further reading

Dirks, T. (1996) 'Film Genres' http://www.filmsite.org/genres.html.
Glaessner, V. (1990) 'Gendered Fictions' in A. Goodwin and G. Whannel (eds) *Understanding Television*, Routledge.
Ryall, T. (2001) 'The notion of genre', *Screen* 11:2, 23–6.

4 REPRESENTATION

In this chapter we consider the important concept of representation in examining media texts. We look at:

- how the media represent to us the world at large
- the significance and accuracy of such representations
- the use of stereotyping
- how minority groups may be affected by media representation.

Media representation of the world at large

For many of us, the media are an important source of information about the world in which we live. Indeed, it has been argued that the media are one of the chief means by which we reach an understanding of this world. In consequence, many people believe the media are a powerful means of shaping our attitudes and beliefs.

This process by which the media can be said to interpret the world, or external reality, for us is called representation. There is a wide philosophical debate about what constitutes 'reality' and whether, in fact, reality ultimately exists. If, however, we assume, for the convenience of looking at representation, that there is an external reality, then one key function of the media is to represent that reality to us, the audience. The means by which they do this are discussed in Chapter 1 on image analysis, in which we identified a series of sign systems that are used by the media to represent the world.

As we have seen, each medium, such as television or print, is composed of an elaborate system or code, by which it represents the world outside. These codes are often a complex combination of symbolic, iconic and indexical signs (see p. 34). Television, for example, uses iconic images of a world we can recognise, often anchored by spoken language to shape and limit the meanings it is communicating to the audience. The use of iconic images is an important element of the televisual

Figure 4.1 The Eiffel Tower is an instantly recognisable and iconic symbol

message because it has the impact of making the images seem very like the world it represents. The television screen gives the audience a two-dimensional representation of the three-dimensional outside. The image can, therefore, be said to be very 'naturalised' as we have grown up to 'read' two-dimensionality as a realistic representation of what we know to exist in the outside world. A similar argument can be made about still photography. 'The camera never lies', we are told, although we all know that it can and does. Indeed the French film director Jean-Luc Godard described film as truth 24 times a second, alluding to the number of individual frames used to create a second of screen time.

ACTIVITY

Consider a situation in which you have been involved in an argument or fight with a classmate. Imagine you are asked to write a report to describe the altercation to:

continued

How accurate?

Clearly an important debate in any study of the media is about the accuracy of the representation it offers us. What must be borne in mind is that the media offer us a representation of reality rather than reality itself. The information communicated by a media text is a constructed reshaping of the world, in the same way as in the above activity, where you will have reshaped your own experience to communicate it. There are a number of questions that we can usefully ask ourselves when we look at examples of media representation:

■ Can we trust the representation that is being made to be an accurate portrayal?
■ How far have the institutional context and audience expectations determined the nature of the representation?
■ In whose interests is it that the representation is made in this way?

The process by which a media text represents an idea, issue or event to us is called mediation. This is a useful word as it suggests the ways in which things undergo change in the process of being acted upon by the media.

ACTIVITY

Consider an event that takes place and is shown on television, for example, a sporting fixture, protest/demonstration or concert.

■ In what ways is there a difference between being at the 'live' event and watching it on television?
■ Are there qualities that are present in the live event that cannot be experienced through watching television?
■ Are there some things in the televisual representation that may not be experienced by being there?

Figure 4.2 A location interview using only one camera to focus on the interviewee

Encoding is the process by which the media construct messages and it involves re-presenting ideas and events from the world outside into a form that can be decoded by an audience. As we have seen in Chapter 1 on image analysis, the audience has to learn the code in order to take meaning from a media text. Once this has been learnt, however, the process of decoding media texts can make them appear extremely natural, as though the process of encoding had not in fact taken place and the audience were directly experiencing reality itself.

Take, for example, a location interview on the television news. Often this will have been filmed using just a single camera. The process of this filming is usually to conduct the interview with the camera framing the interviewee.

What you have is a highly constructed presentation of an event that most people watching television would identify as quite 'natural', simply because the audience have become so familiar with this method of presenting an interview. Note, too, that in terms of fictional dialogue in the cinema and on television the concept of shot/reverse shot is the standard or even 'natural' way of presenting two people in conversation.

Figure 4.3 This interview for *60 Minutes* shows the standard over-the-shoulder shot for interviews. This shot will normally then be reversed and we will see the interviewer from over the interviewee's shoulder when she is asking questions. This is called shot/reverse shot

ACTIVITY

Do all programmes use traditional techniques like shot/reverse shot to make what we see appear seamless? Have you come across other techniques which make us conscious of the fact that the technology being used to create the programme? You should consider for example, the programme *Jordan and Peter: Unleashed*, a chat show in which guests are seen in their dressing rooms talking to the production crew before actually appearing on the programme. How do you think this approach affects the way in which the programme represents the world to us?

Not only are most media texts highly constructed representations of the world, they are also quite carefully selected. In the example of the use of shot/reverse shot, we have considered how a constructed representation can be made to appear natural through simple convention – we are used to seeing it that way and its iconic form convinces us of its naturalness. Prior to the image ever reaching our screens, however, a process of selection has taken place that determines which aspects of the world are chosen to be represented and how these are represented.

As we will see in the case study on news in Chapter 12 (p. 277), a careful selection process takes place that will determine which events on any one day will be reported on television, in the newspapers and on the radio. In putting together a news report, a television news crew will then make a series of decisions about what images and information are going to be gathered by a reporter and film crew to represent a particular news item. Back in the television studio, images and information will be selected (and others rejected) and then combined on an edit suite to produce a representation of the event. These processes of selection may heavily mediate the original event that took place. What we see on our evening news bulletin is a highly refined representation of an event that has taken place, selected and shaped to be represented in a particular way to the audience (e.g. Figure ii).

This process of selection and refinement inevitably involves a large element of simplification in order to produce a text that is clear and manageable enough for the audience to consume. A good example is television highlights of a sporting event, or a report of such an event in a newspaper. Here the process of representation will involve the selecting and highlighting of important details. Inevitably, therefore, those elements that in some way are controversial or dramatic will be included at the expense of more mundane and run-of-the-mill events. As we have noted in the section on narrative (p. 48), dramatic and controversial events usually involve conflict between people. In consequence, it is often this conflict that becomes the main focus of the media's attention in representing the world at large. In this way, a violent tackle, a controversial decision or a brawl on the pitch will almost certainly be highlighted rather than an example of skilful play or sportsmanship.

When we consider popular newspapers, this highlighting of conflict is often called sensationalism. The popular press is accused of seeking to sensationalise events that it represents.

Stereotyping

An important result of the media needing to simplify in order to make a representation is in the production of stereotypes. The process of simplification in order to make events and issues more digestible for the audience in this case is extended to the representation of groups of people. Rather than representing them as individuals, sections of the media use a kind of shorthand in the way in which they represent some groups of people. These groups of people come from all walks of

life, but significantly they are often minority groups (for example, gay men or ethnic groups). What stereotyping does is to characterise whole groups of people by attributing to them qualities that may be found in one or two individuals. These characteristics are often exaggerated, and entire racial groups or nationalities become reduced to single characteristics. For example, the Jewish race and people from Scotland are both characterised as being tight-fisted. Countries and even whole continents are often represented in the media in a stereotypical way. Consider, for example, the most common media representations of Africa, which is often presented through images of starvation and war.

In their book *Media Studies* (1999), Taylor and Willis consider images of youth as examples of stereotyping. They base their analysis on the work of two Cultural Studies writers, Angela McRobbie, who produced an influential study of the influence of the magazine *Jackie* on teenage girls, and Dick Hebdige, who wrote extensively about media representations of youth (see Hebdige 1988).

Youth tended over the latter half of the twentieth century to suffer from a rather negative representation in the media. From the Teddy Boy images and panics surrounding Elvis Presley movies in the 1950s, through mods and rockers, punk and the representation of 'E' and related drug culture today, youth in revolt has always provided the media with ample opportunities for negative representation of young people. Typically, much of this stereotyping has been based on the activities of small groups of individuals whose activities have provided a source of newspaper headlines. Consider, for example, the coverage of black teenagers in South London who are represented as being member of gangs involved in drug culture and violence.

Website Activity 4.1: Conduct research into the ways in which 'young people' can be stereotyped across different media, i.e. television, newspapers and radio. Does it change according to the medium or target audience?

You might like to consider, however, the way in which young people involved in the music industry are represented in the media and how far these representations are deliberately constructed in such a way as to increase their appeal to a young audience. Certainly the stereotype of the 'creative genius' spinning out of control is one that transcends many generations from Jim Morrison through to Kurt Cobain to, say, Pete Doherty. Note too that this seems to be a specific male representation. Although women are often represented as fellow travellers on the voyage of destruction, for example, Kurt and Courtney, Sid and Nancy and Pete and Kate, they are often represented as less than willing victims of male self-destruction.

Figure 4.4 British musician Pete Doherty (C) leaves West London Magistrates Court, in London, 26 October 2007. British rocker Pete Doherty was handed a suspended jail sentence for a string of drug and motoring offences, just two days after vowing to turn over a new leaf. A judge at West London Magistrates' Court gave the 28-year-old Babyshambles singer a four-month jail sentence, suspended for two years

When considering images of how young people are represented, an important factor is the media form or platform through which they are featured. One important change to traditional representations is the fact that young people are now able to represent themselves through social networking sites. You might like to undertake a comparison of the way in which teenagers, for example, are represented in traditional mainstream media such as the popular press and web-based media such as YouTube, MySpace and Facebook.

ACTIVITY

Compare the representations in the media of female rock stars, such as Amy Winehouse and Lily Allen with those of their male equivalents. Do you think the media differentiate their representations of rock stars according to their gender?

Stereotyping is obviously a useful shortcut for media producers to reproduce and represent groups of people in the media. What a stereotype allows them to do is to condense a lot of complex information into a character who is not only easily recognised but also simple to deal with. Minor characters in films are often presented as stereotypes. The unfortunate side effect of this is to dehumanise people by denying them the complex psychological make-up that an individual possesses by reducing them to a few generalised personality traits. As Tessa Perkins has pointed out, some stereotypes are based on truths that can be observed. For example, France has produced many talented chefs and most French people enjoy gourmet food and wine. However, like the rest of us, French people are complex individuals with more to their lives than mere indulgence in food and drink.

ACTIVITY

- Is it possible to find media representations of youth that are positive?
- If so, where are these mostly to be found?
- Do you feel these are accurate representations?

An even more worrying aspect of stereotyping is the way in which it can be used to marginalise and devalue the worth of whole groups of people in society. In addition, it tends to disregard the causes of stereotypical behaviour, making the group a potential scapegoat for broader ills within a society. For example, the stereotyping of some members of ethnic minorities as living all together in crowded and substandard accommodation can suggest that, where this is the case, it is a matter of choice rather than a result of economic and social deprivation.

This use of stereotypical representation can be seen to reflect the power relations within our society; it tends to subordinate certain groups. Often this will involve some element of ridicule by suggesting that certain groups of people are intellectually challenged or more prone to criminal activity than the rest of the population.

ACTIVITY

In the 1970s in America, George Gerbner produced a quantitative survey, using content analysis techniques, to investigate the representation of violence in the American media. One of his findings was that the victims of violence were often minority groups that society considered most expendable.

> Make a list of groups that you feel are most often stereotyped or represented negatively. In what ways can these groups be said to be subordinate within our society, for instance economically or socially?

ACTIVITY

> The end of the twentieth century saw the emergence of so-called 'Girl Power'. Discuss the extent to which this phenomenon represents the emancipation of women and to what extent it can be seen as another form of exploitative representation in the interests of patriarchy (male domination in society).

Another important issue has been the under-representation of people from minority groups in the media. Certainly, television representation of ethnic minority groups and the gay community has increased in recent years. However, some would argue that this is in fact mere tokenism. This implies that the increased presence of such groups is simply to give the illusion of fairer representation, rather than being a genuine attempt to produce a more even balance. Many, for instance, would point to the relative absence of people with disabilities in the media other than in texts aimed at audiences with a disability. People with a disability have traditionally been represented in a particularly negative way by the media. Commonly they are depicted in films as evil and dangerous people intent on causing harm to able-bodied people. For example, consider some of the villains featured in Bond movies.

Website Activity 4.2: Watch some episodes of the popular sitcom *Phoenix Nights* in which Peter Kay plays the lead character Brian Potter in a wheelchair. Then look at the website for the show: http://www.channel4.com/entertainment/tv/microsites/P/phoenix_nights/index.html, and the character guides and images on it. Why do you think the character is represented in this way? Do you feel the representation is likely to be offensive to people with a disability?

The representation of groups, however, is not fixed for ever, and it is possible to observe changes over periods of time. The emergence of specific groups and subcultures is often accompanied by a challenge to existing stereotypes and a challenge to the media to produce more positive representations. It can be argued that this may be linked ideologically to such things as legislation promoting equal opportunities. Some people would argue that these groups remain marginalised; it is simply that the negative representation of them becomes less overt.

It can be argued that there has been a distinct change in the way in which gay men, for example, are now represented in the media. Homophobic representations, although they still exist, are significantly less prevalent than they were. Indeed, there seems in many areas of the media to be a focus on homo-erotic images, for example, in the way in which a figure like David Beckham is celebrated for his style and his physique. The demarcation 'gay' and 'straight' in media representation is perhaps no longer as clear-cut as it once seemed to be, reflecting the complexities of gender and sexual orientation in the twenty-first century. This may in part be due to an increasing acceptance within our culture of diversity. Representations themselves are not only more diverse, they are also much more subject to change. This can to some degree be accounted for by the influence of the web, where the anonymity afforded by online communications allows people to play with their identities, even to the point of changing their gender and sexual orientation at will.

Figure 4.5 David Beckham – celebrated for his style

An important aspect of a study of representation is that of the concept of identity. Our personal identities are to some degree established by the cultural products that we consume. These can determine our value system and beliefs through the perspective they offer us on the world. For many people, celebrities can become role models who, through their actions, determine how they live their own lives. Often these celebrities themselves adopt a persona or other personality to represent themselves to the world at large. The glamour model, Jordan, for example, is represented through two identities which seem at times at odds with each other. Her glamour model image, famous for its large surgically enhanced breasts, is counterpoised by the image of her 'real' self, Katie Price, mother of a child with a disability and wife of Peter Andre. Their lives are played out in the public arena of a reality television show, which seems appropriate given that their courtship was the public property of viewers of *I'm a Celebrity Get Me Out of Here!*

Peter and Katie provide an opportunity to explore a number of issues that relate to gender and more specifically gender relations. The traditional role of men, that of provider for wife and family, has to a large extent broken down as a consequence of economic social and cultural factors. Men, therefore, have found the need to reinvent themselves and the media have played a significant role in doing this. Gender, it is argued, has become a performance meaning that we act out male and female roles, many of which are learned from the media and the celebrities

Figure 4.6 Jordan and Peter Andre / Katie Price and Peter Andre

they feature. Peter and Katie are an interesting example of a celebrity couple in which gender roles are played out to suggest an equal partnership. Neither partner is seen to be dominant in the same way that Posh and Becks are equals with each having their own career. Richard and Judy, presenters of British daytime tv, are another husband and wife team whose media performance makes much of their equal partnership as a married couple.

You will find it useful to look at some examples of how other celebrities have sought to control the way in which their identities are represented through the media. Britney Spears would make an interesting study, given the way in which her identity has shifted from a seemingly puritanical lifestyle in her early career to one of a woman barely able to control her life.

ACTIVITY

Consider the media representation of minority groups:

■ Do you think the high-profile media representation of openly gay figures such as Graham Norton, Julian Clary and Paul O'Grady is a positive development for gay people? You might like to consider how these representations are likely to be read by both heterosexuals and gays.
■ Is there evidence that the representation of other minority groups is changing? You might like to look at minorities such as people with mental health problems, homeless people or economic migrants living in this country. How far is the representation different according to the context in which such social groups are represented?
■ Do you think that there has been any change in the way in which groups from different regions or cities are represented, for example, Liverpudlians or Irish people?

To some extent, the work of many activist groups fighting on behalf of minorities has at least drawn attention to the extent of negative stereotyping. For example, the feminist movement on both sides of the Atlantic has served to highlight the exploitation of women through the media in such forms as page-three girls in the tabloid press, and, more recently, the emergence of 'lad culture', with magazines such as *Loaded* using images of women in an exploitative way. (See also Chapter 11 on Lifestyle magazines.) On the other hand, it has been suggested that our culture has become feminised and that this has resulted in men being forced to adopt feminine behaviour, because of the pressures on them to be 'politically correct'. Modern-day celebrities and role models such as David Beckham are celebrated because they have 'feminine' qualities. Ironically, Victoria Beckham has been criticised for being too aggressive and 'pushy', traits considered inappropriate for women.

The pressure, both cultural and legislative, to be politically correct can be seen in the ways in which the representation of minority groups has changed. However, there has been an inevitable backlash in which being politically incorrect has become of focus for some media output. This is apparent in a programme like the BBC's *Little Britain*, in which Matt Lucas and David Walliams portray a range of 'British' characters in ways that can be seen as 'incorrect'. Of course, comedy may be seen as safe vehicle for this approach, as it allows the defence that this is not deliberately offensive but is rather an ironic commentary on contemporary cultural values and the collective British neurosis. In this case the context is of prime importance. If a character like Vicky Pollard, portrayed in *Little Britain*, were to appear in a storyline in *Coronation Street*, there might be a wholly different response to her. There was also considerable controversy over comments by Jade in *Celebrity Big Brother* in 2007.

It is also argued that the advent of 'lads' mags such as *FHM* and more recently *Zoo* and *Nuts* represents a male response to the influence of feminism. Lads, unable to cope with emancipation of women, have been forced to retreat into the fantasy world portrayed in these magazines of readily available and undemanding women.

Figure 4.7 Fat Fighters in *Little Britain* – what does this representation of a slimming club tell us about representations of beauty in the media?

It is important to note that there are sections of the media where the pressure to create positive representations has been taken on board. Advertising for Dove products (http://www.dove.co.uk/uk_en/uk_en/index.html) has challenged the idea of an 'ideal' body shape for women; indeed, it has created marketing materials that celebrate the diversity of shape and appearance that women possess. Interestingly, these products are directed specifically at a female market. You might ponder whether products aimed at other markets are likely to move in such a direction.

Certainly it is an interesting exercise to compare some of the stereotypical representation from the recent past with today. For example, *Carry On* films or 1970s television sitcoms such as *Mind Your Language*, frequently rerun on cable and satellite networks, were much more overtly sexist and homophobic than programmes today. However, many people would argue that the difference lies in the extent to which such negative attitudes are made manifest.

ACTIVITY

Choose a group of people that you consider to have been negatively represented in the media. Can you identify any members of the group who feature in the media and can be said to present a positive representation? For example, you might like to consider Victor Meldrew or Miss Marple as representatives of elderly people.

In the introduction to this book, you will have read about the way in which the attack on New York in September 2001 had a significant impact on the media. This has brought to the fore an important issue of representation which relates to the phenomenon of Islamophobia. The idea that an organisation like Al Qaeda could bring about such death and destruction on a city so closely associated with the power and might of the Western world has a profound impact on both the United States and Europe. Although in this country, the Blair government went to some lengths to make a distinction between terrorism and Islam, such a demarcation was not so readily made in some quarters of the media.

Islamophobia is a fear of Islam and a subsequent hatred of Islam and Muslims. The portrayal of Islam is that of a violent political movement, associated with attacks on Western democracies rather than as a religion. Such a representation associates Muslims as 'outsiders' within British culture, in some way inferior to and at odds with Western values. They are stereotyped as primitive and barbaric, especially in their treatment of women. Such hostility inevitably leads to discrimination and alienation, in much the same way as the stereotyping of other ethnic minorities. A key issue is the lack of a platform for Muslim groups to represent

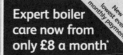

Figure 4.8

Figure 4.9

their own views and opinions about these issues. The control of the media is such that any representation of the Islamic world is largely through the eyes of the white, Christian, western media.

To some extent, opportunities have opened up for the Muslim world to take greater control over the way in which it is represented. The web, for example, provides opportunities through such sites as Islam OnLine for a direct representation of Islamic culture and values. Similarly, the television station Al Jazeera offers a different perspective on the Islamic world from that of mainstream Western media. Of course, the circulation of the information contained on these sites tends to be quite limited and has as its chief audience Muslim people rather than the broader mass audience that most media outlets address.

Post-colonialism is a cultural theory that offers us some perspective on the way in which the Western media control how other countries and groups of people are represented. Post-colonialism concerns itself with the way in which the national identities of colonies can be reclaimed after colonial oppression has ended and colonies have retrieved their independence. Just as Western cultures physically subjugated people in the colonies through force and subjugation, it can be argued that this oppression still takes place through the way in which the Western media represent their cultures and religions.

further reading

Whitehorn, K. (2000) 'Same Old Story', *Guardian*, 1 December.

MEDIA
INTERTEXTUALITY

In this chapter we look at the concept of intertextuality and explore
its role in Media Studies through:

- mimicry
- parody, pastiche and homage
- marketing of media texts
- the treatment of fictional soap opera stories in the tabloid press
- reviews of media texts in other media forms
- media performers as brands.

One of the pleasures that audiences experience in the consumption of media texts
is the joy of recognition. One form of this pleasure comes in recognising the
reference in one media text to other media texts. This process of referencing is
called intertextuality. In a media-saturated culture like Britain today, opportunities
for intertextual reference abound. With so much airtime to fill and so much space
in print and digital media formats, it is inevitable that the media should look to
itself for opportunities to generate material to fill up these spaces. New ideas are
seen as a precious commodity and media producers are inevitably keen that they
get maximum mileage from both new and existing ideas. A new television programme might once have filled the slot that it was allocated in the schedules, for
example, a one-hour prime-time slot. In today's multi-channel 24-hour television
environment, producers are keen to utilise such a programme well beyond its
immediate scheduled slot. Discussion of the programme on breakfast television
is likely to precede the screening in the form of interviews with the stars on the
GMTV sofa. Where possible, follow-up programmes will be spun off in such forms
as *Big Brother's Little Brother*.

Theories of intertextuality suggest that within a postmodern cultural context,
audiences inevitably read individual texts with an awareness of other texts to which
they might relate. In our reading of *The Simpsons* (see p. 96) we bring our cultural
experience of both other animated programmes and films as well as our knowledge

of situation comedy and the conventions by which that genre communicates with us, the audience.

Mimicry

This interdependent relationship between texts can take a number of different forms. It often transcends both genres and media forms so that a text created in one particular medium will be used in some way in another medium. Advertising and music videos are two genres that rely heavily on the use of intertextuality to achieve a particular effect. Often this borrowing of a text to link it to a second one is stylistic. This means that a text will mimic or otherwise copy certain stylistic features of another text. Usually this is done in order to create a particular impact, although there may be instances where this borrowing may seem simply a matter of convenience to give a music video, for example, a particular look. For the reader of the image, however, the connotative power of the original text is likely to be carried through into the new text.

An interesting example of intertextuality is the series *Secret Diary of a Call Girl* screened on ITV2 in autumn 2007 as part of a themed evening which the channel called XXL Thursdays. The programme has its origins in a book of the same name, the author of which was one Belle de Jour. The book itself was published as a result of a successful blog which published under the name of Belle de Jour, which purported to be a true account of the daily life of a high-class prostitute. At its most popular, 15,000 people a day were logging on to the site and the blog was chosen by the *Guardian* as its blog of the year in 2003. There was a great deal of speculation in the quality press about the identity of Belle de Jour, with *The Times* on one occasion claiming to have unmasked her, although her identity remains a secret. The star of the television series which caused some controversy was Billie Piper, once a pop singer, who had launched a successful career in the *Dr Who* series on BBC television. Belle de Jour became one of first examples of web-based product translating into mainstream television. 'Belle' also contributed a regular column to the *Daily Telegraph* up until 2006, entitled 'Belle de Jour's Naughty Notebook'.

Belle de Jour takes her name from the title of a film directed by Luis Buñuel and starring Catherine Deneuve, who played the role of a married woman who worked during the day in a Parisian brothel. The film, based on a 1928 novel written by Joseph Kessel, was released amid some controversy in 1967.

Parody, pastiche and homage

The postmodern critic Fredric Jameson has suggested a differentiation between *parody*, which aims to mock an original in a critical way, and *pastiche*, which he suggests is merely a stylistic mask. Pastiche simply uses images in an empty surface way in order to sell products. Parody for Jameson has substance; pastiche is merely a matter of imitating.

In the introduction to this book, we discussed the significance of postmodernism in any study of the media. You may find it useful to look back at that section in light of some of the ideas about intertextuality. Specifically, one of the concepts mentioned is *bricolage*, the French word for 'do-it-yourself'. The word also carries a more negative connotation of 'patching up'. As you will see, there is an obvious relevance to the idea of recycling earlier texts to produce 'new' ones. For example, the idea of sampling existing pieces of music and mixing them to create new ones is typical of this notion of bricolage. Some people would argue that this recycling represents an act of great creativity, while others would suggest that it is a symptom of the fact that people have run out of ideas, what Jameson calls 'the failure of the new'.

Certainly the insatiable demand for media texts in the postmodern, media-saturated world requires a large degree of recycling simply to meet this demand.

ACTIVITY

Watch a segment of output from MTV or a similar music channel.

■ How many of the videos that you encounter make some reference to other media texts you have come across?
■ How many of these can be said to be parody?
■ How many are pastiche?
■ What criteria have you used to distinguish this?

Obviously, parody can only be effective through our knowledge of the text or genre of text being parodied. We take a delight in the recognition of the elements being parodied, in what is called the 'shared cultural knowledge' which enables us to enjoy through recognition the relationship between the texts.

Similarly, some texts work through the idea of homage. Homage suggests respect for a particular text, acknowledging the power and importance of the original text by imitating it. Homage is commonly experienced in the cinema, where a director may deliberately create a scene, or even a whole film, in which the intertextual elements combine to pay respect to an earlier creation. The work of Alfred Hitchcock is frequently referred to in this way, through, for example, the work of directors such as Brian De Palma. *Film noir* is another cinematic style that is often imitated in contemporary cinema. Recent examples of *film noir*, sometimes referred to as neo-noir, such as De Palma's film *Black Dahlia* (2006), starring Josh Hartnett and Scarlett Johansson, have paid homage to the Hollywood genre that dominated the cinema in the 1940s and 1950s.

The series *The Simpsons* provides a particularly good example of how a television genre, in this case the situation comedy, can be parodied by the creation of a

Figure 5.1 *The Simpsons Movie* (2007)

sitcom family in the form of an animation. The programme employs many of the codes and conventions of the situation comedy format to satirise the lifestyle of middle America. First broadcast in December 1987, it has run for 20 years and in July 2007 a feature-length film *The Simpsons Movie* was released.

ACTIVITY

How can we distinguish homage from imitation or even plagiarism? Consider the many films that have simply copied the successful style of others.

What films have you seen that you think actually develop the style and themes of the original to which they relate?

Marketing of media texts

One area of the media in which intertextuality is important is in the marketing of media texts. In order for a media product to be promoted successfully, it is often advertised extensively. Some of this advertising will naturally be placed alongside existing products of a similar nature and form. Trailers on television and radio for programmes to be shown later in the schedules are a typical example of this. Even the early evening news is used to trail programmes later in the evening by thinly disguising them as news items. Examples of this include upcoming documentary 'exclusives' and even football matches or other events to be televised that evening.

further reading

Taylor, L. and Willis, A. (1999) *Media Studies: Texts, Institutions and Audiences*, Blackwell.

6 MEDIA IDEOLOGY

In this chapter we:

- consider the concept of ideology
- explain the nature and function of ideology
- assess its significance in studying the media.

Belief systems

As suggested in previous sections, as humans we experience a need to make sense of the world and the events that take place in it. One important way of doing this is through our consumption of media texts. It is often argued that all media texts are in some way ideological. On one level, ideology is the system of beliefs that organises the way in which we view the world and the events that take place in it. It follows, therefore, that in our consumption of media texts, we will be subjected to the ideological views of the producer of the text.

Ideologies come in a variety of different forms. Perhaps the most prevalent and obvious examples are the political and economic systems that govern the way in which people live their lives. Capitalism is an ideology that emphasises the importance for people in a society to be free to create wealth by setting up and running their own businesses. Marxism, on the other hand, is a belief system that considers that capitalism exploits the labour of the workers and argues that the state should own and control wealth creation and distribute it fairly among the population as a whole. Clearly these two ideologies are in conflict.

Religion, it can be argued, is an ideology in which an organised system of beliefs and values defines to people how they should live their lives and what constitutes appropriate behaviour. The stained-glass windows in a church, for example, traditionally portray a worldview and a set of values (symbolised by parables, for example) designed to instruct the local people in how to live their lives in a righteous and morally responsible way.

Figure 6.1 This stained glass window tells a story

Today the media have to a large degree replaced stained-glass windows as sources of ideology. Media messages, as we have seen, are constructed. In this process of construction, selection and shaping take place in order to represent the world outside. This selection and shaping reflect the value system of the originator of the message. An important question we need to ask when considering the ideology that lies behind a media message is this: 'In whose interest is it that we perceive the world this way?'

ACTIVITY

Consider a number of texts in which family life is depicted. These might include magazine articles and pictures, radio, television and print advertisements, and feature films. You could consider situation comedies such as *My Family*, whose narratives focus on everyday family life.

■   Are there consistent elements in the way families are represented? For example, do they tend to have two parents of the opposite sex?

Researchers such as the Glasgow Media Group have undertaken investigations that reveal that television news reporting on industrial disputes often depicts strikers as a disruptive force in society that needs to be resisted. This Marxist perspective sees such a representation as doing a good deal of ideological work to reinforce the belief that it is wrong to take industrial action. Ideologically we are being encouraged to see capitalism as a system that is basically fair and just. Workers who exercise their democratic right to withdraw their labour to achieve social justice through better pay and conditions are seen as disruptive and anti-social. Ideologically they are seen to represent subversive forces that threaten the very fabric of society.

As the vast majority of people in this country are workers, many of whom are likely to be dissatisfied with their pay and conditions, it can be argued that such a view is in the interests of those people who hold power within our society and who benefit from keeping workers on low pay. In a democracy, the people who hold power and rule over us have to do so to some extent with our consent. In this way, it can be argued that the media persuade people to act in a way that is not in their interests or the interests of the class to which they belong. Forces do exist that are capable of coercing people into behaving in certain ways – the police for example, or in extreme cases the armed forces. Generally, people have to be persuaded to allow other people to exercise power over them. Some see the media as a powerful tool to ensure the co-operation of the population in accepting the norms imposed by the ruling elite.

Hegemony is the concept used by the Marxist critic Antonio Gramsci to describe how people are influenced into accepting the dominance of a power elite who impose their will and worldview on the rest of the population. Gramsci argues that this elite is able to rule because the rest of the population allow it to do so. It can be argued, therefore, that the ideological role of the media is to persuade us that it is in our best interests to accept the dominance of this elite.

The American commentator Noam Chomsky argues that popular culture can be used to divert people's attention from real issues such as their conditions of employment; it is only the intellectual and educated classes in society, largely the professional classes, who must be persuaded to agree with the ideological values of the ruling elite.

ACTIVITY

- Make a list of some of the mass-media texts that could be viewed as a diversion from real issues and social conditions. In what ways do you think these texts act as a diversion?
- Which texts do you think are aimed at Chomsky's educated classes? Do you think there are any media texts that will appeal to both groups?

Such view of the ideological function of the media can at times appear to suggest that a conspiracy is taking place. It gives an impression that there is a collective viewpoint among the media and it is the function of individual media texts to perpetrate a specific ideological viewpoint. Supporters of such a view would argue that much of the influential mainstream media are in the hands of a relatively small number of people. They point to the ways in which politicians keep on the right side of media moguls such as Rupert Murdoch, whose support for one or other political party is said to have determined the outcome of the general election over at least the past 25 years.

An alternative viewpoint suggests that audiences are far more resilient to the influence of media. A liberal pluralist stance on this issue would argue that in Britain today there are so many different media 'voices' that the power to influence opinion in this way is quite limited. Not only is there a saturation of mainstream 'voices' vying for the attention of the audience, but also a democratisation of the media through the opportunity for individuals to contribute their own views, often in the form of web-based technologies. This might take the form of blogs or podcasts or alternatively it might be public feedback that people are invited to leave at the end of a story on a newspaper website. In this context readers can leave their views on anything from a major news story to a sports story in the form of football transfer gossip.

One way in which ideology can be seen to work through the media is by means of repetition. One isolated story of an asylum seeker represented as an unnecessary drain on our national resources is unlikely to make a huge difference in our attitudes to immigration as a social issue. However, when newspaper headlines and television reports repeatedly represent the issue in this way, there is a cumulative effect which is likely to influence the way we view it. Similarly, repeatedly seeing celebrities represented in expensive clothing, 'enjoying a fun lifestyle', is likely to influence the social aspirations of many people who see such a lifestyle as highly desirable and a reward for winning celebrity status.

Big Brother

Let us look at a particular example of the way in which the media can be seen to shape our attitudes in order to accept what is best for the elite in power.

The idea of 'Big Brother' has always had strong negative connotations in our society. The freedom to go about one's daily business without being spied on has been considered a fundamental human right. In his novel *1984* (which was subsequently made into a film), George Orwell offered a nightmare vision of a society in which a citizen's every move was watched, leaving little opportunity to oppose the oppressive power of the state.

Figure 6.2 It has been estimated that there are in excess of 4 million CCTV cameras operating in the UK

Today, however, nearly every public building and every town centre has surveillance cameras that watch every move of the people who occupy these spaces. The majority of people accept the presence of the cameras, and many would argue that they serve the public good as they act as an effective deterrent against crime. Clearly there has been a shift in consciousness on the part of the population from the paranoia of the Big Brother idea to the acceptance of the concept of surveillance. An important mechanism by which this change has been brought about is the media. Programmes such as *Police, Camera, Action!* make extensive use of footage from such cameras. These clips are often accompanied by a commentary from a reputable media personality, such as a newsreader, extolling the advantages

Figure 6.3 Shows like *Police, Camera, Action!* use the footage from many CCTV cameras

of the cameras in detecting crime. Commonly we are presented with a chase in which cameras, for example, in a police helicopter, offer the audience a privileged vantage point from which to observe the chase, which leads to the arrest of the criminals. As the narrative unfolds, we are positioned to identify with the forces of law and order as they use this sophisticated equipment to keep crime off our streets.

The ideology behind surveillance cameras is an example of how the media can be used to shape social attitudes and gain the acceptance of a population for something that may seem to be against their interests. It also demonstrates how ideologies do not remain fixed or static. In many respects, the media are part of a battleground in which different power elites fight for supremacy in terms of the acceptance of their ideas.

The concept of ideology is closely allied to that of representation. One way in which ideology works through media texts is by the simple process of repetition. This is particularly true of repeated representations across media forms, which can have the effect of naturalising a way of seeing an issue so that it seems that no other interpretation is possible.

So changed is the ideological meaning of 'Big Brother' that it was used as the title of one of the most talked-about television programmes at the beginning of the twenty-first century. A group of people locked in a house, trying to win a prize by staying the longest, became the focus of the nation's attention. The filming of their every action provided voyeuristic entertainment for the nation and the media, beginning with the first series in the summer of 2000. Instead of Big Brother watching us, we took our pleasure from watching *Big Brother*.

Ideology and gender

You will have probably realised that one way of viewing ideology is in terms of the power relations within a society. As we have seen, the concept of hegemony is one of the ways in which one group of people can maintain power over other groups through their co-operation rather than by means of coercion. You might like to consider this idea in relation to minority groups within British society.

As we have seen, family life is nearly always depicted as being a happy and desirable state, with married couples bringing up children. On the other hand, consider the negative representation of people who do not go out to work and earn a living. They are called scroungers and are depicted as people who live off the backs of other people who work hard for a living. Single mothers, for example, have often been demonised in this way.

The effect of these representations is cumulative and, as we saw with stereotypes, they deny the complexity of human existence and reduce it to a simplistic issue of right or wrong. This can be seen in terms of going to work and using your earnings to support your family being 'right' and being unemployed and not being able to support your family being 'wrong'.

ACTIVITY

What do you think is the ideological work of game shows and quiz programmes?

An interesting and useful way of looking at ideology is through its impact on minority groups within society. Despite the ground won by the feminist movement in the emancipation of women, it is generally accepted that we still live in a patriarchal society, that is, one dominated by men, who retain most of the power. Clearly it is not in the interests of women to occupy a position of inferiority to men. However, the ideological work of the media is such that women are represented so as to accept this subordinate position as being both natural and inevitable and in some way 'right'. If we were to make a list of typical depictions

Figure 6.4 Harrison Ford, 65, in *Indiana Jones and the Kingdom of the Crystal Skull* (2008). How many successful, working, 65-year-old actresses can you think of? How many are in action or adventure films?

of women in the media, we would find a preponderance of images in which women are positioned in a domestic situation; as objects for the pleasure of men and as partners to men.

An interesting comparison can be made with the way in which ageing Hollywood stars are depicted. Generally when a female star ceases to be 'young and attractive' she is seen in fewer and fewer screen roles. She is then replaced with the latest and most attractive young starlet. Male stars, however, go on well past their youth and prime, many working into their old age.

One inference we can make from this is that women in Hollywood movies are seen to be of interest only when they are young, attractive and sexually desirable. In an important essay on the image of women in the cinema, 'Visual pleasure and narrative cinema' (1975), Laura Mulvey uses ideas based on psychoanalysis to argue that the main source of visual pleasure in the cinema is the voyeuristic male viewer enjoying the image of the female body. In order for a woman to experience pleasure from the film, she has to position herself in a similar role to that of a male viewer enjoying the spectacle. Ideologically, it can be argued that this positioning aims to persuade women that by occupying a role similar to that of the women on screen, they will become desirable and attractive to men, thus reinforcing a woman's subordinate position within a patriarchy.

In this way, the ideological function of many media texts is to identify for women how they should perform within a patriarchy. Magazines aimed at young girls contain articles and features on how to look attractive and to suggest ways in which to develop relationships with boys. Ideologically, it is clearly the premise that happiness for a young girl is to be found in the arms of a male partner. Similarly, the output of both television and magazines aimed at women suggests the importance of their domestic and childbearing roles. Women who are able to juggle the demands of a career as well as these other duties are celebrated. Men on the other hand are only expected to be successful in their jobs.

Angela McRobbie in 1983 made a study of a magazine called *Jackie*, which was popular with teenage girls. She wrote how girls were being introduced into the sphere of feminine consumption. It can be argued that magazines of this type work ideologically to define for their audience those domestic roles of wife and mother that they should accept and embrace.

Another ideological impact of the media is through what is known as 'moral panic'. This is basically a scare story, often with little basis in truth, which serves to persuade people of the need for drastic action to cure a social ill. Horror videos, dangerous breeds of dog, asylum seekers, and the recreational use of drugs have all been at the centre of moral panics. This panic is often orchestrated by the tabloid press and has the ideological impact of people demanding immediate action, usually to ban the availability of such things, without any rational consideration of whether this is an appropriate reaction or not. More recently moral panics have emerged in the media in relation to gun and knife crime, particularly within inner cities. (See also section 'The "effects" debate and moral panics' in Chapter 7, p. 135.)

Speaking of way in which the government uses propaganda about drug abuse in the United States, Noam Chomsky said:

> **One of the traditional and obvious ways of controlling people in every society, whether it's a military dictatorship or a democracy, is to frighten them. If people are frightened, they'll be willing to cede authority to their superiors who will protect them: 'OK, I'll let you run my life in order to protect me,' that sort of reasoning.**
>
> **So the fear of drugs and the fear of crime is very much stimulated by state and business propaganda.**

(Noam Chomsky interviewed by John Veit in *High Times*, April 1998; see http://www.chomsky.info/interviews/199804--.htm)

It is clear that the media play a role in shaping our ideas and attitudes. What is much less clear is the extent to which they do so and perhaps, more significantly, how the technological changes that are taking place in the way in which we communicate are likely to influence the degree to which the media are able wield this power.

further reading

Dyer, G. (1982) 'Conclusion' in *Advertising as Communication*, Methuen.
Klein, N. (2001) *No Logo*, Flamingo.

7 MEDIA AUDIENCES

In this chapter we look at:

- how audiences are made up and how our engagement with media forms is patterned and determined
- ways in which audiences are becoming increasingly segmented
- terms such as 'hypodermic needle theory', 'uses and gratifications', 'mode of address' and 'situated culture'
- some of the issues around the 'effects' debate
- 'passive' and 'active' views of the audience and how audience participation is increasing.

Different types of audience

In one sense everyone is part of the audience in that we are all, to some degree or other, exposed to media texts. However, it can sometimes be difficult to stand back and think about the different ways in which our daily lives interact with the media. It is well worth considering the extent to which, in an average day, we will be part of many different audiences for a wide range of media (see website activities I.1 and I.2 in the Introduction). This may include being part of a radio audience in the morning as we get ready for college, school or work, watching breakfast television or reading the newspaper, listening to music on an MP3 player, logging on to read our emails and surf the web, sharing photos or texting friends on our mobile phones, or glimpsing advertising hoardings as we travel to school, college or work.

Throughout the day we will be, either consciously or unconsciously, exposed to different media products – becoming part of many different types of audience. As we mentioned in the Introduction, it may be as part of an audience of over 9 million people all watching the same episode of *EastEnders* at the same time. Or it may be as part of an audience sitting alone in our cars listening to the same radio show, or as one of 300 people watching a film together in a cinema. It can also be through

Figure 7.1

the more personal and private consumption of MP3 players, newspapers (either local or national), or magazines, or through the one-to-one communication of texts or email. We may work in an environment in which a radio is on in the background, or somewhere – for example, a hospital or a shop – that has its own radio station. We may also have access to a computer at work or whilst studying where we can listen to a radio station (according to the Radio Advertising Bureau (RAB) at any given time 20 per cent of Internet users are listening to the radio – see http://www.rab.co.uk/rab2006/showContent.aspx?id=1425). Or we may receive up-to-date RSS news feeds from newspapers or news agencies.

Why are audiences important?

There are several reasons why audiences are important. The first is perhaps the most obvious.

■ Without an audience, why would anyone create a media text? What is the point of a film that no one sees?
■ Audience size and reaction are often seen as a way of measuring the success (or otherwise) of a media product. One of the reasons why we say that the *Sun* newspaper is successful is because it sells over 3 million copies a day and is read by nearly 12 million people.

- Audiences who buy media texts are providing income for the media companies that produce them.
- Much of the media available to us, however, are free or subsidised; they are financed by advertising, and the advertisers want to know that they are getting value for money. In other words, they want to know how many, and what types of people are seeing their advertisements.
- As the media become more central to our lives, so many people want to know how we use the media, what we understand of what we consume, and the effects that the media have on our lives.

How have audiences changed?

Concerns about the size and impact of the media on audiences, the 'effectiveness' of advertising, and how audiences interrelate with the media, have been with us since the development of a 'mass' audience at the beginning of the twentieth century.

We know that the media are constantly changing, and this means that audiences, too, must be changing, partly as a result of the changes in media technology but also because of the changes in the way we live our lives and because we as individuals change. Cinema audiences in the 1950s wore special glasses to watch such films as *It Came from Outer Space* (1953) and *Creatures from the Black*

Figure 7.2

Lagoon (1954), which were made with special 3D effects that made the monsters seem to come out of the screen to attack the audience. Although this was seen as a gimmick in the 1950s and the films quickly disappeared, there has been a reappearance of 3D effects in recent years, especially through the growth of IMAX cinemas, where, once again, audiences wearing special glasses can see characters and objects appearing to fly around in space in front of them. Soon, it is predicted we will have access to 3D television programmes.

The word 'broadcasting' implies a 'few-to-many' model where a small number of broadcasters transmit programmes to a 'mass' audience of perhaps more than 30 million people all watching or listening to the same event, at the same time, participating in the same experience. The 1966 World Cup final attracted a television audience of 32 million viewers, while the wedding of Prince Charles and Lady Diana in 1981 attracted 39 million. It is estimated that over 2 billion people tuned in to watch artists and concerts from *Live Earth* in July 2007 and, perhaps more significantly, there were over 10 million live online video feeds from the concerts distributed around the world. Increasingly, new technology is resulting in a 'many-to-many' model through social networking sites and peer-to-peer (P2P) file sharing over the internet.

Today we have a very wide range of broadcasting and press services available to us. Radio and television, in particular, have moved away from the original ideas of addressing a large 'mass' audience. Today the concept is one of narrowcasting, where programmes are aimed at specific, specialist audiences in a way that is similar to the range and variety of magazines available in a newsagent. There is now a wide range of specialist channels and stations aimed at small and specific markets that might be defined on the grounds of age (Classic FM, Disney, or Angel Radio in Havant, where they refuse to play any music recorded after 1959), gender (the digital television channels Dave or NUTS), interests (most obviously sports channels, but also television channels such as National Geographic, UK History, Sky Arts or Teachers TV) or ethnicity (radio stations such as Sunrise in London and Bradford or television channels such as PCNE Chinese, Bangla TV or Channel East, aimed at Chinese or other Asian audiences). All of these television and radio stations, magazines and newspapers (both local and national) are now supplemented by websites that offer a more specialist range of services for consumers (see, for example, http://angelradio.moonfruit.com/ 'Snap...Crackle...but no pop').

This change from 'broadcasting' to 'narrowcasting' partly results from the development of new digital technologies that are increasingly becoming part of our ordinary domestic lives. These include products such as DVD players and recorders, computers (both at home and at school, college or work) and cheap satellite and cable television receivers. For instance, once upon a time it was the norm for a household to have only one television set, often placed in the living room and usually with the furniture organised around it. Before that it was not unusual for households to have just one radio (or wireless) set that would also have been placed in the living room and the furniture arranged around it. The illustration on the cover of the *Radio Times* (Figure 7.3) represents a view of how families were thought to consume radio in the 1930s and 1940s.

Website Activity 7.1: Researching the way people used to consume the media.

In the Introduction we asked you to measure the amount of media hardware you have in your household. As you will have discovered, today most households have several radios and televisions spread around the house, perhaps in bedrooms as well as in the living room, maybe in the kitchen and, in the case of radios, in cars and as part of hi-fi systems or MP3 players. Many homes will also be able to receive radio and television programmes through their personal computers. Part of the reason for this growth in hardware is that personal computers, television sets and radios have all become both increasingly cheap to buy, more compact in size, and can offer a growing range of functions and services. When colour television sets first came on the market, they cost the equivalent of several weeks' wages, whereas today they represent less than one week's wages. Radio receivers, television screens and MP3 players are becoming smaller and smaller and can now be incorporated into other technology such as mobile phones. As more and more of our lives become linked with media consumption and as more and more of our peers have several radio and television sets, so there can be a pressure on us as consumers to buy more and more of these products – especially when we are told that each new piece of technology is better than the previous one. In the Introduction we also asked you to consider how quickly the media hardware in your household has changed and what has happened to older hardware such as cassette decks, record players or CRT-televisions. Increasingly, advertisers try to persuade us that up-to-date hardware is an important part of who we are and our 'modern' lifestyle.

ACTIVITY

Compare the cover of the *Radio Times* in Figure 7.3 with the covers of current listings magazines to see what types of images are used today (see also Chapter 6 on media ideology). In what ways are the images on today's listing magazines different to those from the *Radio Times* in 1949? What assumptions do the images on the listings magazine make about the audience today and how they consume television?

Figure 7.3 *Radio Times* cover, 30 September 1949

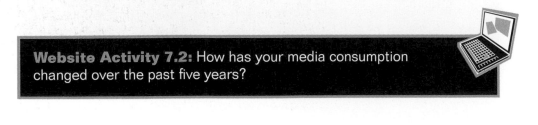

Website Activity 7.2: How has your media consumption changed over the past five years?

Some of the changes you may have identified in the ways in which we consume media products will have come about because of the increase in services available to us. When television first started it was broadcast for only a few hours a day, mostly in the evening, and the BBC had something called 'the toddlers' truce', when television closed down at teatime, after children's television, to allow parents to put their children to bed. On Sundays broadcasting was very limited because it was assumed that most people would be going to church services or wanting religious programming.

Now we have several hundred television channels that broadcast 24 hours a day. Part of the reason for this is that television companies now recognise that there are many different groups of audiences who watch television at different times of the day and want different types of programmes.

'Martini media'

Today the rate of change is becoming faster and it is difficult to predict what our domestic media will look like in ten years' time. Mark Thompson, the current Director-General of the BBC, when launching the BBC's plans for a digital future, talked of the new world of 'Martini media' where viewers and listeners want to pick 'n mix their programmes 'anytime, anyplace, anywhere' (see www.bbc.co.uk/ pressoffice/speeches/stories/highfield_ft). 'We', the audience, are increasingly becoming members of various communities who, probably for some of our time, will watch or listen to BBC programmes but not necessarily when they are transmitted. Today we can re-listen to radio broadcasts or view again television programmes over the internet. We can time-shift with DVD and hard-drive recorders, and tomorrow we will have access to 'tv-on-demand', possibly through our mobile-phone-cum-MP3 player. It is increasingly difficult in an age of Electronic Programme Guides (EPGs) and online broadcasting to know exactly when, how or why members of audiences may consume a particular television programme. This not only raises questions for public service providers like the BBC but also for the more traditional, terrestrial providers who have largely survived financially on the basis of delivering large cohorts of audiences to advertisers.

The 'free' audience for programmes such as *The Premiership* or *Match of the Day* is likely to decline as more and more football clubs offer their own subscription channels, like Manchester United's MUTV, or because of the growth of 'interactive' digital channels such as the Sky Sport channels or Setanta Sports, which offer the viewer a choice of camera angles, instant replays and additional information about players and teams. It is also possible to select your own 'news story' on digital news channels, while travel channels offer the opportunity to book holidays as well as giving weather details from around the world.

We are also becoming more reliant on the mobile phone instead of Radio 1's *Chart Show* to give us the latest record charts (which today also include sales of music 'downloads' as well as the number of actual records sold) and we will be able to download and play the latest releases and order tickets for concerts at the same time. When the Chemical Brothers' album, *Push the Button*, was released, over 275,000 people sampled the tracks by pressing the red button on their television remote controls during advertisements for the album that were broadcast in shows such as *The Simpsons* and *Soccer am* (see http://www.thinkbox.tv/server/show/ConCaseStudy.10).

However, there are some observers who are concerned that those who are less affluent may end up with an inferior and limited, but 'free', choice. The popularity of the BBC Freeview digital service suggests that there are a large number of people who want access to digital services but do not want the range that is on offer via the subscription packages. BBC's Freeview can also be seen as an attempt to 'marry' new digital services with the BBC's public service broadcasting remit. Freesat offers the same service but for those who are unable to use their rooftop aerial.

Part of the change that has occurred over the years reflects the way in which the technology that produces media texts has changed. The introduction of such innovations as the 'Steadicam' or high-definition portable digital video-cameras has made news, documentaries and 'live' programming much more 'action-packed' and attractive to viewers. There was a vogue a few years ago for investigative programmes that used small hidden cameras to expose various malpractices. Consider, for example, the technology required to produce a programme like Channel Four's *Big Brother*, or the way in which video-phones are used in the reporting of the Iraqi and Afghan wars.

Another example of how our patterns of consumption have changed is cinema attendance in this country.

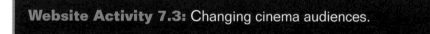

Website Activity 7.3: Changing cinema audiences.

How is audience consumption patterned and determined?

We have already mentioned how we, as audiences, use different media at different times of the day. It is worth spending a little more time exploring the relationship between our patterns of media consumption and the routines of our daily lives. One indication of the extent to which we now live in a media-saturated society is the degree to which our routine daily activities are interlinked with the media.

Many of us wake up in the morning to the sounds of a radio rather than an alarm clock. We may possibly have gone off to sleep with the same radio playing and set to its 'sleep' function. Many televisions also have the same feature, although it may be harder to imagine drifting off to sleep part way through a television

Figure 7.4

programme or a film (intentionally at least!). We have also already mentioned breakfast television, which many of us now take for granted as a way of getting the latest news over our breakfast or whilst getting ready for school, college or work. We may also check our emails or texts before setting off to work, school or college.

The programmes we watch and/or listen to in the morning often have regular features or segments that are broadcast at the same time each day. In this way we are able to measure our progress each morning by their regular appearance, for example, the news headlines, reviews of the day's newspapers or spoof 'wake-up' calls made to unsuspecting members of the public.

It is interesting to reverse the equation and consider to what extent the media *organise* our daily routines rather than just fitting in around them. Some people will refuse to go out in the evening or to answer the telephone or speak to visitors until their favourite programme has ended. Mid-morning television shows encourage housewives to sit down with a cup of coffee and relax after getting the family off to work and/or school. Increasingly, television programmes ask us to phone or text in during certain times to win prizes, join in a vote or offer our opinion.

ACTIVITY

Consider your own daily/weekly routine and the manner in which the media interweave with it.

Consider too the extent to which your consumption of the media fits around your schedule or whether your schedule is to some extent shaped by your media consumption. Do you, for example, sometimes plan your activities around particular media output?

If you look at the radio or television schedules, you will notice that particular categories of audiences are addressed and particular genres of programmes are featured at particular times of the day. We are all familiar with the notion of 'peak viewing time', but it is perhaps more interesting to look at the schedules outside this period to see what types of audience are being addressed, say, between 9 am and lunchtime on a weekday on the different channels or on a Saturday or Sunday morning. One of the 'battlegrounds' between mainstream television channels such as BBC2, ITV1 and C4 is the early evening slot between 5.00 pm and 7.00 pm. There has been fierce competition between programmes such as *The Weakest Link*, *Deal or No Deal*, *Golden Balls*, etc.

ACTIVITY

Look at the current schedules to see what programmes are currently being broadcast and then consult the BARB website to see which of these shows is the most popular. Try to identify who the audience is for these shows and why the shows are so popular. Why do you think the television companies think this is an important slot to 'win'?

Website Activity 7.4: Looking at the TV schedules.

Popular media such as television and the press try to make the most of special occasions like royal or sporting events. They attempt to turn these occasions into rituals in which the media play a central part. The idea of a typical Christmas Day that centres around the television is one example – it is assumed that the family cannot fully celebrate Christmas without watching the Queen's Speech, film premieres and special editions of popular programmes.

Sporting events such as the World Cup or the Olympics are other occasions on which we, the audience, are encouraged to celebrate the success (or otherwise) of our teams through our participation in a 'television event' that often has special theme tunes (*Nessun Dorma* for the 1990 World Cup is perhaps one of the best-known examples) and a special presentation studio for links and interviews. The normal schedules may be changed to highlight the importance and uniqueness of the occasion. There will probably also be special 'souvenir' editions of television listings magazines or newspaper supplements in which we can get background information and keep a record of the progress of the events.

One of the reasons why media companies like to turn these occasions into rituals is that by packaging them in this way, they hope to attract larger audiences than normal. These packages can then be sold on to advertisers. Another reason is that, as pay-per-view becomes increasingly available, it is a way of making these broadcasts look 'special' and worth paying extra money for. This is increasingly the case with sporting events such as world championships in, for example, cricket, rugby, boxing or golf.

ACTIVITY

Imagine that you have been asked to give a presentation on the costs and benefits of various television and radio packages.

- Compare the prices of the television licence and the various costs of digital television and radio packages.
- Highlight what you consider to be the main benefits of each one and the main disadvantages.
- In your presentation say which is cheaper and explain which you think offers best value.

Increasingly, telephone and broadband services are being included in these packages, why do you think this is?

Who is the audience?

Many commentators suggest that in any text there is an implied audience, and that the producers of media texts have a 'typical' audience member in mind when they start to create a text. (Look at Chapter 13 on production.)

Ien Ang, in *Desperately Seeking the Audience* (1991), discusses the manner in which media producers and institutions view audiences as an 'imaginary entity', as a mass rather than as a set of individuals. They will, however, often have a 'typical' audience member in mind when they produce their texts.

In the 1980s, trainee ILR (Independent Local Radio) presenters were supposed to have had an imaginary person, 'Doreen', whom they were told to consider as the 'typical listener'. Presenters were told about her age, her likes and dislikes, her habits, her household and her husband. They were told that Doreen is 'typical'. She is educated and intelligent but may only listen to the radio with half an ear and does not necessarily understand long words or complicated discussions. They were told that this does not mean that Doreen is stupid and should be talked down to, but that they should make sure that she understands and is engaged with what is happening on the radio. They were encouraged to address Doreen and her husband personally, as if they knew them.

Academic research, however, has produced another version of this 'imaginary entity'. In *Understanding News* (1982), Hartley identified seven types of what he called 'subjectivities' that are used by media producers to help define the social position of the individual audience member and to engage with him or her:

■ self-image
■ gender
■ age group
■ family
■ class
■ nation
■ ethnicity.

Fiske, in *Television Culture* (1987), added four more:

■ education
■ religion
■ politics
■ location (geographical and local).

However, Hartley acknowledged that sometimes these categories can get mixed up or can conflict with one another; for instance, some notions of nationhood and some types of ethnicity (Hartley 1982: 69). It is also not clear to what extent these subjectivities are equal or whether in particular circumstances some may be more influential than others.

These categories are useful in identifying the way in which individual members of mass audiences are identified both by themselves and by media producers and advertisers. Fiske, talking about television, says that it 'tries to construct an ideal subject position which it invites us to occupy, and, if we do, rewards us with . . . the pleasure of recognition' (Fiske 1987: 51).

ACTIVITY

Using the subjectivities above, try to construct a profile of an 'ideal viewer/ reader' for a particular programme or /publication. Consider what clues to this type of person there are in programmes such as *Newsround* or *The Bill* or in a newspaper like the *Daily Express*. Apart from the categories already listed, consider also the likes and dislikes the 'typical' members of these audiences might have, their interests, their taste in clothes and music, the types of books and/or magazines that they consume.

- Give your 'typical' viewer a name and a place to live.
- Compare your profile with those produced by others. Discuss and account for similarities and/or differences.

'Television doesn't make programmes, it creates audiences' (Jean-Luc Godard)

Advertising is important to a whole range of media products because these products are financed by advertising revenue or are subsidised by the revenue that advertising brings in. The media therefore spend a lot of time and money looking at the circulation and ratings of their products.

Even if you pay for some media products, the advertising can still have subsidised the price and made the product cheaper for you to buy. Take a local weekly newspaper such as the *Wiltshire Times*, which costs 60p a copy and is probably considered a good buy for that price. It will have lots of local information, stories and photographs. However, if we look through the *Wiltshire Times*, we see that nearly 40 per cent of it is made up of advertisements, either for such products as cars, computers or shop goods, or for job vacancies, private car sales and other services (classified ads). One of the reasons why people buy this newspaper is to obtain the information contained in the advertisements. If we want to buy a new car, find somewhere local to live, or see what is on at the cinema, we can look through the advertisements in our local paper and see what is available.

The cover price of the *Wiltshire Times*, 60p, probably represents about 15 or 20 per cent of the true cost of printing an edition of the paper. Without the advertising the reader might have to pay about £3 a copy, and at that price it is unlikely that the *Wiltshire Times* would sell many copies. A few years ago there was an enormous growth of free local newspapers that were financed purely through their advertising revenue. The *Wiltshire Times* has a circulation of about 19,000, but the company that publishes it also publishes several other local newspapers, both free and paid for, whose circulation varies between 20,000 and 50,000. It also has a website: http://www.wiltshiretimes.co.uk/news/

Similarly, if you buy magazines, you are certainly not paying for the full cost of producing them. The advertising revenue is probably paying up to three-quarters of the production costs.

The attraction for the advertiser is that these media outlets provide an opportunity to advertise their products to particular social groups of people. In relation to the

Figure 7.5

Wiltshire Times, it is a group of people defined by the particular area in which they live. The newspaper will probably have a lot more additional information about its readers in terms of demographics – age, social class, gender, income – similar to the 'subjectivities' that Hartley and Fiske identified. The newspaper will have spent a lot of time and money trying to identify and categorise its readers so that it can then 'sell' these readers to its advertisers.

You may think that this does not apply to the BBC because it does not take advertising. Certainly it is true that at present on its main channels the BBC does not have 'paid for' advertising, but it is moving into other types of services and many BBC programmes are available on digital channels via subscription, and many of its magazines, for example, *Top Gear* and *Gardeners' World*, carry commercial advertising.

The BBC is also in competition with the commercial channels in an attempt to prove its popularity and to justify the licence fee. If the BBC's audience share falls below a certain level, the criticisms of its licence fee increase. (See 'Public Service Broadcasting (PSB)' in Chapter 8 on institutions, p. 163.)

Being able to identify both the size and type of their audience is very important for both the BBC and commercial media. There are various organisations who carry out this research and whose findings are sold to media companies. Currently BARB measures the audiences for the five terrestrial channels and all the digital channels. According to BARB, its ratings are based on the use of 5,100 panel homes, representing about 11,500 viewers. As the way we consume television is changing with the introduction of many more digital channels, 'narrowcasting', 'time-shifting' (recording programmes and watching them later) and the 'shuffling' of programmes (when they are repeated several times a day or over several days), television companies and BARB will need to develop ways of measuring much smaller but more specialised audiences (there is more information regarding viewing figures and statistics at http://www.bfi.org.uk/filmtvinfo/gateway/ categories/statistics/).

Both NRS (National Readership Survey) and ABC (Audit Bureau of Circulation) carry out a similar function for the newspaper and magazine industry, producing circulation figures, but using different methods. ABC measures the sales of newspapers and magazines, whilst NRS interviews a sample of approximately 40,000 people about their reading habits. RAJAR (Radio Joint Audience Research) also uses the sample method and compiles both BBC and commercial radio listening figures. All these organisations have websites that contain up-to-date figures as well as explaining how they carry out their research (http://www.nrs.co.uk; http://www.abc.org.uk; http://www.rajar.co.uk).

Another industry-based organisation that offers detailed information regarding newspaper circulation and readership is JICREG – the Joint Industry Committee for Regional Press Research (http://www.jicreg.co.uk/about/index.cfm).

Website Activity 7.5: Local newspaper readership

According to the Radio Advertising Bureau, all commercial radio stations have a clearly defined core target audience – those who are at the centre of its market and who, it is hoped, will become station 'loyalists'. Around this core are other, secondary, listeners.

All of these organisations use the same categories for classifying audiences. These are based on the National Readership Survey's social grades used in advertising and market research. This divides the adult population of Britain into six grades and identifies the types of occupation that each grade represents and (as at 2005) the percentage of the population that fits into that particular grade:

A   Higher managerial, administrative or professional 3.8%
B   Intermediate managerial, administrative or professional 22.1%
C1   Supervisory or clerical, junior managerial, administrative or professional 28.9%
C2   Skilled manual workers 20.6%
D   Semi-skilled and unskilled manual workers 16.2%
E   Casual labourers, unemployed, state pensioners 8.4%

Sex, age and ethnicity are also important. Age is generally divided into the following categories:

<15
15–24
24–35
35–55
55>

(For more detailed information on how the National Readership Survey categorises the British public, see its website http://www.nrs.co.uk/open_access/open_methadology/index.cfm.)

Research within ethnic minority groups published by Ofcom in June 2007 found that

> **consumers from ethnic minority groups are among the most enthusiastic and technology aware consumers of communications services in the UK . . . [however] they watch less TV – especially the biggest traditional channels and those with internet are more likely to have broadband and to use and depend on a mobile phone than the rest of the population.**

http://www.ofcom.org.uk/media/news/2007/06/nr_20070621

The statistical information provided by organisations such as BARB and RAJAR is then supplemented by more detailed and qualitative data about audiences. This is often carried out by advertising or marketing companies for particular broadcasters and media companies, and focuses on the audience's lifestyle, their habits, opinions and sets of values and attitudes. Advertising companies claim that they can segment audiences on the basis of 'socio-economic values' such as:

Survivors   Those who want security and like routine
Social climbers Those who have a strong materialistic drive and like status symbols
Care givers   Those who believe in 'caring and sharing'
Explorers   Those for whom personal growth and influencing social change are important.

Thinkbox is the television marketing body for many of the main UK commercial broadcasters and aims to help advertisers get the best out of television. They offer their clients profiles of various audience types such as 'Stylish singletons (independent, single, career-minded women in their 30s); Technophiles (enthusiastic pioneers of new technology) and Tweenies (brand-conscious 10–12 year olds) . . . Flourishing Fifties, Wise Guys and Yummy Mummies.' (Although you have to register, you can get more detailed information about these groups at http://www.thinkbox.tv/server/show/nav.00100d00a.)

These socio-economic groups may be given a variety of names (see, for example, the Insight Social Value Groups at http://www.businessballs.com/demographics classifications.htm), but they are all based on the work of the American psychologist Abraham Maslow and his idea of a 'Hierarchy of Needs' (see Figure 7.6). Maslow suggested that we all have different 'layers' of needs and that we need to satisfy one before we can move on to the next. In other words, we all start at the bottom of Maslow's hierarchy, having basic physiological needs such as food and shelter for our survival. We can then move up the hierarchy to the level of safety needs, probably to do with having a regular income, from a job for example, which guarantees us a regular source of food and shelter – perhaps being able to pay the rent or mortgage. The next level is to do with belonging to a social group, whether it be our family, work colleagues or peer group. In fact most of us belong to a variety of different social groups, for example, as students, family members, social groups, work groups and so on. Our esteem needs are to do with wanting to gain the respect and admiration of others, perhaps through the display of status symbols such as expensive consumer goods. Maslow argues that many people stop at particular levels and only a very few reach 'self-actualisation' at the top of the hierarchy. These are the people who are considered to be in control of their lives and to have achieved all their goals.

Advertisers are increasingly using ideas like Maslow's and are combining both demographics and lifestyle categories in an attempt to be more effective and efficient in how they target particular groups of people. They are trying to sell their products in a way that meets the target audience's perceived needs. (There is

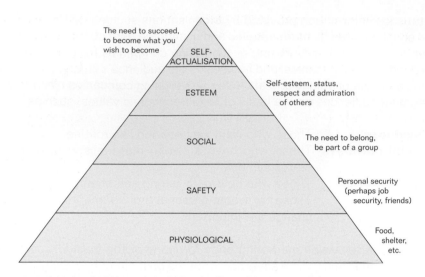

Figure 7.6 Maslow's Hierarchy of Needs (from Maslow 1943)

more information on Maslow's Hierarchy of Needs at http://www.businessballs.com/maslow.htm.)

Website Activity 7.7: 'Pitching' a film.

> **We must get away from the habit of thinking in terms of what the media do to people and substitute for it the idea of what people do with the media.**

(Halloran 1970)

The history of audience research is a story of the shift from the view of the audience as passive to one that views the audience as active in its relationship with media texts.

The Hypodermic Needle theory

The Hypodermic Needle theory suggests that the media 'inject' ideas into a passive audience, like giving a patient a drug.

Some of the earliest academic studies of media audiences appeared in the 1920s and 1930s and looked at what we understand as the 'mass media' – cinema, radio, popular magazines and newspapers – as they became increasingly available to the majority of people in Europe and America. In these early studies the audience itself was seen as a 'mass' audience – a mass of people, all together, consuming the same product and receiving the same 'mass' message. This seemed to be particularly effective when the Nazis in Germany and the Communists in the Soviet Union used the media as a propaganda tool. They appeared to be successful in making their ideas dominant and 'injecting' large numbers of people with their messages.

The Frankfurt School was made up of German Marxists who, in the 1930s, saw the success of Nazi propaganda and later, in 1950s America, of commercial television. They thought that the media were a force for pacifying the population and restricting and controlling public and cultural life by injecting a 'mass culture' that functioned as a distraction from the mundanity of ordinary daily life. Members of the Frankfurt School, including Theodor Adorno and Max Horkheimer, suggested that the American culture industries, in particular commercial television and popular cinema, moulded people into a standardised, passive state of being that allowed them to be easily manipulated.

Although in America most of this manipulation was carried out by advertising and the drive for consumerism, they suggested that, as had happened in Germany, the mass media could also be used to manipulate people into accepting particular political ideas such as capitalism. They believed that these culture industries worked against democracy and restricted people's choices and actions. (A more recent version of this argument has been put forward by Noam Chomsky, see p. 168 in Chapter 8 on media institutions.)

This view of the media seemed to be reinforced by Orson Welles's *The War of the Worlds*, broadcast on American radio in 1938. The programme, based on the book by H.G. Wells, was broadcast as part of a regular weekly drama slot but was produced to sound like a series of news reports and news flashes about the invasion of America by Martians. The programme appeared to include interviews with people in authority such as politicians and police officers and contained instructions for people to evacuate their homes. Many people did in fact believe that the broadcast was a real emergency and did drive out of New York State. The programme caused considerable panic and also attracted considerable criticism and complaints for being 'too realistic'. It is a good example of the power and 'authority' that the media had at the time in the minds of radio listeners. Many commentators have suggested that today we are too sophisticated to make the same mistake but a spoof broadcast of the BBC programme *Ghostwatch* on Halloween in 1992 fooled many viewers into believing that they were seeing real paranormal experiences on television. The campaign to 'name and shame' paedophiles by the *News of the World* is also perhaps a reminder that we still give the media too much authority and credence.

With the introduction of commercial television and in particular advertising, the idea of 'injecting' the audience with a message seemed even more relevant. It was thought that advertisers could make people buy particular products or brands of products merely by repeating the message often and loudly – the 'hard sell' approach. Vance Packard in *The Hidden Persuaders* (1957) identified many of the ways in which advertisers attempted to manipulate audiences. C. Wright Mills in *The Power Elite* (1956) suggested four functions that the media perform for audiences:

■ to give individuals *identity*
■ to give people goals and *aspiration*
■ to give *instruction* on how to achieve these goals
■ to give people an alternative if they failed, *escapism*.

However, studies of the various political advertising campaigns in America in the 1940s and 1950s suggested that the audiences were not so passive and did not just accept what the advertisers or the programme makers said. Rather, in terms of political advertising, audiences focused on those messages that reinforced their existing beliefs and tended to dismiss those that contradicted their established ideas. This suggested that audiences selected the messages that they wanted to hear and ignored others. The media's effect seemed to be one of reinforcement rather than of persuasion.

Uses and gratifications theory

Research then led to a view that audiences, rather than being simply a 'mass', were composed of different social groups, with particular sets of social relations, and a variety of cultural norms and values. Several American researchers, including Paul Lazarsfeld and Elihu Katz, concentrated on providing evidence that audiences were not simply one large, gullible mass but that messages put out by the media were in fact being received by a complex mixture of different groups and that media texts were themselves mediated by these social and cultural networks. The audience was now being seen as playing an active role in the interpretation of the meaning of particular media texts.

Uses and gratifications theory was an important shift in the study of how audiences interacted with texts and was developed by Blumler and Katz in 1975. They suggested that media audiences make active use of what the media offer and that the audience has a set of needs, which the media in one form or another meet. Through a series of interviews with viewers, they identified four broad needs that were fulfilled by viewing television:

■ **Diversion** A form of escape or release from everyday pressures
■ **Personal relationships** Companionship through identification with television characters and sociability through discussion about television with other people
■ **Personal identity** The ability to compare one's own life with the characters and situations portrayed and to explore individual problems and perspectives
■ **Surveillance** Information about 'what's going on' in the world.

Uses and gratifications theory is seen to have some merit as it supposes an 'active' audience that to some extent provides its own interpretation of the text's meaning.

However, as a means of understanding the complex relationship between the audience and the creation of meaning, it can appear to be rather simplistic in its reading of how we the audience/reader actually work with a text. One of the main problems with uses and gratifications theory is that it assumes that the media somehow identify these needs on behalf of the audience and then provide the material to meet or gratify them. It is difficult, for example, to image what the 'need' was that resulted in a television show such as *The Office* or *Heroes*. An alternative interpretation could be that we, the audience, create these needs as a response to the material provided by the media, and that we could have many other needs that are not identified, or met, by existing media texts.

In fact many of our 'uses' and 'pleasures' can be seen to be 'making the best' of what is available and putting it to our (the audience's) use, which may be different from the one that the producer intended. For example, consider the unexpected popularity and fashionableness of many cheap daytime television shows, such as *Deal or No Deal* or *Ready Steady Cook*.

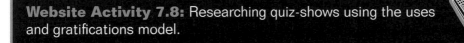

Website Activity 7.8: Researching quiz-shows using the uses and gratifications model.

It is worth thinking a little about the different ways in which we tend to consume different media. The term 'situated culture' is used to describe how our 'situation' (daily routines and patterns, social relationships with family and peer groups) can influence our engagement with and interpretation of media texts.

If we compare our consumption of films and television, there is an obvious difference between the two in that television is generally part of what Raymond Williams (1974) described as a 'flow'. By this Williams meant that television was a constant stream available to us in the home that we can turn on or off at will, like a water tap in the bathroom or kitchen. Sometimes we have it on as background or, as is the case for many elderly people, as a form of 'company'. On other occasions we may turn the television on in order to 'share' our watching with others, particularly with sporting events or perhaps soap operas. This may be a way of sharing companionship or, like *The Royle Family*, a way of being a family.

This, Williams suggested, means that our reception of television programmes, and the media in general, is mediated through our domestic, situated culture. It means that *who* we are, our sense of our own place in the world, our views and beliefs, as well as *where* we are in terms of our social location, all influence our responses to the media.

Watching a film, in contrast to television, is generally a more carefully chosen and focused activity. A visit to the cinema requires a series of conscious decisions such as deciding to go out to the cinema, choosing who to go with, at what time, to which cinema or multiplex, and which film to see. Watching a DVD or video also involves a set of deliberate choices such as deciding which DVD or video to rent, paying money, putting aside the time to watch the film, perhaps choosing particular companions to watch it with. Even a film on television is often chosen in a much more deliberate way than the rest of the television's 'flow', which is often watched 'because it is on' rather than as the result of a series of deliberate choices.

ACTIVITY

Think about the last time you went to the cinema. List the series of decisions that you had to make. How did you make your decisions? Refer back to some of the earlier activities in this section that are about patterns of film consumption. How do you and your friends consume this medium?

Jeremy Tunstall in *The Media in Britain* (1983) has suggested that the way in which we consume the media can be divided into three levels: primary, secondary and tertiary.

Figure 7.7 Primary media – the cinema

Primary media is where we pay close attention to the media text, for instance in the close reading of a magazine or newspaper, or in the cinema where we concentrate on the film in front of us.

Figure 7.8
Secondary media –
the car radio

Secondary media is where the medium or text is there in the background and we are aware that it is there but are not concentrating on it. This happens most often with music-based radio but also when the television is on but we are not really watching it; maybe we are talking with friends, eating or carrying out some other activity. This could also include 'skimming' through a magazine or newspaper, waiting for something to catch our eye.

Figure 7.9 Tertiary
media – walking past
a poster

Tertiary media is where the medium is present but we are not at all aware of it. The most obvious examples are advertising hoardings or placards that we pass but do not register.

ACTIVITY

Tunstall's ideas are based on 'traditional' media such as film, television, radio or newspapers. In what ways do you think they can also be applied to more recent digital technologies such as the web, our use of mobile phones, blogging etc.?

Mode of address

Mode of address refers to the way in which a particular text will address or speak to its audience.

Researchers have looked at the way in which the media 'address' or 'position' their audiences in relation to an event, person or idea (see Chapter 2 on narrative). Audiences can be positioned by the viewpoint used both verbally and visually to create a relationship between the text and its audience. Expressed verbally, this can include words like 'I' used by the narrator or broadcaster, 'you' when address- ing the viewer or listener, and 'it' or 'they' when referring to an event, third person or idea. Visually this positioning can be maintained by using camera angles, where the camera follows the action in a particular way or follows a particular person. Editing the flow and sequencing of shots can also position the audience to the extent that they become observers who see more than the participants and are spectators placed outside the action. For example, this occurs in a crime drama where the audience is given 'privileged' information about who committed the crime, or in a soap opera where someone is lying or has a secret.

The modes of address used in broadcasting are often informal, conversational and open ended because they are consumed in the private domestic world of the home. To create the necessary sense of intimacy, presenters talk to the audience as if they were individual members whom they know personally (see discussion on 'Doreen', p. 121). Although these modes of address are largely motivated by the producers' sense of their audience, sometimes they are determined by the institution's own sense of itself. For example, the BBC might consider itself to be representing the nation at a time of crisis and therefore may present its material in a particularly solemn and dignified manner.

Gendered consumption

There has been much research on how gender affects our consumption of the media. Studies such as Hobson (1982) and Gray (1992) suggest that women prefer 'open-ended' narratives like soap operas, whereas men prefer 'closed' narratives like police dramas (see Chapter 2 on narrative). Soap operas are con- sidered popular among women because they conform to what Geraghty (1991) calls 'women's fiction' and share certain common conventions:

- They have strong female lead characters.
- They focus on the private, domestic sphere.
- They deal with personal relationships.
- They contain an element of fantasy and/or escapism.

(See Chapter 3 on genre.)

Other research, such as Radway's (1984) study of a group of readers of romantic novels and Stacey's (1994) work with women cinema-goers from the 1940s and 1950s, also explores this notion of escapism or 'utopian solutions'.

These studies suggest that women audiences welcome romantic texts as a means of reasserting positive aspects of their lives. Radway suggests that heroines in romantic novels are seen as victorious because they symbolise the value of the female world of love and human relationships as being more important than fame and material success.

'Utopian Solution' is a term taken from Dyer (1977), who suggested that entertainment genres are popular because of their fantasy element and the escapism that they provide from daily routines and problems. He suggested that particular genres such as musicals or westerns offered particular types of utopian solution.

Males are considered to prefer factual programmes such as news and current affairs, although, as Morley (1986) notes, many men may watch soap operas but are not prepared to admit it. Mulvey (1975) suggests that most Hollywood films are based on the idea of a male viewer and that the camera shots and editing are 'positioned' from a male perspective. This she calls the 'male gaze', which automatically positions women as passive and as objects.

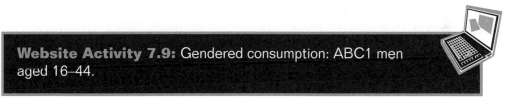

Website Activity 7.9: Gendered consumption: ABC1 men aged 16–44.

All this research suggests the complex nature of the relationships between audience and media text. As you will have read earlier, texts are polysemic (see p. 37) in that they have a variety of meanings, and the audience is an important component in determining those meanings.

The 'effects' debate and moral panics

There has long been concern about the supposedly bad effects that popular culture may have on 'ordinary' people. This concern has grown with the increase in 'mass media' and the availability of cheap fiction books, popular magazines, the cinema, popular music, television and, more recently, the internet.

Figure 7.10

In the 1950s American comics such as *Tales from the Crypt* or *Haunt of Fear*, with their depictions of violence, were seen as dangerous, so a law was introduced called the 1955 Children and Young Persons (Harmful Publications) Act to control which comics were allowed to be on sale in the UK.

In fact we can trace panics about the effects of the media back to the introduction of newspapers in the eighteenth century, when a tax or stamp duty was put on newspapers by the government to make newspapers so expensive that only rich people could afford to buy them.

The term 'moral panic' comes from *Folk Devils and Moral Panics* (2002) by Stanley Cohen. Cohen looked at the media reaction to the fights between mods and rockers at various seaside resorts in Britain during the mid-1960s. His term 'moral panic' came to mean a mass response to 'a group, a person or an attitude that becomes defined as a threat to society'.

Once a threat has been identified, a panic is then often created through press coverage, particularly the tabloid press, and is then taken up by other newspapers and/or television programmes. Newspapers may start campaigns claiming 'something must be done' and then politicians may become involved, offering support to the campaigns, and often legislation is introduced as a result.

In recent years we have had panics over refugees 'flooding' into Britain from Eastern Europe seeking asylum, as well as over dangerous dogs, illegal raves and video nasties. The Columbine high school massacre in 1999 prompted a moral panic about 'goth' culture.

As a result of these 'panics', legislation has been introduced to try to control dangerous dogs, make rave parties illegal, control the activities of asylum seekers, and the classification and distribution of certain types of video. One topical 'moral panic' was the 'naming and shaming' of paedophiles by the *News of the World*.

The moral panic over video nasties such as *Driller Killer*, *Zombie Flesh Eaters* and *The Texas Chainsaw Massacre* in the early 1980s led to the Video Recordings Act of 1984, which limited the kinds of videos on sale in this country (see the section 'Regulation of the media', p. 171). Other moral panics can be more subtle, for instance the campaigns over unmarried mothers who, it is claimed, get pregnant for the welfare benefits, or the panics about supermodels and 'heroin chic', which, it is claimed, encourage young girls to diet and can result in anorexia.

Perhaps the best-known case is the murder of James Bulger in 1993 and its association with the film *Child's Play 3*. In this case neither the prosecution nor the police presented any evidence to support the supposition that the two boys who had killed James Bulger had actually seen (yet alone been influenced by) this film.

The two boys came from socially and environmentally deprived backgrounds. Jon Venables had been referred by teachers to a psychologist because at school he banged his head against a wall to attract attention, threw objects at other children and had cut himself with scissors.

Figure 7.11 *Child's Play 3* (1991)

Even if it had been proved that the two boys had seen *Child's Play 3*, it is difficult to know how the court could have separated the influence of this video from all the other factors that made the two boys who they were. It was the judge in the case who, in his summing up, made the connection, which was then taken up by the tabloid press and MPs. This eventually led to the law being changed so that the British Board of Film Classification now has to take into account the influence of videos as well as their content.

There has been a large amount of research to try to identify the effects of the media on audiences, particularly in relation to violence. However, such research tends to be either inconclusive or contradictory (see, for instance, Barker and Petley 2001). Part of the problem with any attempt to prove the effects of watching violence or sex on television, video or film is trying to isolate the effect of the media from all the other factors that are involved in shaping us as individuals – family, home, education, religion, peer groups and so on. In America there were several cases of supposed 'copycat' killings after the release of the film *Natural Born Killers*. In fact many of those convicted of murder already had a history of violence before seeing the film.

Two of Britain's worst murder cases were the shootings of 16 schoolchildren and their teacher in Dunblane by Thomas Hamilton in 1996 and the murders of elderly women carried out by the doctor Harold Shipman over a number of years. In neither case was there any suggestion or evidence at all that Hamilton or Shipman had ever watched any violent videos.

Much of this 'effects' debate seems to assume that somehow if we, the audience, watch a violent film then we will carry out violent acts. This seems very simplistic in view of the complicated relationship that we, as audiences, have with the media. The most we can possibly say with certainty is that people with violent tendencies may watch violent videos, but that does not mean that everyone who watches violent videos is (or becomes) violent.

One of the moral panics today is focused around access to the internet. Over 60 per cent of adults in this country now have access to the world wide web, and it is available in schools and public libraries. There does perhaps need to be a debate about how media like the internet are controlled and monitored, but perhaps the real difficulty lies in deciding who should be in charge of regulation. Many people are probably fully in favour of censorship – as long as they are the ones who make the decisions!

ACTIVITY

What do you understand by the term 'moral panic'? By referring to one or more specific examples, such as the *Manhunt 2* computer game mentioned in the Introduction (see p. 13), illustrate how the media can be said to be responsible for creating moral panics.

The effects of advertising

One of the most important debates surrounding the influence of the media is the effects that advertisements may have both on us, the audience, and on those who rely on advertising for their income, namely the media producers.

As adverts are often consumed as tertiary media, it is very difficult to assess the effect of advertising and the extent to which people are affected by the advertisements to which they are exposed. In the section on moral panics, we discussed the difficulties in trying to isolate the effect the media may have from other influences on us – such as parents, education, peer groups or religion. This is perhaps even more difficult in the case of advertising, as we often are not consciously aware of advertisements, in that we may skim past the adverts in a magazine or newspaper or fast-forward through on a DVD or film.

One of the pieces of evidence to suggest that advertising works is the fact that companies spend so much money on it. According to some commentators, up to one-third of the cost of a bar of soap or up to 40 per cent of the price of a tube of toothpaste may represent advertising costs. Remember that, for example, about £20 billion is spent on marketing and advertising each year.

Arguments in support of advertising

- It finances a whole range of media and provides us with a wide range of choice in terms of the media available to us.
- It can be seen as an essential part of a modern-day, consumerist society and is a very effective way of informing us about new products.
- It stimulates consumption, which benefits industry, increases employment and leads to economic growth.
- Over the years advertising has been a very effective way for government and its various agencies to provide public information about safe sex and the use of condoms, the dangers of drinking and driving or, more mundanely, changing telephone codes. The government is one of the major advertisers in the UK.
- Sponsorship is an important source of funding for many sporting and artistic events.
- The advertising industry provides many people with employment.

ACTIVITY

The media fix their advertising rates according to the size of their audience and its age and social profiles. The rates are highly negotiable depending on numerous factors, including possible large discounts.

continued

Using industry sites on the web such as BRAD (http://www.brad.co.uk/info/) and the companies' own websites, research the rates charged in various national and local newspapers across a range of television channels and on the radio. Which medium is the most expensive? Why do you think this is? Which medium do you think would be best for reaching an audience made up of yourself and your peers?

Arguments used to criticise advertising

These are perhaps a little more subtle and complicated, as the following list suggests:

- Advertising creates false hopes and expectations.
- It works on our insecurities.
- It promotes unrealistic and dangerous role models.
- It can influence the content of media texts.
- Advertising revenue can direct programming.
- Advertising revenue is the foundation of new newspapers.

'Advertising creates false hopes and expectations'

Commentators such as C. Wright Mills in the 1950s and organisations such as Adbusters (http://www.adbusters.org) are critical of the consumerist nature of our society for this reason. They suggest that advertising excludes the less wealthy and creates a 'must-have' society (advertising on children's television is often cited as one of the main examples of this). Advertising, combined with easily available credit, means that some people may buy products which they cannot afford. This then may lead them into debt or criminal action to try to obtain those goods that are made desirable to us through advertising (ram-raiding is cited as an example).

'Advertising works on our insecurities'

The work of John Berger (1972) has been used by many people to explain the way in which advertising works upon the individual. Berger suggests that advertising works upon our insecurities and our need to feel 'esteemed' in the eyes of others by implying we are less than perfect if we do not own a particular product or look like the models in the advertisements. The advertisement implies that if we buy that product, we will look like the models or lead the type of life shown in the advertisements. Advertising is always working on our insecurities and making us constantly aspire to something new.

Figure 7.12 Adbusters spoof advertising

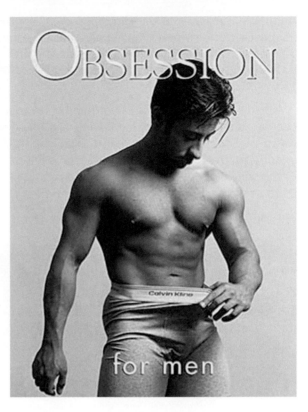

> The purpose of publicity is to make the spectator marginally dissatisfied with his present way of life. Not with the way of society, but with his own life within it. It suggests that if he buys what it is offering, his life will become better. It offers him an improved alternative to what he is.
>
> All publicity works upon anxiety. The sum of everything is money, to get money is to overcome anxiety.

(Berger 1972)

'Advertising promotes unrealistic and dangerous role models'

There has been a considerable amount of debate in recent years over the effects of 'super-waif' and 'heroin-chic' images of models in glossy magazines. It is claimed that the constant representation of ultra-thin models in both fashion spreads and advertisements has led to an undermining of girls' self-esteem and to eating disorders.

An article published in the *British Medical Journal* in 2000 by Jones and Smith suggests that between 1 and 2 per cent of women between the ages of 15 and 30 suffer from some kind of eating disorder and that this is directly attributable to the images that appear in fashion and 'lifestyle' magazines (see also Chapter 11 on lifestyle magazines).

(We had wanted to show an illustration of an advert for Kellogg's Cornflakes that used a 'super-waif' type of model and suggested that eating Kellogg's Cornflakes was a way of staying slim but also remaining healthy. However, perhaps because of criticism that Kellogg's received as a result of this advertisement and because of the sensitivity of the whole issue, the company would not grant permission for us to use the advertisement.)

ACTIVITY

Look through back copies of newspapers and magazines and collect examples of these types of advertisements and articles about the issue of female representation. You can also access early advertisements at http://www. hatads.org.uk/

- Can you identify any change in the portrayal of women over the last few years?
- Do men and women view this issue differently?
- To what extent do you think that this is a 'moral panic'?

Write a report or prepare a presentation outlining the main arguments in this debate.

OR

Collect a range of advertisements for slimming and/or fitness products.

- Who are the target audiences for these advertisements?
- What (if any) insecurities are they playing upon?
- Do they offer a wide range of body types?

'Advertising can influence the content of media texts'

Some commentators suggest that advertisers can influence the content of media texts, although there is very little direct evidence that this takes place in the British media.

One notable example is from the 1960s when *The Sunday Times* Insight team were investigating the links between cigarettes and cancer. Tobacco companies threatened to cancel their advertising if the investigations were published. The then editor, Harold Evans, published the investigations and the cigarette companies did pull their advertising (a considerable amount in those days) but eventually returned to *The Sunday Times* because it was a particularly effective means of targeting their desired group.

What is perhaps of more concern is the relationship between programme content and sponsors of programmes. This is an acknowledged issue in America but generally has not been considered as such in the UK.

ACTIVITY

According to Williamson, 'Advertisements are selling us something more than consumer goods. In providing us with a structure in which we and those goods are interchangeable, they are selling us ourselves' (Williamson 1978).

Choose one particular product or service and illustrate the range of ways in which advertisers have attempted to make it desirable for consumers.

It is undeniable that advertisers do have considerable power over the media in which their advertising appears. In the 1980s the *Sport* and the *Star* ran a joint newspaper but the *Star*'s main advertisers, household names including Tesco and Sainsbury's, were unhappy at being associated with the types of stories, features and pictures that appeared in the *Sport*. They threatened to cancel their advertising if the joint venture continued. The *Star* then pulled out of the venture with the *Sport* to safeguard its advertising revenue.

'Advertising revenue can direct programming'

Many commentators feel that Channel Four has become less radical and adventurous over the years and suggest that this may be the influence of advertising revenue. When Channel Four started broadcasting it had a number of quite (for the time) radical programmes, some with fairly small audiences, and could not fill all its advertising space. Gaps would appear on the screen in the commercial breaks with a notice saying that 'Programmes will continue shortly'. Since Channel Four has been allowed to keep all its advertising revenue instead of having to pass it on to the other commercial television companies, some commentators suggest that there has been a general shift towards more popular programmes that attract younger audiences and so raise advertising income.

Most commercial radio stations tend to offer the same mix of music and presenter 'chat' because they know that this will attract the largest number of the 15 to 25 year olds that advertisers want to target. A commercial station that initially attempts to offer something different, as did London's X-FM, Jazz FM or Kiss, often quickly changes its format to reach a more popular market.

ACTIVITY

Look at the schedules for Channel Four. Can you identify the way in which different audience 'segments' are packaged together? To what extent do you think that the present Channel Four schedules offer something that is 'innovative'?

OR

Carry out a survey of the radio stations that are available in your area.

- Group them under particular types of programming and the audiences that they are aimed at.
- Think about which groups (if any) are not represented by these radio stations. Why do you think this is?

'Advertising revenue is the foundation of new newspapers'

Newspapers such as *Today*, the *Post* and the *Sunday Correspondent* all started up in the 1980s but folded in the 1990s because they could not attract sufficient income from advertising. This may have been as a result of fierce competition in the newspaper market or because the products were not good enough to attract high circulation figures, but in the case of the *Sunday Correspondent*, a left-wing newspaper founded in 1989 and lasting less than one year, it is possible to argue that there was a conspiracy behind its demise, which happened after advertisers withdrew their support. Other radical magazines such as *Red Pepper* or the *Big Issue* struggle to survive because of the lack of advertisers willing to invest their money in these publications.

Audience participation

Recently there has been a paradigm shift in the way in which members of the audience interact with media producers and their products. Until recently producers and broadcasters had created the content of television programmes, newspapers, magazines, etc. for audiences largely to passively consume. Now, however, due to the growth of 'user-generated-content', this is rapidly changing and 'real people' are increasingly becoming actively involved in the production and content of television programmes. At the same time, readers and listeners are being encouraged to contribute to radio programmes, newspaper and magazine articles as well as online activities such as, for example, posting photographs, writing reviews or joining in votes.

Once upon a time it was only certain privileged types of people (politicians, experts, presenters) who appeared on our screens. If the public were seen, they were tightly controlled and mediated through the use of presenters (as in documentaries) or a quiz-master. (Even the early quiz and entertainment shows relied upon various types of 'expert' or personality – for instance the BBC's *What's My Line?*, *Juke Box Jury* or *Brains Trust*.) It was largely with the introduction of more American-type quiz shows on ITV in the 1950s that 'ordinary people' started to appear in front of cameras and then usually only to answer a well-rehearsed and tightly controlled set of questions.

Today, however, the public, ordinary people like us, are increasingly the stars of the shows. A recent popular genre has been the talent show where 'ordinary people' become stars (*How Do You Solve a Problem like Maria?*; *Any Dream Will Do*; *Strictly Come Dancing*; *The X Factor*). Another popular genre is the 'makeover' show, where ordinary people change their looks (*What Not to Wear*; *How to Look Good Naked*), their homes or gardens (*Home Front* or *How Clean*

Is Your House?) or try to reorganise their lives and families (*Supernanny*; *The House of Tiny Terrors*; *Help Me Help My Child!*).

Television companies are increasingly looking for 'ordinary people' to participate in shows. The BBC website http://www.bbc.co.uk/showsandtours/beonashow/ lists shows that are currently looking for participants, for example, *Sex . . . with Mum and Dad* where the BBC is looking for 'young adults aged between 16–20 and their parents to discuss attitudes towards relationships'. The BBC claims to 'help teenagers and their parents address relationship issues and promote discussion in a positive and constructive way' and to 'offer advice and support to families in order to resolve their individual concerns'.

ACTIVITY

Visit http://www.bbc.co.uk/showsandtours/beonashow/ and think about:

- Why might the BBC be considering producing such a show, for example, will it be popular?
- How does it fit with the BBC's public service remit?
- Why might people wish to participate in the programme. Is it because it offers '15 minutes of fame'? Or perhaps because the show offers professional support and advice?
- Think also about why the BBC might have chosen that particular title for the show and when and where you think the programme might be broadcast.

You can also visit the websites of other television production companies such as Channel Four (http://www.channel4.com/microsites/T/takepart/index.html) or http://www.livingtv.co.uk/extrememakeover/ and see which programmes are offering the opportunity for ordinary people to participate.

Increasingly, television producers are putting participants in these shows under some kind of pressure to increase tension and, some commentators argue, to make the participants behave in more extreme ways and therefore to be 'more entertaining'. A recent example has been the controversy surrounding Channel Four's *Big Brother* and *Celebrity Big Brother*. When this happens there is a question over the extent to which ordinary people are being empowered or merely exploited for commercial reasons.

There are many possible reasons for the increase in ordinary people appearing on television. One explanation is that they are a lot cheaper to use than professional entertainers and presenters. They may also help the audience at home identify with the participants and the programme and they may help to encourage audience loyalty through their familiar situations and characters.

As more viewers switch to digital television (the analogue services are to be switched off by 2012), so we can interact more with the programmes or choose from a range of different screens. According to Thinkbox,

> **Statistics from Sky show that 93% of SkyDigital households interacted with their TV between January and June 2006. Viewers of all ages . . . will now press red with confidence, in part thanks to the increasing amount of interaction offered by programme makers . . . ITV, for example, reports that three million viewers now press red on Coronation Street every month and spending up to 10 minutes within the interactive service.**

(For further information and some examples of interactive television adverts go to http://thinkbox.tv/server/show/ConCaseStudy.637.)

There has been a lot of coverage recently about Web 2.0 – the concept of using the web as a dynamic platform, where users become participators, contributing and sharing with a wider community (the 'many-to-many' model we discussed earlier, see p. 114). Web 2.0 is becoming a generic term describing this behaviour and the technologies that enable it. One of the main ways of doing this is through the use of wikis. A wiki is a collaborative website which can be directly edited by anyone with access to it. Wikipedia, the online encyclopedia, is probably the best known. However, this technology is increasingly being used as a way of enabling people like us to participate in the designing of media products. For example, *Where are the Joneses?* (http://wherearethejoneses.com) is an interactive fictional comedy made by the production company responsible for television shows like *The Mighty Boosh*. Members of the audience are encouraged to influence the storyline either by writing scripts or by suggesting new characters. The audience can also keep up with the storyline and the characters through the video-sharing site YouTube, social network sites MySpace and Facebook, photo site Flickr and various blogs. The characters in the comedy even have their own Twitter feeds, updating fans via mobile phone (see http://technology.guardian.co.uk/news/story/0,,2122547,00.html).

Figure 7.13 The car bomb at Glasgow airport 2007, taken by a passer-by

Like other news organisations, BBC News encourages members of the public to send in material from the scenes of news stories. The BBC tries to incorporate content from its viewers and listeners such as Figure i from the 7 July 2005 bombings in London, discussed in the Introduction or the photograph of a vehicle being driven into the Glasgow Airport's Terminal One building in June 2007 taken by Thomas Conroy and sent to the BBC (Figure 7.13). On its 'Have Your Say' website, the BBC says 'News can happen anywhere at any time and we want you to be our eyes. If you capture a news event on a camera or mobile phone, either as a photograph or video, then please send it to BBC News' (http://news.bbc.co.uk/1/hi/talking_point/default.stm).

Traditionally newspapers and magazines have had a Readers' Comments section; sometimes it is as traditional as a letters page or the *Sun*'s Dear Sun – 'The Page where you tell Britain what you think.' The new technologies are making it much easier for us, the audience, to also become producers and to submit material for publication.

The magazine *Nuts* works hard to encourage reader participation. It asks its readers to send it letters, emails, texts or jpegs. There is a competition for letter or spam of the week where the winner receives a year's supply of Durex. Women can also send in photographs of themselves and the (presumably) male readers can then vote by text, online or email for the one who they think should become a future bedroom babe. Readers are asked to get their 'girl' to submit raunchy confessions and each week's winners' stories are published and they get a £50 prize. (See the profile of *Nuts* in Chapter 11 on lifestyle magazines, p. 239.)

ACTIVITY

Read Chapter 11 on Lifestyle Magazines and then look through a sample noting the ways in which the magazines try to get their readers to contribute to the articles and features. Why do you think this appeals to (a) readers and (b) the magazine editors?

Think about the mode of address and the way in which readers are addressed. What assumptions do you think are being made by the magazine editors regarding their target audience? Do you think this trend improves magazines? If yes, in what ways? If no, why not?

ACTIVITY

Go to the Zuda Comics website at http://www.zudacomics.com/?action=the_deal where they are asking people to help create a 'web comic' using jpeg technology. They are asking for examples of comic strips and say that they may eventually be published. Why do you think the company is making this offer?

Surf the website and think about the mode of address used and what this suggests about the way in which Zuda Comics envisage their audience. Think about the 'Zuda community': what does this mean? And why is the company using this term?

And finally . . .

Let us return to *The Royle Family* (Figure 7.1) as this programme highlights many of the key themes in this section on media audiences and how audiences interact with media texts. In one episode of the situation comedy, the family members settle down after Sunday lunch to watch the BBC's *Antiques Roadshow* but instead of admiring the antiques, they bet on how much they are valued at, and the family member who is nearest takes the winnings.

This episode is a good example of how the fictional family members are using a programme as a means of both entertainment and diversion from the mundane routines of daily weekday life as well as bringing themselves together as a family and sharing in the experience of betting on the antiques. Their particular use of the programme, to see who can best guess the value of the antiques, is their own 'negotiated' meaning of the programme, but one that is shared by all the members of the family. Their 'situated culture', the family together, affects the meaning of the programme, and their social background affects their interpretation of what the notion of 'antiques' means – not something to own but a way of sharing pleasure, gambling and winning money.

We could also say that the members of the Royle family are making quite an astute comment on the *Antiques Roadshow* itself – middle-class people bring out their antiques and pretend surprise when told how much they are worth – but actually the money 'value' of the antiques is the whole point (and attraction?) of the programme. So really we could say that the Royle family is getting to the hub of the programme and exposing its hypocrisy.

The Royle Family is now ten years old and it is worth speculating how the family would consume television today or in the near future. For example, would four generations of one family still all sit around in one room watching one television set? Would they continue to watch a 'live' programme such as *Antiques Roadshow*? How would the newer technologies such as Freeview or a Sky box, DVDs or interactive services change the way they 'consumed' television programmes?

It may be that *The Royle Family* captured a particular mode of television consumption that has already become history.

further reading

Williams, K. (2003) *Understanding Media Theory*, Arnold.

8 MEDIA INSTITUTIONS

In this chapter we:

■ investigate the ownership of media institutions and consider the role of public service broadcasting in an increasingly commercial and globalised media environment

■ look at how media products are distributed and paid for by audiences

■ consider the ways in which media institutions are controlled and regulated

■ look at globalisation and the way that the internet is changing how we view and access the media.

As we mentioned in the Introduction, wherever you go in the world it is almost impossible to avoid the media. There are few areas in the world that do not have some kind of newspaper (even if it is only a news-sheet). There is barely a country that does not have a television station, and if it does not have one of its own, then it is generally possible, via satellite, to receive pictures broadcast from a neighbouring country (although in some countries this might be considered a crime). The web is now available throughout the world, although the degree of access may vary widely between countries.

The media have, in many ways, challenged our conventional notions of national identity. We can watch television from many different countries, listen to foreign radio stations, read overseas newspapers and now, with even more ease, access as many websites as we wish from all over the world through the internet.

Website Activity 8.1: Media ownership.

Figure 8.1 Distribution of food and supplies, Iraq 2003

Ownership: commercial media institutions

We also mentioned in the Introduction to this book that it is important to remember that media texts are not fortunate accidents and that usually profit is the motive in producing them. The vast array of media artefacts available is not simply the product of circumstance and a few altruistic people. There are undoubtedly some media texts produced by people who feel that they have something to say or who anticipate a gap in the market that should be filled. However, as a general rule, people with money do not launch a new newspaper or magazine because they feel sorry for our lack of awareness of what is going on in the world. Nor are they concerned that we have too much leisure time. In fact the vast majority of media texts are produced by media institutions to make money.

There can be little doubt that there is the potential for enormous profit in the media world. There is equally the potential for financial disaster. What works for one company may not work for another. But certain ideas about media institutions remain constant.

One common idea is the 'conspiracy theory' of Media Studies. This is the popular and common idea that a small group of multimedia tycoons is busy trying to take over or amalgamate with every other media company available, so that in the end this group will end up with more power to control what we know about the world, with all that this implies politically and socially. News Corporation and/or Microsoft are usually cited as examples.

There are, however, no hard and fast rules that can be applied to the media anywhere in the world, although it is the case that in many countries the government owns or controls the major mass media. In situations like this the media are often used purely for propaganda and informational purposes. It is interesting to note that when such governments are threatened by public uprisings or military coups, one of the first targets for the protesters is these very same radio and television stations – which demonstrates how important control of the media can be. In 2003 in post-Saddam Iraq, the coalition forces set up an American-based television service and there was an enormous expansion of independent newspapers and radio stations expressing views that had been suppressed by the previous government.

One of the issues that has to be dealt with by those who study or take an interest in the media is the fact that much of the media is largely in the hands of a small number of multinational companies. Companies such as Time Warner, Sony, News Corporation and Viacom are major players on the world media scene. In Britain there is a small number of companies that dominate the media industries but compared to American and Japanese companies, they are relatively small.

ACTIVITY

How do media corporations make themselves recognisable to different markets?

Consider the corporation websites below and analyse the ways in which they present themselves around the world.

http://www.bbc.co.uk/
http://www.cnn.com/
http://www.foxnews.com/
http://news.sky.com/skynews/home

Not all media companies are large players but historically a pattern has emerged. Whenever a new technology is invented or discovered, companies have been formed, or existing companies have been forced to try to take advantage of the benefits and profits that the new technology offers. However, it is often the case that no one is quite sure what those benefits might be, and that there is no guarantee that profits will be made. For instance, when CDs first came into production, they were marketed on the premise that they produced 'better' quality and that they would last forever and that anyone who owned vinyl records should therefore replace all their collection in the new CD format. The major record companies then started to reissue their back catalogue of records in CD format, in effect re-selling the same product (often as a 'special edition') to consumers who already had a copy of the album albeit in a different format. Yet today the CD appears outmoded as we increasingly access music digitally either through our PC or else through an MP3 player.

Very much the same has now happened with the arrival of the DVD to replace the video cassette and which in turn may eventually be replaced by hard drive recorders and MP4 players.

Figure 8.2

Each new technology has been hailed as an improvement on existing technology, a boon to consumers and a way for producers to get rich (often fairly quickly). Risks have been taken, some companies have fallen by the wayside, but others have survived and prospered. For instance, all the major American film studios started off as small independent companies. Each found a particular niche for itself. Warner Bros, for instance, were famous for the realism of many of their films, whilst MGM were famous for the escapist nature of their product. Both managed to build on their success. However, there were film companies that were not able to respond quickly enough to the demands of the audience, or indeed to the threat of new technologies. These companies no longer exist (for example, RKO Radio Pictures). Embracing the new technology seems to be the most effective way of responding to the threat of new media technology.

Website Activity 8.2: EMAP case study.

A good example of this is the way that the major record companies have eventually responded to the 'illegal' downloading of music files off the internet. Outlawing this activity through the courts has not prevented it happening – indeed, this has probably given it free and extra publicity. Eventually many of the majors have had to set up their own download sites, where, for a small payment, music files can be downloaded legally.

Recently the internet has become a place for small entrepreneurs to start up independent companies. If successful, they may make a profit or indeed be bought out by the majors at considerable financial gain to the owners. According to Gauntlett (2000) there are many entrepreneurs who have become millionaires by developing 'free' websites that people want to visit. The attraction of these websites for advertisers is that they enable them to target very specific groups defined by age (such as social networking sites like MySpace or Bebo), by interest (such as the Interactive Investor website), by musical taste (for example, http://www.iLike.com)

or through search engines and directories such as Yahoo or Google. Online advertising is expected to grow at about 20 per cent per year until 2011, when it is estimated that it will account for 15 per cent of the world's advertising market.

However the 'value' of these new websites is not necessarily in the income they bring in from advertising or sponsorship but the potential that they have. One such example is Facebook, founded by Mark Zuckerberg when he was 19, which was valued in 2007 at £15 billion, mainly on the basis of the estimated 27 million active 'friends' registered with the site (6.5 million users in the UK as at September 2007). In 2007 Microsoft paid US$ 240 million for a 1.6 per cent share in Facebook, attracted by its advertising potential.

However, the collapse of some major internet companies demonstrates that there is just as strong a likelihood that the internet will not end up being the money-making machine that some people hoped it might become. It is estimated that in 2002 one in five of all dot.com start-ups went bust.

Website Activity 8.3: Web studies 2.0.

In the 1950s both the American film industry and the British radio industry dismissed television as a medium that would not last. In America they then tried to combat it by making films that could only be seen at their best at the cinema. This goes some way to explaining why there were so many 'epics' made in the 1950s – large-scale Biblical stories as well as a multitude of big-budget musicals. These were initially popular but then audiences grew tired of too many similar products and as a consequence these companies watched their revenues dwindle as audiences decided they preferred to stay at home. It was only later that the successful and more thoughtful film companies (and producers) realised that television networks, as well as movie theatres, needed product. They then diversified into television production as well.

Nowadays, almost every television programme we see, particularly those of American origin, has the logo of a major film and television production/distribution company at the end of its final reel. Thus Fox, Columbia TriStar, Warner Bros and Paramount are all involved in large-scale film production as well as in production for television.

ACTIVITY

http://www.fox.com/home.htm
http://www2.warnerbros.com/main/homepage/homepage.html
http://www.paramount.com/
http://www.columbiatristar.co.uk

Types of ownership: horizontal and vertical integration; convergence

Horizontal integration

Horizontal integration involves the acquisition of competitors in the same section of the industry. One example is the ITV network, once 13 separate companies, which is now just one company, ITV, following the merger of Carlton and Granada at the end of 2003. It might be possible for one company to seek to control all of the market – a monopoly position – but most capitalist countries have laws to prevent this happening.

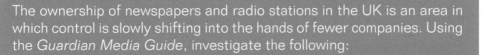

ACTIVITY

The ownership of newspapers and radio stations in the UK is an area in which control is slowly shifting into the hands of fewer companies. Using the *Guardian Media Guide*, investigate the following:

- Who owns the national daily newspapers?
- Who owns the Sunday national newspapers?
- Who owns the majority of the UK commercial radio stations?
- What are the advantages and disadvantages of the horizontal integration process to (a) the consumer and (b) the producers?

BSkyB, 39 per cent owned by News Corporation, is one of the UK's most aggressive commercial television companies. In 2007 the Competition Commission, the UK's key antitrust regulator, said it believed that BSkyB's 18 per cent holding in ITV, the UK's largest free-to-air commercial broadcaster by sales, was anticompetitive. It is widely though that BSkyB bought into ITV to stop Richard Branson, his Virgin Media company and NTL from taking over ITV, one of BSkyB's main competitors.

When in 1999 BSkyB attempted to buy a controlling interest in Manchester United Football Club, the government intervened to prevent the takeover on the grounds that there would be a clash of interests when the question of football coverage on television came up for auction later on in the year (for further

information on this and other media-related mergers and acquisitions see http://
www.competitioncommission.org.uk/rep_pub/reports/1999/426sky.htm #full).

Vertical integration

Vertical integration is when companies want to control the three main areas of
production, distribution and exhibition and involves one company having the ownership of every stage of the production process, thereby ensuring complete control
of a media product.

An example of vertical integration is the Fox Entertainment Group. This is an
American company that is owned by News Corporation. If at one time during
the late 1970s and early 1980s Twentieth Century Fox was a Hollywood film company that had perhaps seen better times, it is now (again) one of the major
massmedia companies worldwide. Famous originally as a film-production company,
Fox Entertainment now produces, develops and distributes television and film
programming through its Fox Film Entertainment and Twentieth Century Fox units.
It also owns the Fox Television network in the USA, has interests in cable television
channels and major-league sports teams, and owns a chain of cinemas in the USA.
But it does not end there. News Corporation is also a worldwide media organisation
with part-ownership of many satellite and cable channels across Europe and Asia.
The company owns several newspapers, notably in the USA, Australia and the UK.

There are various websites that details the holdings of the major media companies although they tend to focus on American companies; see, for example,
http://www.nowfoundation.org/issues/communications/tv/ mediacontrol.html
or http://www.cjr.org/resources/.

The advantages of this type of global ownership are many. A film produced by Twentieth Century Fox can be shown in Fox-owned cinemas, publicised in News Corporation newspapers, then shown on Fox-owned television channels. All media associated with Fox can give the product publicity in one shape or form. It is interesting to note that Fox became joint producer of the film *Titanic* at a point when it was about to become known as the most expensive film ever made – and perhaps a financial disaster. The very fact that it received such notoriety before its release is now seen as a very clever 'hype' – it became a film that everyone wanted to see, and the rest is history.

ACTIVITY

Select a film produced by Twentieth Century Fox for exhibition in the UK (you can find a list of these on the website http://www.foxmovies.com). Research the many different ways it is brought to the attention of an audience through the use of other media companies associated with Fox and News Corporation. Remember, bad publicity is often as useful as good publicity.

Also consider what additional tie-ins are used to promote the film, for example, links with fast-food chains, toy companies, mobile phone companies and/or computer game manufacturers.

Multiplex cinemas grew from the principle of vertical integration. A multiplex cinema can have as many as 30 different screens in one building. Immediately there are benefits to the owner in terms of costs. Only one or two projectionists are needed and a minimum number of staff (who may well be working on the kiosks as well). Heating, lighting and cleaning costs can be kept to a minimum and even advertising costs kept low. The major point is that if people arrive to see a film and it is sold out, they are unlikely to just go away. Having made the effort to get to the cinema, they are likely to see another film that is showing at the multiplex instead. At the same time, they are likely to buy food and drink at vastly inflated prices.

Consider, also, the choice for the consumer. On one level the multiplex offers a wide range of films, and a particularly popular film can be shown on several screens at once and only one print of the film is actually needed (there need only be a slight time delay between screenings). But what happens to a film that might not be quite so popular and is perhaps a risk in terms of profitability? It makes sense for the multiplex owner not to bother showing such a film, since the job is to make money, not necessarily to cater for the minority film-goer. There are of course independent cinemas in existence in the UK and other countries. But even they have to make a profit to continue their existence. It can be argued, therefore, that a system that appears to offer more choice can often lead to less choice.

Figure 8.3

In terms of issues of ownership, what this implies is that decisions about what is available to media audiences rest in the hands of a few media companies. They, of course, have to answer to their shareholders and the financial institutions that have invested in them. Media companies are not altruistic, they can take risks, but their responsibilities to investors and shareholders suggest that they are very unlikely to do so.

Commercial television is bound to its owners and shareholders. It is financed by advertising. Therefore the onus on all commercial television channels is to gain as large an audience as possible. This then makes their programmes attractive for advertisers, who, on the whole, want to show their advertisements to as large an audience as possible. A popular programme attracts a large audience, who will then see the advertisement. Thus the concern is to make and broadcast popular programmes, especially during peak viewing hours. Of course there are times when audiences are necessarily small, such as the period between lunchtime and tea-time, when most people are at work, college or school. However, advertisers have responded to this by targeting audiences quite specifically (see Chapter 7 on audiences).

The problem with this is that commercial television ends up beholden to three masters – the audience, the advertisers and the shareholders. The primary concern becomes to produce programmes that will gain the maximum number of viewers. And the evidence suggests that, in order to do this, schedules tend to become full of soap operas, quiz shows, docu-soaps and reality television shows such as *Big Brother* and *Dancing on Ice*.

Convergence

Convergence means that the new media technologies are all coming together and most hardware is now multi-functional. Television has become a medium through which one can shop, bank, and even send and receive emails through a telephone cable link-up. The phone has become a piece of hardware through which one can still talk but can also send text messages, voicemail, emails and connect to the internet as well as being a camera and MP3 player. The radio is still a radio, but few units are simply just radios – most are again multi-functional, including MP3 and CD players, or at the very least alarm clocks and digital radios that enable listeners to access a whole range of additional services.

Sky has produced a piece of hardware, called Sky Plus, that sits on the television set and enables viewers to skip over adverts and even pause 'live' television. It has the capacity to record hundreds of hours of television. But more interesting is the fact that viewers can key in certain words and the box will then automatically watch out for programmes featuring these words. Thus viewers can select pro- grammes they want recorded or search for different types of programmes, or indeed particular actors or genres. In addition, part of the Sky Box package also includes broadband internet access (with video-on-demand) as well as telephone services (see also http://allyours.virginmedia.com/whychooseus/index.html).

Figure 8.4 The modern desk is cluttered with technology

One consequence of this increased convergence is that media companies are increasingly able to synergise their products. Synergy means the way in which media companies sell or promote the same or similar products across more than one medium. (See chapter 9 on *Heroes*.) An example of this would be the merchandising of a game that may be linked to a popular film and its characters, such as the *Lord of the Rings* strategy board games. Synergy can also refer to the way in which media companies tie together similar aspects of their production and distribution services. For example, regional BBC centres may have one newsroom that supplies news for a variety of different outlets, including local radio and television as well as online and national channels.

Figure 8.5 Sky Plus Box

KEY CONCEPTS

Public Service Broadcasting (PSB)

Despite the increasing concentration of media ownership, there also exist many people in all media fields who remain committed to the notion of choice and independence. Organisations such as the Voice of the Listener and Viewer (http://www.vlv.org.uk/) and the Campaign for Press and Broadcasting Freedom (http://www.cpbf.org.uk) see the wave of deregulation that has taken place, in this country in particular, as not necessarily being in the public interest. They therefore argue strongly for an element of public service broadcasting (PSB) to be preserved.

The concept of PSB was adopted in this country in the 1920s. The most obvious example of a PSB organisation is the British Broadcasting Corporation (BBC), which was founded in 1926 initially as a radio service, though it was later to involve the then new medium of television. The fundamental principle behind PSB was to provide a service for all members of the community, with what Lord Reith, Director General of the BBC in the 1920s, called a duty to 'inform, educate and entertain'. For the payment of a yearly licence fee, the public received a national radio service, which was joined by a television service after the Second World War. Originally, all households that owned a radio had to buy a licence. Later, ownership of a television meant the purchase of a television licence was obligatory as well. Nowadays the two licences have been merged into one – but it is still a legal requirement to have a television licence if a household owns one or more television sets.

What is interesting about the concept of public service broadcasting is the philosophical stance underpinning it. In a media world in which often the central concern is profit, shareholders and aggrandisement, there can still exist, and be room for, an organisation created to serve a nation, rather than to make money from the nation, financed by a licence fee and, in theory, available to all.

ACTIVITY

Access the BBC Trust website (http://www.bbc.co.uk/bbctrust/) where it claims that 'it ensures the BBC provides high quality output and good value for all UK citizens and it protects the independence of the BBC.' Read through the remit and various activities of the BBC Trust and design a short presentation on the main aims and activities of the BBC Trust. To what extent to you think the Trust is successful?

It is important to note, however, that the notion of performing a public service is not unique to the BBC. All terrestrial television organisations have written into their charters an element of public service – usually that they should provide some kind of news programme and an element of educational programming, although it is important to note that these regulations are very much looser than they were when the first commercial television station started broadcasting in 1956.

Underpinning the concept of PSB is the belief that all members of the community have a right to programming that appeals to them. And of course soap operas and game shows do not appeal to everyone. If 9 million people are watching *EastEnders*, then an equal if not larger number are not. This is not to say that popular genres do not have a place in PSB, but that a balance needs to be struck between entertaining popular programmes and those that might not have such a direct appeal but that still have a potential audience. Since the PSB channel does not have to gratify advertisers and shareholders, the opportunity arises to make and show programmes that are not necessarily going to be large ratings winners, indeed minority interests have specifically to be catered for under the remit of PSB.

This is part of the argument used currently by television companies such as Channel Four and ITV that as they also have a PSB remit, they should also be entitled to a share of the income levied via the licence fee.

It is also important to note that PSB is not unique to this country. It exists in one form or another in most European countries. Even the USA, where television is dominated by powerful networks showing advertisements as often as they can, possesses PSB channels. However, these channels tend to be funded by sponsorship and donations from members of the public rather than by a general licence fee and rely heavily on BBC-produced programming.

By 2012 all television broadcasting in the UK will be digital and the choice of television programmes available to viewers is expected to become even larger. Many people now find that they no longer watch any programmes presented by the BBC. So, not surprisingly, there is a groundswell of opinion that, if they do not watch BBC programmes, why should they continue to pay their licence fee? This has increased pressure on the BBC to produce programmes that will attract a large audience, if only to justify the payment of the licence fee. The conundrum then turns full circle as people who are committed to the notion of public service television start to complain because, they would argue, public service broadcasting is simply becoming a replica (and perhaps not a very good one) of commercial television, which of course is ostensibly free. (It should also be noted here that of course commercial television is not free. Millions of pounds are spent by companies in this country every year producing and showing adverts on television. It can be argued that ultimately we, the consumers, pay for those adverts in the cost of the products that we are being enticed to buy.)

Inevitably this has sparked off a further debate, with some critics arguing that the BBC should not be spending money on services that are very similar to those offered by other commercial channels. BBC Three, for instance, is designed to appeal to a predominantly teenage audience – an audience that is in theory already well catered for.

Others would argue that the BBC needs to change because of the changes that are taking place in the broadcasting environment. The licence fee does not cover the full cost of the BBC's television and radio programming. Already the shortage of funds has been highlighted by the loss of several sporting fixtures that up until a few years ago could be watched free of charge on the BBC, such as Test Match cricket and English international football matches.

The large investment in television, particularly by satellite and cable companies, has been reflected by the enormous sums these companies are prepared to pay for sporting fixtures. It seems inevitable that, to pay for this investment, audiences not only will have to subscribe to certain satellite/cable channels but may well have to pay an extra amount to watch particular major sporting fixtures.

ACTIVITY

Examine the current television schedules and attempt to identify which programmes or segments of programmes fall into the category of education/information and which fall into the category of entertainment.

- Do any patterns emerge?
- Are some channels more educational or entertainment than others? Suggest reasons for this.
- What are the advantages and disadvantages of PSB for a) consumers b) producers?
- Are there alternatives to the television licence fee as a means of financing the BBC?

This is already the case on some digital channels with the advent of pay-per-view (PPV) television. At present this mainly occurs for recently released films, but certain sporting fixtures, notably boxing and wrestling, have also been transmitted as PPV events and digital television allows for each premiership football club to own and run its own television channel to show its own fixtures. Sport on Sky has had a great deal of investment money put into it by News Corporation and is seen as a loss leader to get audiences to subscribe to Sky channels. Once we could watch the occasional game on the BBC for nothing; now we have to pay a monthly subscription and perhaps extra for particular matches or films – all this in addition to a licence fee that is compulsory.

Alternative media

Alternative media organisations exist as a counterpoint to everything that has been mentioned above. Not everything in the media world is about market domination, large-scale target audiences, big business and enormous profit.

Companies and organisations do exist that attempt to make a positive virtue out of being small and, perhaps most importantly, out of being independent and countering mainstream views (see for example, http://www.iraqbodycount.org/).

If an organisation is run on essentially democratic grounds, and has a policy of independence, then the genuine voice of an artist or writer is more likely to flourish. For example, in the music industry, particularly in the UK, pop music has flourished and with it the creation of, for example, girl and boy bands – many of which seem to follow a well-worn formula. A band or musician/singer who produces material that does not 'fit' the major record companies' notion of what should or should not be released may not get a contract and might never be heard. Thus independent record labels – small, with low budgets and few overheads – have given artists the opportunity to produce material. There might not be such a large publicity machine working for them, nor instant access to radio and television play, but there is an audience out there who have rejected the product of the mass-media organisations and keep a lookout themselves for product to purchase, often through the medium of music fanzines or, as the success of the Arctic Monkeys demonstrated, through social networking sites such as MySpace. In 2007 both Radiohead and The Charlatans released their latest albums online, bypassing traditional record companies and their distribution and promotion services. Increasingly, albums by established artists are available free, or very cheaply, online (see for example, www.freealbums.blogsome.com or the article http://www.businessweek.com/magazine/content/07_44/b4056094.htm?chan=search).

ACTIVITY

Take two media products, one mass market and one significantly alternative – for instance a football magazine and a football fanzine, or a mainstream music paper and a music fan website.

- What are the differences?
- What are the similarities?

Concentrate particularly on:

- the content
- the style

This is also true in the world of football. For years football fans have paid their money at the gate, supported their team and developed a sense of ownership. Yet the run-of-the-mill football programme is frequently an anodyne affair – glossy pictures, many advertisements, but rarely any genuine discussion of football, the team or financial affairs. The increase in the number of football fanzines was very much a phenomenon of the 1990s. It reflects many people's dissatisfaction with the typical football programme or magazine available on the mass market – a product that cannot help but be tied to the sponsors' and the owners' point of view and is unlikely to rock the boat or court controversy.

Recently the major football clubs have developed their own websites and in some cases their own television stations, for example, http://www.arsenal.com/index.asp; http://www.mcfc.co.uk/; http://www.avfc.co.uk; http://www.mfc.co.uk/page/Home/0,,1,00.html.

ACTIVITY

Access a range of the sites mentioned above and consider the sponsorship that they have. Notice the different media outlays that are involved in football. Sponsors include an airline company, phone network companies, alcohol, online betting, insurance companies, etc. Why do you think these companies choose to invest in football teams? Do you think these companies set high standards for the supporters? Should a child be wearing a shirt advertising alcohol and online betting when they themselves should not be concerned with such products?

Manufacturing consent: Noam Chomsky

We have tried to outline the process by which major media conglomerates seemingly have a stranglehold over much that media audiences are consuming. Although our emphasis is on the film industry, this is also the case in many other media industries.

It is in this area that the works of Noam Chomsky are particularly relevant. Noam Chomsky is particularly interested in the social and political implications of the mass media and their ownership (see also Chapter 12 on news). The basic premise of much of his writing on the media is as follows:

Figure 8.6 Noam Chomsky

- Society is made up of two different classes of people.
- The top 20 per cent represents the professional class, those who feel they have a stake in the decision-making processes in society, professionals such as judges, lawyers, teachers and intellectuals. Many of these people have a genuine interest in politics and the rudiments of power that are associated with their positions. They like to think that they have some influence on the way things are run and governed. It is also the case that this group is (in general) the one with the most financial influence in society. They represent the dominant ideology in American society.
- Then there is the remaining 80 per cent, whose main function is to work and follow orders, usually at the bidding of the top 20 per cent. Their interest in politics tends to be minimal, as long as they are housed, fed and have enough money to finance their leisure time.
- The top 20 per cent, the group with the money and power, is also likely to contain those individuals who are involved with or who actually own the media or have a strong influence on their artefacts and content. This is one of the ways in which hegemony can be seen to work (see p. 268).

Chomsky argues that the media, especially the large multimedia companies, have one prevailing motive apart from profit and that is what he calls the 'Manufacture of Consent'. Essentially, Chomsky argues, the media today are involved in a two-pronged process.

The first process is to ensure that the top 20 per cent of the population are satisfied, and this is achieved by maintaining their position as policy-makers, in control of some of the rudiments of power. The issue is one whereby the media help the government to remain on a path that keeps this elite content and feeling that their position in society is of some worth, whilst continuing to ensure the lifestyle and political attachments of this elite. Most of the media are therefore inevitably interested in maintaining the status quo, as is, frequently, the power elite; often the power elite and the media elite are the same group of people.

This means that much of the time the government and the elite are involved in an alliance – but only when it suits them. Obviously issues can and do arise on which the government and the elite disagree. For instance, towards the end of the Tony Blair government in the middle of 2007, even normally sympathetic newspapers turned against him, particularly in the area of personal morality and the Iraq war. This can be seen as an example of the media acting as the spokesperson for this elite and 'taking on' the government. But by and large the media can wield a considerable amount of power because, certainly since the Second World War, every government has been dependent on the media to get into office. Not for nothing was Rupert Murdoch's *Sun* able to boast that it had won the election in 1992 for the Tories. And indeed the same newspaper certainly also helped the Labour Party get into power in 1997.

A more recent example of the complex relationship between the government and the media in Britain can be seen in the reporting of the Iraq war in 2003. The media were allowed a considerable amount of access to the activities of the military in Iraq. Many reporters were 'embedded'; in other words they joined the military and lived and worked alongside them. This meant that the journalists and film crews had access to military activities and could often report from the front line. However, it also meant that the military were able to keep watch on the media and to some extent control what they saw and could (or could not) report on. There was some criticism that these embedded reporters, especially those from the American media, were not as objective or as critical of military action as they should have been.

On the other hand, there was strong disagreement between the Labour government and the BBC over the reporting of the war and in particular the way in which the war was justified by Tony Blair. This argument mainly revolved around the BBC reporter Andrew Gilligan, the suicide of the Iraqi arms expert Dr David Kelly, the 'dodgy' dossier, used as the basis for going to war, and the role of Alastair Campbell. The government also accused the BBC of being anti-war in some of its reporting, but, as Figure 8.7 shows, research carried out by media academics at Cardiff University suggests that the BBC was less prone to be critical of the government and the war than was Channel Four. The campaign by the government

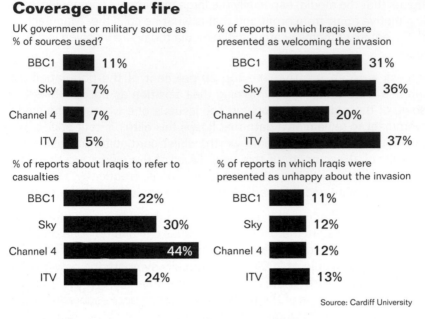

Coverage under fire

UK government or military source as % of sources used?

BBC1	11%
Sky	7%
Channel 4	7%
ITV	5%

% of reports in which Iraqis were presented as welcoming the invasion

BBC1	31%
Sky	36%
Channel 4	20%
ITV	37%

% of reports about Iraqis to refer to casualties

BBC1	22%
Sky	30%
Channel 4	44%
ITV	24%

% of reports in which Iraqis were presented as unhappy about the invasion

BBC1	11%
Sky	12%
Channel 4	12%
ITV	13%

Source: Cardiff University

Figure 8.7 'Coverage under fire', *Guardian*, 4 April 2003

eventually led to the resignation of the BBC Director-General Greg Dyke, the sacking of Andrew Gilligan, a government inquiry and subsequent publication of the Hutton Report. (You can access the key points of the Hutton Report at http://news.bbc.co.uk/1/hi/uk_politics/3437315.stm.)

Chomsky argues that part of the hegemonic function of the media is to keep the remaining 80 per cent of the population happy – a concept called 'bread and circuses' – with a diet of celebrity gossip, sport, soap operas and light enter-tainment that they can read and watch without too much challenge. This could be seen as a rather cynical view, certainly one that might make us feel rather uncom-fortable. On the other hand, the counter-argument would suggest that this is a very generalised view that shows no understanding of the pressures under which those in the media world work – it also in itself seems quite elitist at times, assuming as it does that the 80 per cent are in fact compliant in some way – which is not always the case.

It can therefore be seen that the media have vested interests: to maintain the ideological status quo, to co-operate with the government (whenever possible) and to make money. Chomsky argues that this process is a form of control in a democratic society.

Regulation of the media

The UK media industry is more regulated than many in the rest of the world and every major medium in this country has some form of regulation protecting the public in one way or another. As Julian Petley points out in 'The Regulation of Media', the dominant view that Britain enjoys a largely free media is contradicted by the fact that there are over 50 pieces of legislation in place to restrict media freedom. These include the Contempt of Court Act, the Obscene Publications Act and the European Convention on Human Rights. Amongst the most commonly invoked are the law of libel and issues of personal privacy. There have been many famous cases in recent years involving Jeffrey Archer (against the *News of the World* and the *Star*), Elton John (against the *Sun*), BP's Lord Browne (against the *Daily Mail*) and Naomi Campbell (against the *Daily Mirror*). Petley argues that unlike in the United States, in Britain,

> **there has never been any domestically created, statutory, legally enforceable right to freedom of expression . . . In law, journalists are not regarded as society's watchdogs . . . Similarly, newspapers and broadcasters are treated . . . in exactly the same way as any other commercial organisation.**

(Petley 1999: 144)

In 2003 several of the existing regulators were replaced by one unified body, the Office of Communications, better known as Ofcom (information about its duties can be found on the website http://www.ofcom.org.uk). Other bodies include the Press Complaints Council (PCC), the Advertising Standards Authority (ASA) and the British Board of Film Classification (BBFC).

Self-regulation and the press: the Press Complaints Commission (PCC)

The Press Complaints Commission was set up in 1991 to replace the Press Council, itself introduced in 1951 as a means of curbing the then perceived power of press barons like Lord Beaverbrook. The Press Complaints Commission like its predecessor is a self-regulatory organisation; in other words, it has been set up by the newspaper industry itself and has no legal powers. It has a Code of Conduct that newspaper owners, editors and reporters (in theory) adhere to (this can be accessed at http://www.pcc.org.uk/cop/practice.html). However, if a newspaper flouts this Code of Practice, the PCC has only limited ways of punishing it. If the PCC upholds a complaint it will ask the newspaper to print the adjudication or an apology but cannot fine the offending newspaper.

The newspaper industry is keen to avoid the introduction of a 'proper' regulatory body with legal powers to impose fines. They argue that this would represent a threat to the freedom of the press and so would ultimately be anti-democratic. The government is unwilling to take on the newspapers by trying to impose such a regulatory body, as governments need the support of national newspapers, especially in the run-up to elections. It seems likely therefore that the current situation of newspaper self-regulation will remain in place.

The press, as with other branches of the media in Britain, are an important part of our democracy and in theory the principle of free speech should be protected to allow journalists to call to account those in positions of power and authority. For this to work, however, the press needs to maintain standards of accuracy and individual privacy. This is a delicate balancing act that requires considerable finesse but in the case of the newspaper industry, Petley argues, the PCC with its creed of self-regulation offers nothing more than 'the newspapers' insurance policy against the threat of statute law'. For an interview with Sir Christopher Meyer, the current director of the PCC, see http://media.guardian.co.uk/mediaguardian/story/0,,2185643,00.html.

In addition to the libel laws, there are a number of other legal statutes that impact upon what a newspaper can and cannot report. These include the Official Secrets Act, which prevents the publication of information (usually official papers) that might jeopardise state security. The government of the day can also, after consideration, issue a 'D Notice' to editors of newspapers suggesting that in the interests of the state security information might be withheld. Newspapers seldom breach a D Notice. One increasingly problematic area legally for newspapers relates to the reporting of information about people who are likely to be charged with criminal offences. Clearly a newspaper is able to write about the arrest and charging of a person accused of a crime. However, many are tempted to publish further background information that is likely to interest their readers. The danger is that in doing so the newspaper may influence the trial of the person when it takes place ('prejudice a fair trial') because the jury might have read information that would prejudice them in coming to a fair verdict. In extreme cases a newspaper may even be prepared to pay those involved in a trial to secure the rights to their stories once the verdict is announced. (See also Chapter 12 on news.)

The cinema: the British Board of Film Classification (BBFC)

The BBFC was originally set up by the film industry itself to bring uniformity to standards of film censorship imposed by the many disparate local authorities. The BBFC then became a regulatory body with an ambiguous relationship with the industry and the audience (see http://www.bbfc.co.uk/).

No entertainment organisation wants to become involved in legal battles because litigation is notoriously expensive and the publicity that court cases attract can backfire. At the same time all entertainment organisations have a genuine sense of what audiences might want and they also have to make a profit. A film, especially one made in the USA, has an average cost of US$100 million, which is a considerable investment.

The essential role of the BBFC is to classify films, videos and DVDs, assessing their suitability for public and private viewing across various age ranges. There is a range of certificates that can be given to film and video material. This system is particularly helpful for the exhibitors of films (the cinemas) because they feel safe in showing material without the threat of legal or other action being taken against them in terms of the nature of the material being shown. However, there have been times when this was not the case. *Crash*, a film directed by David Cronenberg and released in 1996, was banned by Westminster City Council despite being given an 18 certificate by the BBFC. Members of the Licensing Committee decided to ban the film from cinemas in their area because they felt that it was an immoral film that might actually inspire 'corrupt and depraved' behaviour in those who saw it. (It is interesting to note that since that time the film has been shown repeatedly on one of the Sky movie channels without a whisper of protest being heard.) Cinemas within the Council's boundaries simply did not show the film.

At the heart of all classification undertaken by the BBFC is the attempt to protect children from material that might be harmful to them, and also to protect the public at large from material that might deprave, harm or corrupt. This obviously pertains, in the main, to material of a sexual or violent nature.

Classification is not the only issue. There have been occasions when the BBFC have refused a film or video a certificate because it breaks their guidelines. This

Figure 8.8 *Crash* poster (1996)

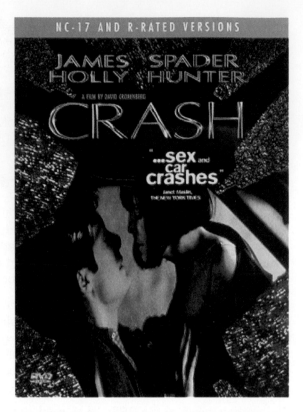

in turn has led to a debate about the nature of classification and whether it should be read as a form of censorship.

The nature of the job is such that there are in fact no formal qualifications needed to be a classifier. However, classifiers tend to be well-educated professionals. There is no evidence that any members of the film industry's target audience (for instance 18 to 25 year olds for a horror film) sit as classifiers. The BBFC says it recruits from the late-twenties age group upward because it thinks that the level of maturity required to assess some of the very disturbing material viewed by classifiers has not yet been acquired by a lower age group. However, films are tested, usually by distribution companies, with target audience screenings to see how well they are received.

Recently we have seen the introduction of the 12A certificate. This was a direct consequence of parental and exhibitor unhappiness at the discovery that the film *Spiderman* was going to be granted a 15 certificate – thereby preventing its natural audience from having an opportunity to view the film. It is interesting to note quite how many films have been granted this 12A certification since – there has clearly been a response to public pressure and an awareness that what children might see on the television (or indeed on video/DVD) is treated in a far more liberal manner by parents and guardians than by members of the BBFC.

Regulation and advertising

The degree to which advertising is regulated and controlled gives some idea of the importance, and potential influence, that it is considered to have. There is a range of organisations whose role is to make sure advertisements are not causing offence or breaking the rules. Many parts of the industry also have their own 'advisory' codes on what is acceptable in terms of advertising. The Broadcast Advertising Clearance Centre (BACC) (see http://www.bacc.org.uk), for instance, is a non-statutory body that takes responsibility for 'checking' all television and radio advertisements, although it is Ofcom that has the legal responsibility for regulating all commercial radio advertising.

Terrestrial television advertising is limited to an average of 7 minutes per hour during the day and 8 minutes per hour during the evening peak time. On satellite and cable channels the average is 9 minutes per hour. On some types of programming, for example, religious services, currently no advertising is allowed.

There have been strict controls on the advertising of health products, medicines and medical services since commercial television was introduced in 1955. However, over the years there has been a gradual loosening of the restrictions. As a result of concerns over AIDS (acquired immune deficiency syndrome) in the 1980s advertisements for condoms became acceptable.

The Advertising Standards Authority (ASA), an industry organisation, regulates advertising across all media. It operates a voluntary code (the CAP code, available at http://www.asa.org.uk) and is responsible for the 'Legal, Decent, Honest & Truthful' campaign.

Benetton

Any discussion of advertising has to acknowledge the impact that the campaigns of Benetton have had over the years, whether it be its images of a newborn baby, a dying AIDS patient or Mafia victims.

The AIDS patient advertisement was refused by several magazines, including *Marie Claire*, *Woman's Journal* and *Elle*, as well as *J-17* and *19*. This advertisement, like many others, was referred to the ASA, which recommended that this, like many of Benetton's other advertisements, be withdrawn. However, the controversy itself gave Benetton plenty of publicity.

These campaigns have succeeded in making Benetton a household name, which was the intention of Luciano Benetton and Oliviero Toscani, the founders of

Figure 8.9

the campaigns. Their advertisements have generated a lot of debate, and you can make your own contribution to this debate via the Benetton website (http://www.benetton.com).

Children

One of the most tightly regulated and controversial areas of advertising concerns children. There are many restrictions on the content of advertising aimed at children, the types of advertising that can be seen by children, as well as guidelines on how children may be portrayed in advertisements.

Ofcom stipulates that advertisements should not mislead, particularly in relation to games and toys. Advertisements must not make 'direct exhortations' to children to ask their parents to buy products for them, should not employ methods that 'take advantage of the natural credulity and sense of loyalty of children' and should not imply that a child will be 'inferior in some way or liable to be held in contempt or ridicule' if they do not own the product.

Many of these rules are the result of parents complaining about 'pester power', the amount of pressure put upon them as a result of advertising aimed at children, particularly in the run-up to Christmas. Toys may be demonstrated 'in action' on television but in real life often require additional components or perhaps need expensive batteries to operate in the manner shown on television.

The ASA recently announced new rules about the way in which food products can be advertised on TV (see http://www.asa.org.uk/asa/news/news/2007/New+food+advertising+rules.htm). According to the ASA, the rules have been tightened in response to government and public concern about the increase in childhood obesity and the future health of the nation. As a result, TV advertisements for food products that are classed as high in fat, salt and sugar (HFSS) will not be shown in or around programmes that hold particular appeal for children up to 16 years of age.

The advertising industry is aware of these concerns and debates surrounding advertisements aimed at children and there are several industry-based initiatives that attempt to promote a more responsible attitude to children's advertising. (See, for example, Mediasmart http://www.mediasmart.org.uk and the Advertising Association's site http://www.childrensprogramme.org.) There are also several academic surveys that focus on the issue of advertising and children; see, for example, http://www.aber.ac.uk/media/Documents/short/toyads.html.

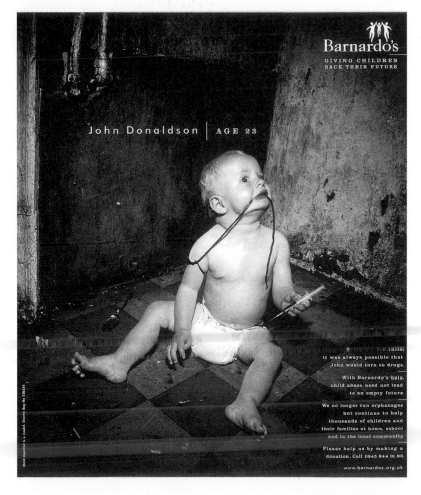

Figure 8.10

In October 1999 Barnardo's launched a newspaper campaign that caused some controversy. Figure 8.10 shows one of two advertisements featured in the campaign that were referred to the ASA. The other one, 'Martin Ward', featured a boy on top of a high-rise block of flats about to jump off. According to Barnardo's website at the time:

> **the current communications campaign challenges outdated views of Britain's biggest children's charity. It positions the organisation in the forefront of the fight to build better futures for disadvantaged, abused and troubled children. Though the advertisements are hard-hitting, the message is one of hope – that Barnardo's can help children overcome childhood deprivation and avoid futures like these. While Barnardo's work has evolved to encompass all the key issues affecting the lives of disadvantaged children, young people and their families, the public image of the organisation has not kept pace with this development. Research shows that the majority of people in the UK retain an essentially historical view of Barnardo's. They continue to see it as a charity running 'orphanages', or large-scale residential childcare facilities. The image of the organisation remains rooted in its past, epitomised by the 'cottage collecting boxes' once a feature of millions of homes.**

(http://www.barnardos.org.uk)

This is the ASA's adjudication of the Barnardo's advertisement shown in Figure 8.10:

Media: national press
Agency: Bartle Bogle Hegarty
Sector: Non-commercial
Complaints from: Nationwide (28)

Complaint: Objections to an advertisement in the *Guardian*, the *Independent*, the *Independent on Sunday*, the *Observer*, the *Scotsman*, *Scotland on Sunday* and *The Times* for a children's charity. It featured a baby sitting alone in squalid surroundings. Dirt covered the floor and walls; in his teeth the baby held a cord, which was tightened round his right arm to make a tourniquet; in his left hand he held a syringe as if to inject heroin. The headline stated 'John Donaldson Age 23'; the body copy stated 'Battered as a child, it was always possible that John would turn to drugs. With Barnardo's help, child abuse need not lead to an empty future. Although we no longer run orphanages, we continue to help thousands of children and their families at home, school and in the local community'. The complainants objected that the advertisement was shocking and offensive.

The advertisers believed the advertisement complied with the Codes. They said it was part of a campaign to raise awareness of their preventative work with children and young people; the campaign was designed to make people reconsider their opinions about Barnardo's work and the subjects depicted in each advertisement. The advertisers argued that they had not intended merely to shock. They said they had taken the precaution of researching the campaign twice among their target audience of ABC1 adults aged 35 to 55 and their supporters, staff and service users. They submitted the research findings, which they believed showed most people understood the advertisement's message and found its approach effective in changing opinions about Barnardo's work. The advertisers maintained that, because the consequences of drug addiction were potentially devastating, the stark image was justified as a means of raising public awareness of the potential dangers for disadvantaged children; they believed it was an effective way of making the point that Barnardo's could help keep them safe. Their consumer research acknowledged that some people found images of alcoholism or drug abuse upsetting. They nevertheless maintained that an image based on the innocence of a child and potential pain in adult life communicated the message that Barnardo's was a contemporary charity with modern perspectives on child development. The advertisers submitted extracts from published research, which showed that disadvantaged and abused children were particularly vulnerable to emotional and behavioural problems in later life; they provided recent survey results that showed that parents and children found drugs worrying and frightening. They asserted that the child depicted had not been put at risk and that the advertisement was made with full parental awareness and consent. The advertisers said they had monitored public responses to their advertisement; they had received more supportive responses than complaints. The *Independent* said they had received less than five complaints and considered that the advertisement would not cause serious or widespread offence to their readers. The *Guardian* said they believed their readers would understand the advertisers' message and they had received no complaints. The *Scotland on Sunday* said they regarded drugs very seriously but considered that Barnardo's advertisement was compelling and justified. They said they had received no complaints. *The Times*, the *Scotsman*, the *Independent on Sunday* and the

continued

Observer did not respond. The Authority noted the advertisement had offended or distressed some readers. It nevertheless acknowledged that the advertisers had intended to convey a serious and important message. The Authority considered that they had acted responsibly by conducting research among their target audience to ensure the message was understood and unlikely to shock or offend. The Authority noted the picture of drug abuse was directly related to the advertisers' preventative work with children and considered that the target audience was likely to interpret the image in the context of the accompanying text. The Authority accepted the advertisers' argument that they had not intended merely to shock. It considered that, because the advertisers had used the image to raise public awareness of the seriousness of drug abuse and the action that could be taken to prevent it, the advertisement was unlikely to cause either serious or widespread offence or undue distress and was acceptable.

Adjudication: Complaints not upheld.

Media imperialism

Media imperialism is the idea that powerful and wealthy countries can exercise economic, cultural and social control over others through control of media industries or their output.

Since the events of 11 September 2001, the demand for information about news and events is more global than it ever used to be. This is a demand for information not only about news and politics but also about other areas of human activity such as sport and entertainment. The world of the domestic or parochial television or radio station is changing very rapidly as media institutions, in order to deal with worldwide audience demands, have discovered that they need to look beyond their own borders.

Again money plays a big part. Take, for example, US television and film production. An American film or television series such as *Friends* or *Lost* is made for an American audience on what often amounts to a tremendously well-organised and efficient conveyor-belt/studio-system production line, after much money has been spent on research and testing audience satisfaction with the product. Test audiences tell the producers whether they like, or even understand, the product. Characters are removed if test plays suggest they are not popular. It is not uncommon for the ending of a film to be changed after testing. Yet the majority of American film and television products make their money on the domestic front. It is important to remember that the production costs, based on what in many cases amounts to a factory system, are relatively cheap – relatively, considering the size of the American audience in the first place. If the production company recoups all its costs and makes a good profit on the show's distribution in America, any extra income from sales abroad is therefore 'extra' profit (see Chapter 9 on *Heroes*).

Often a television company in any other part of the world will often find it cheaper to buy American ready-made programmes than to make them itself. Again the notion of the loss leader comes into play here. In the first instance these non-American companies can purchase the product relatively cheaply, especially if it is an old programme (*Star Trek* and *I Love Lucy* are perennial favourites). However, should that programme prove to be popular, then the next series will not be quite so cheap (a striking example of this was the escalating price of the television series *Lost* or *The Sopranos*).

It is also worth noting that nowadays many products come in packages. If the television company in question wants to purchase a very popular American series that all its rival networks are also interested in buying, then it will often have to purchase other less successful or less popular series made by the same producers at the same time. Naturally, once a television company has bought a series, it will show it anyway. If it is not a great ratings winner, then it can be used as early-afternoon or late-night filler material.

There are two reasons why some governments are worried by this trend. On one level this process can have a retrograde effect on the home market in terms of developing domestic production, talent and culture.

Figure 8.11

result, in 2007 companies including BBC, ITV, Channel Four and GMTV were all found guilty of manipulating competitions, votes and phone-ins. Ofcom found GMTV guilty of 'gross negligence' and 'widespread and systematic deception of millions of viewers' and fined the broadcaster £2 million. Ofcom also fined the BBC £50,000 over an incident in which a girl on a studio tour was persuaded to pose as the winner on a *Blue Peter* competition.

It is hard to speculate on the extent to which this interactivity will affect the ways in which we consume the media. However, new hard-drive player/recorders are said to offer the potential for each consumer to organise and select his or her own particular menu of entertainment. These machines contain a computer hard-drive that can store many hours of television digitally and when played back it can skip advert breaks. Like a VCR, this technology can record live or pre-programmed television and can also suggest particular programmes based on the owner's viewing habits. It is connected to the telephone so can send viewing information back to marketing firms. Instead of 'broadcasting', these new recorders will mean 'narrowcasting' – in effect making the 'old' mass audiences increasingly fragmented. (See Chapter 7 on media audiences.)

Much of this technological revolution is driven by companies who see it as an opportunity to sell us consumer products – games consoles, online services (both for goods and for services), 'edutainment' software on CD-ROM or DVD, and interactive and subscription services that we may be willing to pay extra for – as well as the hardware necessary to access them. The companies will be targeting those who can most easily afford to buy these new products. Those who cannot afford the new hardware or subscription charges will perhaps be excluded, and we will develop a 'digital underclass' or 'information-rich/information-poor' societies.

Currently most countries in the world have some kind of internet activity, but it is only used regularly by about 18 per cent of the world's population – those who live in affluent, developed societies – and most of these users are white, male professionals.

However, these statistics need to be considered as a percentage of the population for each area, for example, in the USA over 70 per cent of the population are online. In Africa, although the number online has doubled over the last five years, it is still less than 5 per cent of Africa's population, and this varies considerably between such extremes as South Africa (with over 10 per cent of its population online) and Ethiopia (with less than 0.2 per cent of its population online). Ethiopia has a population larger than that of Britain but has only one ISP (internet service provider), which is state-owned. In Britain there are at least 245 ISPs, most of which are commercially run.

Conclusion

A recent survey by Google claimed to show that we now spend more time surfing the net than watching television:

> **the average Briton spends around 164 minutes online every day, compared with 148 minutes watching television. That is equivalent to 41 days a year spent surfing the web: more than almost any other activity apart from sleeping and working.**

(file:///C:/Documents%20and%20Settings/Philip/Desktop/3rd%20ed/Internet%20&%20television%20use%20report.htm)

ACTIVITY

Conduct research to try to verify the Google survey. You may want to ask a sample of people from a range of ages to determine how internet usage varies across the age range; then ask your respondents to keep a short record of the hours they spend watching television and surfing the internet over a 'typical' week. Display your findings so that you can share them with your peers. Did your findings corroborate the Google survey? If not, how can you explain the disparities?

One of the difficulties in studying or writing about the media is that the media world is constantly changing. This change may be fairly superficial, for example, in terms of what is this week's most controversial television programme or the current bestselling 'lads' magazine. Often, however, these changes are the result of developments in technology, and the rate of these technological changes is speeding up. As we have suggested, one of the biggest changes taking place today in the media is the development of the internet.

This means that by the time you read this book, many of the examples and scenarios discussed in it will have changed or moved on. It also means that it is increasingly difficulty to talk about British media because so much of the media in Britain comes from outside our geographical borders. The way in which the media in Britain reflects the increased multi-culturalism and globalisation of our culture and everyday lives makes it an interesting and dynamic subject to study. However, because it is constantly changing, it is especially important that you, as a student of the media, keep up to date with the latest developments in ownership, regulation, competition and new technology. A good way to do this is to regularly access the *Guardian*'s media website at http://media.guardian.co.uk/.

further reading

Curran, J. and Seaton, J. (2003) *Power without Responsibility: The Press and Broadcasting in Britain*, Routledge.
Franklin, B. (ed.) (2001) *British Television Policy: A Reader*, Routledge.
Gauntlett, D. (2004) *Web studies*, Arnold.
Media Guardian (2007) *Media Directory*, Guardian Newspapers.

part 2

INVESTIGATING MEDIA

BROADCAST FICTION: HEROES

9

In this chapter we use the series *Heroes* as an example of an American-based fictional television series. We will examine *Heroes* using a variety of key concepts, exploring issues such as:

- genre
- codes and conventions
- representation
- institution
- audience.

Figure 9.1 *Heroes*

Stokes suggests that it is a basic human characteristic to tell stories about ourselves, about the world and about the people and phenomena that we encounter. Stokes suggests that 'Narrative also conveys the ideology of a culture, and it is one of the means by which values and ideals are reproduced culturally' (Stokes 2003: 67).

Television drama fiction programmes are at the heart of the broadcasting schedules and are heavily dependent upon real and fictional narratives, for example, it would be interesting to conduct an analysis across a day or a week's peak-time viewing on television to see what proportion of the programmes are fictional or factual. Drama fiction is, however, an expensive genre and as audiences become more sophisticated, drama fiction requires greater and greater investment. This is perhaps one of the reasons why many of our most successful fictional dramas and narratives are American and particular companies, such as HBO (part of Time Warner), have become associated with 'high quality' television fiction such as *Sex and the City*, *The Sopranos*, or *Six Feet Under*. These types of programmes are popular with audiences and often attract publicity for the channel that broadcasts them.

However, there is a difficulty when it comes to analysing these types of programmes, in that we often choose those that we particularly enjoy and end up producing an analysis that is little more than 'why I like xxx'. We need to be able to distance ourselves from our favourite fictional programmes, separate the 'fan' bit of ourselves and instead subject the programmes to critical scrutiny.

This involves looking at a range of issues, for example:

- Knowledge, application and evaluation of **film and media language** (e.g. the analysis of image, sound and music; mise-en-scène, sets and settings; visual techniques [editing, camera positioning, lighting, etc.]; generic conventions; non-verbal codes [basic semiotics]; iconography, etc.)
- Issues of **audience** (audience positioning; target audience; the programme's assumptions about the audience; possible audience readings and evaluations; conditions of reception); your own reading and evaluation of the text, and the major cultural and subcultural influences upon this)
- Issues of **representation** (e.g. of gender, race, nationality, region, heroes, villains, historical periods, etc.). Debates around the fairness, accuracy, function and purpose of particular representations
- **Narrative** issues (e.g. study of specific narratives; comparison of different narrative structures and techniques; major differences between film and television narratives; types of television fictional narrative – soaps, series, serials and single narratives; influence of genre on narrative; influence of conditions of viewing; narrative openings and closures; use of character and actors in narrative; techniques of audience engagement and identification)
- **Institutional** issues (influence of film/broadcasting institutions upon texts; differences within film and broadcasting institutions, e.g. Hollywood vs. non-Hollywood; public service vs. commercial broadcasting; influence of finance,

marketing and distribution upon the production and reception of texts. Debates around aesthetic value, profit, public-service values etc.)

■ Questions of, and debates around, **values and ideology**.

Below is an example using the American fictional television drama series *Heroes* (series 1).

Heroes premiered in 2006 on NBC in America and in 2007 in the UK on the digital Sci-Fi channel. When the series transferred to BBC2, it attracted audiences of over 4 million. (Excerpts from the series can be found at http://www.bbc.co.uk/drama/heroes/episodes.)

Heroes can ultimately be seen as a science fiction programme (hence its premier in the UK on the digital Sci-Fi channel) which follows the generic conventions of films such as *Men in Black* or *X-Men* and television series such as *Buffy the Vampire Slayer*, *The X-Files* or *The Twilight Zone*.

Codes and conventions

Heroes is a complex, carefully constructed multimedia product that relies on a very sophisticated audience that is able to 'read' the variety of signs, codes, conventions and references contained in each episode. It is a prime example of bricolage, where the signs or artefacts of one or more styles or genres are borrowed to create something new. At the same time, part of the series' attraction is that it contains some basic, 'mythic' narratives familiar to many science fiction texts, i.e. the fight between good and evil (although it is not always clear who is good and who is evil), 'ordinary' people being put into extraordinary situations (for example, where they have to save New York City from an apparently 9/11-type catastrophe), the conflict between authority, order and anarchy (although again it is not clear on which side of this conflict the various 'heroes' are) and the fear of conspiracies and a too-powerful (secret) government organisation.

Science fiction iconography is used as part of the title sequence which occurs several minutes after the show has started in the form of a total eclipse of the earth whose relevance (if any) is not explained. There is also a quick flash of light that is again unexplained but ominous. This is usually accompanied by a voice-over saying mock-mystical phrases such as 'Is it evolution that takes us by the hand?' The premise of the series, that ordinary people develop super-human powers, perhaps through evolution, is also a key characteristic of the science fiction genre.

Each episode is usually made up of a number of short scenes that may (or may not) be interconnected as they follow the storyline of the various 'heroes'. The series is very dependent upon the comic book, science fiction genre with short, sharp scenes that seem to replicate the image of a comic book. There are several overarching story lines all going on at once that are somehow interconnected but this connection is usually not clear to the viewer and is one of the programme's main sources of engagement and suspense.

One difference between *Heroes* and a comic book is that it is not possible to peek at the end to see how things work out. This means that the viewer is in a constant state of uncertainty, waiting to see what happens next, which story line will be featured in the next scene, and how the (complex) narrative will develop.

Each scene is short, lasting approximately 2 minutes, and usually ends with some kind of climax. The *mise-en-scène*, whatever appears in the actual film frame, is carefully constructed to reinforce a continual ominous sense of threat or uncertainty. Most scenes seem to take place indoors where the lighting is low, the spaces appear cramped, and the shots are often multi-angle head and shoulder shots that give little information to the viewer but rather focus on the character and what he/she is thinking or feeling. This helps create an almost continual sense of claustrophobia and underlying danger. Speech is also often jumbled and con- fused, which increases the sense of confusion and disorientation in the viewer. The music used is low-key and ominous, although there is also a modern 'spacy' feeling to it. The music, the lighting, the use of slo-mo, non-diegetic sound and multi-angled filming all contribute to give a sense of 'otherworldliness' to the characters and their activities, especially when using their 'powers' (see, for example, where Peter jumps off a New York building and is caught by his 'flying' brother Nathan: http://www.bbc.co.uk/drama/heroes/episodes/1.shtml).

Special effects are an important part of the way the series is constructed and made to appeal to its audience. There is even a spin-off weekly series called *Heroes Unmasked* (http://www.bbc.co.uk/drama/heroes/unmasked/) which is broadcast on BBC2 after each episode. This explains how the series has been made, the actors chosen 'after a worldwide search' and the special effects created. It is a little ironic that this show demonstrates the falseness of what we see and shows us how the use of stunt artists, post-production editing and the insertion of computer-generated imagery (CGI) help create the illusion of the action we see on our screens. Rather than destroy the illusion, this series seems to add to the whole 'mystic' of *Heroes* by emphasising how clever and cutting-edge it is.

Heroes is a difficult text to analyse as it confuses the traditional roles of 'hero', 'villain' etc. and it is therefore hard to apply the structure suggested by Propp (see Chapter 2, p. 55). However, the notion that we discussed early that 'conflict is central to the functioning of narrative not least because it is conflict that invites us, the audience, to take sides' (p. 55) is an important element in driving the narrative of *Heroes* forward.

Representation

Most of the main characters in *Heroes* are male with a range of young/old, black/white, good/evil characters. The characters appear to be more complex than the female characters with more ambiguous traits. Nathan, for example, appears to be very protective of his brother Peter, but this may be due to the damage Peter could do to Nathan's political aspirations. Matt is a failed policeman whose marriage is not working out and who steals some diamonds.

The central character of Mohinder is, like his father, an Indian university professor and could perhaps be seen as part of a general stereotype of people of Indian-descent being hard-working, intelligent and at the cutting edge of new technology. The scenes where Mohinder returns to India are perhaps some of the least realistic of the series. (The whole series is shot in television studios in Los Angeles.)

The two Japanese characters, Hiro and Ando, are shown in a slightly comical way as they try to adapt to life in America and in particular to Las Vegas and New York. The scenes of their lives back home in Japan show them as stereotypical 'company men' working in large impersonal offices (although Hiro is eventually revealed as the son and heir of the man who owns the company – who is himself a rather sinister character). Both Hiro and Ando are depicted as very innocent.

There are several male characters who, in varying degrees, are seen as bad and/or evil: Isaac the artist who paints the future but only when under the influence of drugs; DL, Niki's husband who is an ex-criminal but tries to look after his son when Niki is in jail; Mr Bennet (he doesn't seem to have a first name); Claire's father, whose intentions, whether good or evil, are unclear; and Sylar the serial killer, responsible for some gruesome murders. The male characters seem to have more depth and variety to them. They are allowed freedom of action, both good and bad, which does not seem available to the female characters.

There are two main female characters in the first series, both blond, white, young and attractive. Niki has an alter-ego (her dead sister called Jessica) and between them they are both violent and sexual. Niki is shown early on in the series as an 'internet stripper' (note, not a porn artist) and Jessica is responsible for some of the most bloody and gruesome killings in the series. Niki is shown as trying to live as a single mother focused on her son's welfare.

The other main female character, Claire, is shown as a young teenager/cheerleader and seems to spend most of her on-screen time wearing a cheer leader outfit and running a lot. Although attractive, the character is not overtly sexual. Claire is shown as being concerned about her 'real' parents as well as the welfare of her adopted mother.

A secondary character, Issac's one-time girlfriend Simone, is played by a black actor and is again young and attractive. She is killed early on in the first series.

Both Claire and Niki as female action heroes can be seen as positive representations, although overall the range of female characters and actors is rather limited compared to the male characters. The female characters are portrayed as trying to maintain 'ordinary' middle-class American lives despite the problems caused by their super powers.

There is a good racial mix in *Heroes* with American negroes, a (mysterious) Haitian, Indians and two Japanese characters. It is interesting to consider why these characters were included: is it to reflect the racial diversity of United States; is it to try to appeal to a racially diverse television audience; is it political correctness; or is it for dramatic effect? It is also worth considering the extent to which these characters do (or do not) conform to racial stereotypes.

Figure 9.2 Hiro in *Heroes*

INVESTIGATING MEDIA

It is also interesting to consider that if the science fiction films from 1950s (*The Invasion of the Body Snatchers* (1956) or *It Came from Beneath the Sea* (1955)) were supposed to represent a fear of communist invasion and *Star Trek* in 1960s was supposed to be a metaphor for America's involvement in Vietnam, what (if anything) is the underlying representation of *Heroes*?

ACTIVITY

Apart from the main 12 characters listed on the *Heroes* website, list the other important characters and try to decide in what ways they are positive or negative representations. For example:

■ How would you categorise the character of Claude?
■ Are there any differences between the male and female characters? If so how do you account for this?
■ Are there any social groups that are obviously missing from *Heroes*, for example, the elderly, gays or native American Indians?

Institution

It is important to remember that *Heroes* is the carefully constructed product of a major multi-national television company, NBC, owned by the US-based consumer giant General Electric (GE). This means that the *Heroes* series have had a lot of money invested in them and that consequently NBC anticipates making a lot of money as a return on its investment. General Electric own a whole range of production companies and television stations in America as well as Universal film studios and theme parks (http://www.cjr.org/resources/).

ACTIVITY

Access the General Electric home page and analyse how the company presents itself. For example, it has various web pages dedicated to 'values' such as community and citizenship: 'Every day, the people of GE seek to improve the world in which we live.' Why do you think the company focuses on this rather than telling us about its products?

continued

On the UK page of its website (http://www.ge.com/uk/) it asks 'What can GE do for you?' and then says: 'GE people worldwide are dedicated to turning imaginative ideas into leading products and services that help solve some of the world's toughest problems.'

Again, try to suggest reasons for this approach to marketing the company. Do you think these statements are supported by the information contained in the website?

It is also important to remember that *Heroes* is being promoted by NBC as a brand, something that has a strong identity through its name and logo or slogan. Establishing *Heroes* as a brand is important financially for NBC because it allows the company to sell many other products under that brand name. The name *Heroes* will become not only associated with the television series but also with the way in which the series is viewed, understood and interpreted by television viewers across the world.

ACTIVITY

One of the most successful brands to develop out of a television series is *Star Trek*, first broadcast in 1966. Using *Star Trek* or another example of your own choice, investigate how the brand has been developed and what products are sold under the brand heading. You might consider videos and DVDs of the television series and films, toys, books, clothing and other items. A good way to start is to look for commercial websites for the brand and then see if there is a shopping or store section (see, for example, http://store.startrek.com/page/collectibles/).

The main NBC *Heroes* website is sponsored by Nissan (see http://www.nbc.com/Heroes/) and offers a shopping facility that includes *Heroes* branded items such as DVDs, T-shirts, watches, a calendar, graphic novels and a lunchbox. The graphic novels can be downloaded from the website as well as being published in hardback. There is currently a second series of *Heroes* as well as a spin-off series *Heroes: Origins*. With its changing cast of characters, potential back-stories and unresolved story lines, *Heroes* should run for several series. If *Heroes* is a success in countries like the UK, then NBC can increase the price it charges for each series as the BBC will not want to lose the programme. (This is similar to other successful television programmes where another television channel has 'poached' the series

from the original broadcaster by paying more for follow-up series, examples include *The Simpsons*, *Lost* and *The Sopranos*.) There are also computer and mobile phone games being developed around the *Heroes* brand.

The fact that the series was created by NBC means that there was a considerable amount of financial investment available for the making of the programmes, especially if we consider that *Heroes* is an 'untested' product rather than a direct copy of other successful programmes within an easily definable genre. This means that NBC were perhaps taking a risk with the making of *Heroes* but that also they could invest heavily in the promotion and marketing of *Heroes* to try to ensure that the risks were as small as possible.

The sponsors Nissan will also have made a financial contribution to the making and marketing of the series; their logo and adverts feature strongly on the websites and Nissan cars are used by various characters in different episodes.

It would be hard for many other, smaller television production companies to emulate this amount of investment in the production and marketing of a new untested series like *Heroes*. Even the BBC, with far more resources than many independent television companies, would be unlikely to take such a risk and is much happier buying something that is a proven success in USA, although this in itself is no guarantee of success in the UK. The BBC also knew that the series was well received when premiered in the UK on the Sci-Fi channel and in fact benefited from 'word-of-mouth' recommendations from those who had seen the series on the digital channel. The Sci-Fi Channel (coincidentally?) is owned by NBC, enabling them again to promote their product in a new country and again lessen the risk of losing money on a new series. It would be interesting (but difficult) to know when the BBC made the decision to buy the series, how much it paid for it, and whether it has also purchased the second (or subsequent) series. Some people argue that there are too many American programmes on British television and that organisations like the BBC should be developing home-grown programmes.

Website Activity 9.1: Audience research into American programming.

The BBC website has an online *Heroes* game and a podcast for the 'Official Radio Show' broadcast on BBC7 as well as a download facility for mobiles to get character profiles, wallpapers and other material sent to your mobile phone (at a cost, of course). This enables the BBC to also make some money out of the series.

In 2007 there was considerable scandal around the use by television companies, including the BBC, of premium telephone lines as a means of generating extra income (see p. 187). However the BBC, like the other television companies, needs to generate extra income, especially as the licence fee is lower than the BBC would have wished.

Outline the main argument for and against the BBC earning additional income through activities such as downloads for mobiles. You might also wish to consider what other commercial activities the BBC undertakes, for example, books and magazines relating to successful BBC series such as *Dr Who*, *The Clothes Show*, etc. Consider the arguments for and against these types of activities by a 'non-commercial' organisation.

Audience

Although when *Heroes* was first broadcast on BBC2 it attracted over 4 million viewers, its audience is now around 2.5 million. BBC3's broadcast of *Heroes* attracts just over 1 million per episode and follows on from the previous episode just shown on BBC2. In effect digital viewers are being allowed to see the next episode one week early. Episodes are also repeated again late at night on BBC2. This means that each episode is broadcast at least three times a week, plus an episode of *Heroes Unmasked*, and seen by an audience of over 3.5 million. By showing each episode first on BBC3, the BBC is using *Heroes* as a means of attracting viewers to its digital channels. You may wish to conduct some research amongst your peers and colleagues to find out when, where and how audiences access and consume a programme like *Heroes*, for example:

- Do they watch it online?
- Do they watch it on BBC3 or BBC2?
- If they watch on BBC2 or BBC3, do they watch it alone? With family? With friends?
- Do they watch the same episode more than once?
- Did they watch the series when it was first broadcast on the Sci-Fi channel?
- What first made them decide to watch the series?

Increasingly, fans, in both the UK and America, communicate with one another through the web where there are several official and unofficial *Heroes* websites.

Originally fan-based websites were seen as a way of empowering audiences who had been previously ignored by mainstream culture. These unofficial websites enabled fans to develop a sense of community and common interest as well as exchanging ideas, gossip and information about characters and narrative development. It was often claimed that these websites helped generate a sense of fellowship and support for fans who may have otherwise felt isolated and/or misunderstood.

Today, however, fan-based websites are officially sanctioned and controlled and are an important part of the marketing and attraction of programmes like *Heroes*. Television companies recognise the importance of these websites and the opportunity they provide to encourage viewers to participate in the programme beyond merely watching it on television.

The official websites (such as http://www.9thwonders.co.uk; http://www.heroes360.co.uk/mainsite) are carefully constructed to enable fans to have the opportunity to become more deeply involved in the brand, its characters, narratives, insider 'gossip' and future developments. For example, it is possible to see trailers for the next series of *Heroes* at http://heroes-spoilers.blogspot.com. This helps to ensure that audiences are 'hooked' on the programme, will remain loyal to subsequent series and continue to purchase the merchandising.

These official websites also give the show's authors and producers the opportunity to develop a more personal and intimate relationship with their (worldwide) audience. One of the recent postings from the show's creators says:

> **I'm sorry that I can't answer all of your questions personally but I will be looking over all of them in the next day or so. It is fans like you that will make this show a success. I need each and every one of you to keep watching and telling all of your friends to watch as well, and we will do everything in our power to make this the best show on television and to honor friends like you.**

ACTIVITY

Access the blog at http://blog.nbc.com/heroes/2006/09/thanks_to_all_the_fans.php and consider the way in which the show's creators try to create a sense of personal engagement with their audience. For example, how do they talk to their fans? What are the issues that are discussed? Who initiates these? Do you think this works?

Hill and Calcutt (2001) argue that sites like these are typical of the ways in which fandom operates. By using websites to create a sense of community, the producers are enabling fans to construct particular identifies for themselves and actively participating in the creation of certain types of meaning for popular cultural texts. Increasingly, the media companies are taking over the idea of fan-based websites and turning them into promotional vehicles.

Fan-based websites originally offered a distinctive way of engaging with popular media texts, whether through expressing one's own personal views, giving information or entering into discussion with other fans. However, increasingly those that participate in the blogs and other web-based activities are viewed as being manipulated by NBC and other mainstream media companies.

There are many other *Heroes*-related websites. Most of them, like http://www.imdb.com/title/tt0813715/board, are hosted by media companies that are trying to sell merchandise to *Heroes* fans. However, it is still possible still to use the web to subvert the programme, for example, the YouTube parody at http://www.youtube.com/watch?v=vVV2ft4-2xk.

ACTIVITY

Run a Google search for fan-based websites for the show *Heroes* (for example, http://www.buddytv.com/Heroes.aspx or http://www.conservativecat.com/mt/archives/2007/05/heroes_on_tv.html) and try to categorise the types of responses that are shown. For example:

- Are they all positive?
- Where in the world do they originate from?
- Are they predominantly from males or females?
- What are the main topics of discussion?
- Do you think these messages are censored or moderated in any way? If so by whom, using what criteria?

Conduct some research amongst your peers, do many of them use these types of sites? If so, why?

Some of the popularity of long-running television series is their familiarity and sense of continuity, although it is difficult to think of *Heroes* offering reassurance or comfort. It is, however, useful to think about how audiences are positioned in terms of a programme like *Heroes*. For example, who are we supposed to identify with, be sympathetic to? Do male members of the audience identify with the male heroes and female members with the female heroes? Do the opinions of your peers and colleagues influence the way you view the programme or its characters? Does the idea of a hero inevitably invite our admiration?

Website Activity 9.2: Marketing of another TV series/film.

And finally . . .

It is worth spending a little time to think about the ideological messages contained within the *Heroes* series. Questions to consider include the following:

- To what extent can the programme be seen to promote American values?
- What is the significance of the threatened destruction of New York and the way that it can be seen to refer the events of 9/11?
- What is *Heroes* saying (if anything) about authority, social order and America's place in the world?
- Why, for example, if the 'heroes' are a worldwide phenomenon, does everyone end up in America?
- What messages (if any) are we the audience being given about the role of individuals in society and the role of a large, anonymous government agency?
- In what ways does *Heroes* promote a positive (or a negative) representation of 'the future' and, in particular, evolution?

Further reading

Creeber, G. (ed.) (2004) *Fifty Key Television Programmes*, Arnold.
Hill, A. and Calcutt, I. (2001) 'Vampire hunters: the scheduling and reception of *Buffy the Vampire Slayer* and *Angel* in the UK' in Rayner, P., Wall, P. and Kruger, S. (2003) *AS Media Studies: The Essential Introduction*, 2nd edn, Routledge.
Stokes, J. (2003) *How To Do Media and Cultural Studies*, Sage.

10 DOCUMENTARY AND ITS HYBRID FORMS

In this chapter we look at the concept of realism and its particular significance to the genre of documentary. We consider:

- the accuracy of the representation
- different types of realism
- continuity editing
- documentary film-making
- the docu-soap
- reality television.

The study of documentary and the many related forms that have emerged from the genre provide a particularly useful means of exploring the concept of *realism*, which is central to much of our study of the media. In Chapter 1 we looked at the way in which the media use sign systems to provide us with a representation of the outside world. We also noted that, because of a prevalence of iconic signs in visual media such as film, television and photography, these representations of the world can appear so natural that we easily see them as real. In this way, audiences may overlook the process of mediation that has occurred in presenting these images to us.

In considering the issue of realism, one of our concerns is to determine just how accurately a media form such as film or television can be said to represent 'reality'. As we noted in Chapter 4 on representation, what the media present to us is always a constructed and edited version of the real world. Any enquiry into realism must always take on board this issue. Similarly, when we look at a landscape painting, we always bear in mind that it is a painting or representation rather than the landscape itself. In both the painting and a media representation, we should always remember that what we are presented with is an illusion of the real world and the events that take place in it.

We can identify just how constructed and encoded the concept of realism is by considering the significance of monochrome, for example, in press photographs or film and television text. Many people associate black and white images with realism. For example, some types of documentary photography or 1960s British cinema, in films such as *This Sporting Life* or *A Kind of Loving*, use black and white photography to depict a gritty realism of working-class life or poverty. As most of us see the world in its full spectrum of colour, there is a fundamental contradiction in the perception of black and white being in some way more real than a Technicolor image. Obviously there is something in our reading of mono-chrome images that makes us perceive its starkness as depicting the world in a more realistic way.

To confuse matters further, it has been argued that there is not one single realism, but that realism in media texts exists in a number of different ways.

Different types of realism

Some media texts may be considered realistic because they contain 'truth' from the outside world. In this way we would identify a news bulletin as realistic in so far as the information it communicates to us is based on a verifiable external reality. In consequence, we could argue that the content of such a text makes it realistic. A similar argument may be made for the realism of documentary films, which, like news, are concerned with offering factual information about external reality. This realism is sometimes referred to as 'realism of content'.

Some media texts may contain material that has little credibility in terms of what we may know of any external reality. Science fiction programmes or action movies are likely to contain material that we perceive as far-fetched or unrealistic. However, the construction of these texts may still be seen as realistic in so far as they are produced in such a way as to remain plausible and to contain detail that we accept as being realistic. For example, the characters, although unreal in appearance, may act out of plausible motives and hence appear realistic. We might ask ourselves the relatively simple question of whether or not we are convinced by the text.

One of the ways in which we judge a text is by its ability to represent reality to us in a convincing way. We expect some degree of verisimilitude or resemblance to things that we know from real life. For example, an anachronism such as motor vehicles appearing inadvertently in a historical drama will create implausibility and can interfere with our ability to believe what we see in the text.

Abercrombie (1996) identifies three different aspects of realism which are useful in our study of this topic. First there is a realism that can be called 'window on the world'. This type of realism makes the assumption that the media offer a view of the world similar to that of looking out of our window. This is the world *as it is*, or at least as it is when we look at it. Such a way of seeing realism of course ignores the complex construction of media output.

A second aspect of realism relates to the way in which narratives are used to create products that are 'real'. In general, realism employs narrative forms that are rationally ordered. The narrative will provide connections between events and the characters who participate in them. Such a narrative provides the audience with a flow of events taking place within a logical sequence.

A third way of looking at realism is how media products are designed to hide from the audience any evidence of the production process. When we look at a media product, we are generally not made aware of the way in which it has been constructed. It contains within it the illusion of realism. The text has been created in such a way as to look real or natural rather than to look as though it were the result of a production process. An example of the way in which media producers work in order to create realistic effects is through the use of the shot/reverse shot technique. This is a film-making artifice that is employed in news reports, documentaries and even dramas. It is a convenient way of filming a dialogue between people so that it will appear on screen as if they are having a normal conversation. This can form the basis of an interview on screen for a news report or a scene in which two actors are speaking to each other.

The technique (illustrated in Figure 10.1) is to shoot the faces of each of the participants in turn. So in the example of an interview on location, the interviewee will be facing the camera and answering the questions posed by the interviewer. If only one camera is being used, as is often the case on location, a second take will have to be made of the interviewer asking the questions. This is often shot over the shoulder of the interviewee. The questions and answers are, therefore, each shot in two separate takes and then edited to give the illusion of a 'natural' conversation between two people. The editor's job is to match up the individual shots of the two participants into a convincing and coherent sequence.

One useful device in creating such sequences is the use of what the industry calls 'noddies'. Noddies are basically reaction shots of an interviewer responding to what an interviewee has said. If you watch carefully, you will see these in news reports and other factual programming. They are, however, not what they seem. Noddies are generally filmed after the interview has taken place, with the interviewer making a variety of facial gestures to the camera. These can then be edited into the sequence to make it look as though the interviewer is showing interest in what is being said. This technique is especially useful when sequences are shot on film cameras with the sound recorded separately, as they can be used to 'patch' sequences where there are technical problems with lip sync.

Continuity editing

As we have seen, an important aspect of realism is the way in which the production process is concealed in film and television and is rooted in the editing process. The use of continuity editing is one method of shaping a text in such a way that it appears natural or realistic. Continuity editing requires that the action on screen should appear 'continuous'. In order to achieve this, the material must be shot

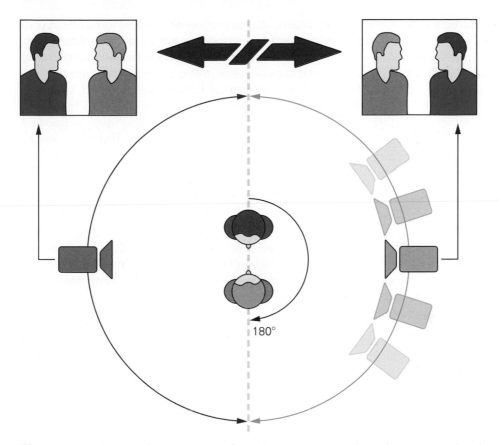

Figure 10.1 The 180° rule – cutting from the green arc to the red arc means the characters switch places on the screen and the sense of continuity may be destroyed

so that the editor can ensure that what we see appears logical; for example, matching the eye levels when using shot/reverse shot for dialogue. The editor must also observe the 180-degree rule, whereby the camera keeps to one side of an imaginary line dividing a scene. This means that the audience has a constant reference point in viewing the action. If the 180-degree rule is broken, the audience will lose this frame of reference and the sense of continuity may be destroyed.

For some critics, discussion of the issue of realism has no relevance in a world in which for many people the media themselves have come to represent the real world. The media no longer simply try to represent the real world; they have in fact replaced it. The French writer Jean Baudrillard (1993) coined the term 'hyper-real' to describe the way in which the media now dominate our perception of the outside world. For Baudrillard, the world of the television represents a reality that is 'more real' than what we can directly experience in the outside world. In this way a media representation becomes a hyper-reality, with the reality encountered in the world itself a pale shadow of this.

To appreciate what Baudrillard means, you might find it useful to think about your own experiences in attending a sporting event or a concert and comparing this with a similar experience of watching a football match or a rock concert on the television. Obviously the first-hand experience of 'being there' and the atmosphere are not readily captured by the televisual experience. On the other hand, television offers a multi-camera view of the event with cameras much closer to the action than most spectators are allowed. Television provides opportunities to pause a replay for an action that you missed, in slow motion or even still frame, as well as the opportunity to hear the views of experts and post-match or post-concert interviews and analysis.

Documentary film-making

Documentary film-making is one area in which the issue of realism is important. As its name suggests, a documentary seeks to document real life. It attempts to replicate experiences in the world in a realistic fashion. So, to some extent, we assess the effectiveness of a documentary film by its ability to convince us that what we are seeing is 'real'.

As a genre, documentary has developed over a period of years but still functions by seemingly holding up a mirror to the world to show the audience what is 'out there'. Clearly this is an oversimplification, not least because there is a whole range of different types of documentary. However, one feature common to all documentaries is the fact that, like all media products, they have to be constructed. Although this construction may be undertaken in such a way as to make the text seem natural and realistic, the same process of selection and shaping has taken place as in a fictional text.

Indeed, there are important areas in which there is a clear parallel between fictional film-making and documentary. Film-makers such as Mike Leigh, for example, in *Meantime* (1984), or Ken Loach in *Raining Stones* (1993), or more recently *The Wind That Shakes the Barley* (2006), create films that have a strong realistic or naturalistic quality. This is in part because of their subject matter. Many of their films are a celebration of the lives of ordinary people. The filmic style contrives to be naturalistic in that there is little evidence of intrusive camerawork or editing. The artifice of film-making is rendered subsidiary to the truth being told on the screen. Similarly, some documentaries will use the reconstruction of events where the original footage is either non-existent or needs to be supplemented by more dramatic sequences. There are also examples of drama documentaries in which real-life events are reconstructed and dramatised to enable audiences to relive the experience. The film *Touching the Void* (2003), directed by Kevin Macdonald, retells the events of a climb to the summit of Siula Grande in Peru. It reconstructs the climb made by Joe Simpson and Simon Yates and features them in the film retelling the story of how Simpson miraculously survived a fall, with two actors, Brendan Mackey and Nicholas Aaron, playing their characters to create dramatic impact.

There are a number of issues that need to be explored in relation to the nature of documentary and of realism. There are also ethical and ideological issues to be considered. If documentary seeks to show us some kind of truth, the process of construction is obviously going to represent that truth from a specific viewpoint. As we have seen, the use of a voice-over narrator is a powerful device not only in determining the response of the audience to a documentary, but also in positioning them in such a way as to limit the readings that are available.

The term 'documentary' was first coined by the Scottish film-maker John Grierson. As well as making films himself, Grierson wrote extensively about film. His essay 'First principles of documentary' written in the 1930s (republished Grierson 1996) argued that the cinema offered important opportunities for observing life and that using 'original' people and scenes were of more value than fictional ones, not least because they were more real. In the essay he describes documentary as 'the creative treatment of actuality'. This definition points to many of the issues that the student of documentary might usefully explore. The idea that although documentary is based in observation of real life or actuality, it can treat this creatively, which suggests that the documentary film-maker is empowered to do more than simply record what is there. For example, you might like to consider if creativity extends to the making of a scene that might not exist in order to achieve a particular impact or effect.

Grierson was zealous about the ability of film to educate people and in consequence the opportunities it offered for social reform. Grierson's films, and others of what became known as the British Documentary Film Movement, are very much a celebration of the life and work of ordinary people: fishermen in the North Sea, coalminers and, most famously, those associated with the transport mail from London to Scotland. *Nightmail*, made in 1936, featured the journey of the mail north from London, set against the poetry of W.H. Auden and set to a score by Benjamin Britten (see http://www.screenonline.org.uk/people/id/454202/).

Documentaries produced by the British Documentary Film Movement were shown in cinemas often as an accompaniment to the main feature. Today television is the main showcase for documentary productions. However, documentary made for first screening in the cinema has made a comeback in recent years. Film-makers such as Michael Moore (*Bowling for Columbine*) and Morgan Spurlock (*Supersize Me*) have released their films in cinemas to a great deal of critical acclaim and controversy. The work of these film-makers offers an interesting comparison with that of Grierson. Both make films from a specific ideological standpoint and use the documentary format as a means of making a specific point. *Bowling for Columbine* (2002) explores the shooting of 12 students and a teacher at Columbine High School in April 1999. Moore unashamedly uses footage to attack the National Rifle Association, which supports the constitutional rights of US citizens to bear arms. His film *Fahrenheit 9/11* (2004) is a direct attack on George Bush and his administration over the handling of the 9/11 attack on New York. For *Supersize Me*, Spurlock lives for 30 days on McDonald's fast food in order to demonstrate the potential damage such a diet can do to a person's health. It is fair to say that neither film-maker is much concerned with offering a balanced view but is making a film to offer a specific interpretation of an issue. (See also Michael Moore's website at http://www.michaelmoore.com/.)

Speaking about his film *Sicko* (2007), which exposes the inequalities of the American healthcare system, Moore said:

> **I made *Bowling for Columbine* in the hope the school shootings would stop and that we would address the issue of how easy it is to get a gun in the United States and, tragically, those school shootings continue. I made *Fahrenheit 9/11* and I said that we'd been led to a war under false pretense. I said it on the Oscar stage and I was booed off. It's my profound hope that people will listen this time.**

(IMDB website at: http://www.imdb.com/name/nm0601619/bio)

Interestingly, Moore's polemical style of documentary-making has led to a number of other film-makers creating documentaries as a riposte to his work. Canadians Debbie Melnyk and Rick Caine, once great admirers of Moore, released their film *Manufacturing Dissent* (2007) as a response to their own concerns about Moore's tactics as a movie-maker. The film purports to show footage shot by Moore in one of his documentaries which they say he deliberately left out of his film in order to create a specific impact. They also show in the film that Moore was evasive about giving them a sit-down interview as part of their film. Other films that have been made as a critique of Michael Moore include *Michael Moore Hates America*; *Celsius 41.11*; *Michael & Me* and *FahrenHYPE 9/11*.

An aspect of the political documentary that you might wish to consider further is the function of websites linked to the documentary or its maker. Websites have

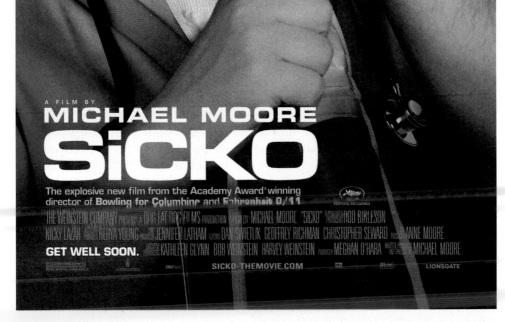

Figure 10.2

long been an important way of promoting films and television programmes. Websites for Michael Moore, however, do more than simply market the product: they are designed to engage the viewer in the activism that the film makers are proposing. This can involve in the first instance signing up to receive information about issues linked to the documentary. Visitors to the site are also encouraged to record their own experience of healthcare insurance as well as being directed to a YouTube site to which they can upload their videos. This involvement of audiences in contributing to media products is called 'democratisation of the media', on the basis that it is broadening participation in the production of the media and offering people an opportunity to put forward their own ideas and responses to issues.

If you check out some of the web activity around film-makers such as Moore and Spurlock, you will find that not only do they promote their ideas (and themselves) through the sites but also that a host of sites that both support and present counter-arguments to theirs have sprung up. Typically a site such as Morgan Spurlock Watch has the specific objective of countering Spurlock's claims by offering an alternative and generally right-wing take on the issues he tackles in his blog, where he describes himself as 'the worst blogger in the history of blogdom' (see http://blogs.indiewire.com/morganspurlock/).

This approach to documentary has become increasingly popular. It is sometimes referred to as 'political journalism' and is often released at the cinema rather than being made for television transmission. Robert Greenwald's film *Wal-Mart: The High Cost of Low Price* (2005) exposes the contrast between the advertising by which Wal-Mart, the largest company on earth, represents itself and what Greenwald considers to be the reality (see http://www.walmartmovie.com/).

The investigative function of documentary has always been important on television as well as at the cinema. A documentary such as *Ghosts of Abu Ghraib* can be an important focus for public opinion when it comes to challenging government policies. In *Ghosts of Abu Ghraib*, film-maker Rory Kennedy investigates the events surrounding the torture of prisoners in Abu Ghraib prison in Iraq and considers how these events tarnished the reputation the US had tried to nurture as a champion of human rights around the world. The documentary consists largely of interviews with prisoner guards involved in the torture, as well as with their Iraqi victims. This approach is a good example of the investigative approach to documentary where the producers seeks to expose wrongdoing, especially of people in a position of trust (see http://www.hbo.com/docs/programs/ghostsofabughraib/index.html).

Another interesting approach to the construction of the documentary is Werner Herzog's film *Grizzly Man* (2005). In this film, released in the cinema, Herzog used hours of footage shot by amateur conservationist and activist Timothy Treadwell. The footage documented the work of Amie Huguenard and Treadwell with Alaskan Grizzly bears, which ended tragically with their deaths when they were attacked and eaten by bears during filming.

Most television documentaries are made by independent companies. The process by which they get made is reliant on the commissioning process by broadcasting companies such as the BBC, ITV and Channel 4. As we have seen, all the major channels have programme slots or strands for documentary output. Each of these strands has its own distinctive features and producers hoping to be commissioned to film a documentary need to determine which it most likely fits into.

A typical BBC strand is *ONE Life*, broadcast at 22.40 on BBC1. According to the website:

> **This strand aims to deliver surprising, high impact 40 minute films which reflect life in contemporary Britain.**
>
> ***ONE Life* has to continually evolve and therefore we are broadening our remit. Multi-narrative, zeitgeist films will become increasingly important.**

The site offers an example of this from a documentary broadcast in its current series:

> **The first film in the latest run, 'The Oldest Drivers in Britain', is an example of an idea which can be funny, quirky and poignant all at the same time. Films like the 'Oldest Drivers in Britain' don't have to be all the same shape, i.e. I don't want to take one subject and intercut three stories, like many traditional documentaries do.**
>
> (http://www.bbc.co.uk/commissioning/tv/network/genres/docs_st rands.shtml)

You might like to compare the demands of the BBC in the commissioning of documentaries with that of Channel 4. The website indicates that they are looking for new and challenging ways of telling stories. They suggest that would-be documentary-makers look at their current documentary output in order to work out 'who we are and what we stand for'. The head of documentaries, Angus Macqueen, goes on to say:

> **We believe these programmes show a commitment to make programmes that are popular and purposeful – all the time pushing the boundaries.**

The department is a microcosm of Channel 4: its output ranges from the very silly to the highly provocative, the angry and emotional to the funny, the popular to the challenging – always seeking out that streak of innovation or discomfort that characterises the Channel. This is the department that came up with *Faking It*, *Wife Swap* and *Jamie's School Dinners* – we are constantly looking to continue that tradition.

Our immediate needs – and they are real – are series for mid 2008/9 – these should be bold events in the schedule – with striking propositions that will get noticed. We are in a period of transition where we do not quite know what comes next: once it was soapdocs, then formats . . . Now what? We are looking for the big and the bold – and hope to foster the conversations that will find them. "

(http://www.channel4.com/corporate/4producers/commissioning/documentaries.html)

Part of the popularity of documentary as a genre is the way in which it allows the audience to get inside other people's lives. We often associate it with the idea of fly-on-the-wall filming techniques, where the participants are seemingly unaware of their being characters in the unfolding drama. Reality unfolds before our eyes, and the function of the camera is simply to capture it. This is not true for a number of reasons. First, there is generally a process that takes place before filming, which is about selecting precisely what is to be filmed. The characters who feature in a documentary will be vetted for their charisma and screen presence long before a camera is ever pointed at them. What on screen seems a spontaneous process in which a film crew simply turns up at someone's house and starts filming is in most cases a carefully planned and constructed piece of film-making. A good deal of planning and preparation is likely to have taken place before the expense of committing a film crew is incurred.

It is very likely that the character featured will have been interviewed by a researcher to determine what he or she will say and do on camera. As most people, when confronted by a camera, will either freeze or ramble on for hours, some prompting as to the most appropriate responses may well be necessary. Similarly, as talking heads (midshots of people just talking) tend to be boring in televisual terms, it is often necessary to set up some activity in order to add visual interest. Note how often people in documentaries are filmed undertaking some domestic chore while their voice is played over the action.

A second key issue with shooting documentary is the extent to which the camera itself necessarily intrudes and determines how people will respond and react. Your

Figure 10.3 Documentaries show people performing an action so that there is something to sustain visual interest

own experience of using video equipment will probably tell you that people 'play to the camera'. There is evidence to suggest that the more accustomed people become to the presence of the camera, the more likely they are to forget that it is there and to act naturally. Despite this, there will always be the tendency for a person to act differently when being filmed.

A third issue is that at the post-production stage, editing will probably be used to cut any of the material that does not fit readily into the narrative or that gets in the way of the flow of the programme.

ACTIVITY

In Chapter 2 on narrative, we emphasised the importance of conflict. Consider the narrative construction of a documentary. How has conflict been presented here? Do you think the conflict has emerged naturally or do you think it may have been contrived for dramatic effect?

- Would you be prepared to be featured in a docu-soap about your family or school or college? What reasons do you have for your answer?
- When you watch a docu-soap are you conscious of people deliberately acting for the benefit of the camera?
- What do you think is the appeal of docu-soaps to media producers?

Reality television

A natural extension of the docu-soap is the use of real-life characters in 'reality television'. Reality TV is not an easy genre to pin down, not least because there are so many variations on a theme. The use of 'ordinary' people, however, might be one of the conventions that help us define the genre, although purists might argue that celebrity variants of the reality shows negate any such attempt to foreground this as a convention. One useful approach to the study of reality TV is to explore some of the many formats into which it has metamorphosised and perhaps to try to predict some of the formats which we are yet to see.

There are a number of factors at play that have made reality TV such a popular genre. Viewing figures suggest that this is the type of programme that people want to watch but equally it might be argued that such is the saturation of reality formats in the schedules, they may not have a great deal of choice. A prime influence over the increasing dominance of the genre is the need to fill airtime. In a digital multi-channel environment, there is inevitably a call for cheaply produced material that will fill as much space within the schedules as possible. Reality TV fits the bill nicely. *Big Brother* not only allows Channel 4 to block out weeks of its summer schedule with extensive coverage, but it also provides spin-off programmes such as *Big Brother's Little Brother*, to be screened on affiliated channels such as E4. A subscription site on the Web allows C4 to generate further revenue from people seeking 24-hour engagement with the inmates of the house.

Programmes like *Big Brother* have been greatly influenced by web-based technologies. The webcam in its many different guises offers opportunities for voyeuristic engagement with the lives of other people. What was once private has now been made public by the exhibitionists who are prepared to use the webcam to allow the world access to all aspects of their lives. The idea of surveillance and, more specifically, people playing with surveillance is an important part of our 'celebrity' culture. *Big Brother* and similar related reality series are in essence a mass media extension of the webcam.

Another quality of web-based technology is its interactivity. Audiences have become used to the notion that they can influence what is on the screen and even determine the outcomes of the narratives that they see. This idea is extended into reality TV programmes through the opportunity of allowing the audience to vote. This might, for example, be to decide who stays in a competition or what 'trial' they are expected to undertake.

Life swap is a common subgenre of the reality TV format. It relies for its impact on the contrasting lifestyle of people from different backgrounds and social class. An example of the life swap format is *Wife Swap* or its celebrity version, *Celebrity Wife Swap*. The title suggests a programme rather more salacious than it in fact is, but the basic premise that couples swap partners for a period of time provides ample opportunity for narrative conflict as the different expectations of couples, particularly in terms of the sharing of domestic duties, usually sets them on a collision course. An edition of the *Celebrity Wife Swap* programme broadcast in October 2007, brought together Pete Burns, famous for his appearance on *Big Brother* and his cosmetic surgery, with Neil 'Razor' Ruddock, hard man ex-footballer and hard-drinking partner of glamour model, Leah Newman. This juxtapositioning of personalities likely to react to one another in a volatile way is the essence of this type of reality TV and has become known as 'car crash television'.

Figure 10.4 *Celebrity Wife Swap*

11 LIFESTYLE MAGAZINES AND TELEVISION

In this chapter we:

- concentrate on 'lifestyle' magazines and in particular those aimed at women readers
- look at 'lads' mags' such as *Nuts*
- examine lifestyle television programmes, in particular cookery programmes.

Figure 11.1 Nigella Lawson

Estimates of the number of magazine titles available in Britain vary between 8,000 and 10,000, of which about half are consumer and lifestyle magazines. According to the Periodical Publishers Association (http://www.ppa.co.uk), people in the UK spend over £2 billion on magazines each year.

ACTIVITY

Go to http://www.ppamarketing.net/public/downloads/circulation.pdf and look at the top ten magazines as measured by their circulation. You will see that only one, *What's on TV*, is 100 per cent 'actively purchased'; in other words, all the others are given away free in one form or another. It is interesting to speculate whether magazines such as the Sky or AA magazines or the periodicals for companies such as Asda or Tesco would be so popular if readers had to pay for them.

- Do you think people actually read these free magazines? If not, how are they consumed?
- What do you think is the attraction for readers of magazines of this type?
- Why do you think these companies seem to be prepared to give away magazines for free?

'Lifestyle' magazines

This is one of the most popular and competitive areas of the magazine publishing market. Although the top 'actively purchased' magazine in 2006 was *Take a Break*, over the past ten years it is lifestyle and celebrity magazines such as *Closer* or *Heat* that have shown the biggest increase in the number of titles available, the number of copies bought and the amount of advertising revenue that they bring in.

According to the Periodical Publishers Association (PPA), 82 per cent of women and 72 per cent of men read a lifestyle or consumer magazine (36 per cent more than read a national daily newspaper).

'Lifestyle' is a very broad category that can include *FHM*, *Gardener's World*, *Catworld* and *Woman's Own*. However, all these magazines are trying to do the same thing, using a consumerism based on particular lifestyles to deliver particular groups of audiences to advertisers. It is interesting, for example, to carry out a simple contents analysis of the most popular lifestyle magazines to determine the amount of advertising that they contain. This advertising will include not only the glossy advertisements and double-page spreads at the front of the magazine but also the smaller advertisements that often appear at the back. It is not unusual to find that over 40 per cent of a lifestyle magazine is devoted to advertising in one form or another.

On p. 114 we talk about 'narrowcasting': as new magazines come on to the market, they are increasingly trying to narrow down the market and provide advertisers with more and more specific reader 'profiles'. Like most newspapers, the revenue that lifestyle magazines get from advertising is far more important than the income they receive from the cover price and individual sales.

Consider what the term 'lifestyle' means. What is it that these magazines offer their readers? On the surface they seem to offer information and advice about certain types of 'lifestyle': what products to buy; where to buy them; the types of goods and services that might be available to someone leading that particular 'lifestyle'. However, as Katz and Lazarsfeld (1955) suggest, the relationship between audience and text is often much more complex and more intimate, offering a range of 'uses and gratifications' for the reader.

Lifestyle magazines often offer their readers not only advice but also a sense of identity, companionship and reassurance. The PPA suggests four main ways in which magazines engage with their readers: through trust, as a friend and advocate; by offering support and help in managing their lives; through status and their sense of position, belonging and confidence; and as a means of participation, as a bridge to interactivity with the wider world (http://www.ppamarketing.net/cgi-bin/go.pl/scaleable/index.html).

One of the features of the lifestyle magazine market over the recent past has been the growth of weekly magazines that have become increasingly popular at the expense of some monthly publications. The launch of *Zoo* and *Nuts*, for example, are given as one of the main causes for the decline in circulation of the 'lads' mag' market leaders *FHM* and *Loaded*, both published monthly. Although *Nuts* may have a lower circulation figure per issue, it publishes four editions to each of *FHM*'s one. However, now even weekly magazines are being challenged by the internet and the magazines' own websites as increasingly readers access the websites but do not purchase 'hard' copies of the magazine.

In recognition of the way in which the target audience, young men aged 16–34, consume the media, advertisers are becoming more sophisticated in the way they try to reach consumers. Magazines are increasingly trying to develop alternative media 'platforms'; so for example, apart from the actual magazine there is a website and visual downloads for mobile phones as well as radio and television stations that can be accessed via both a satellite receiver and a personal computer.

Internet websites can offer high-quality images, interactivity beyond the pages of the magazines themselves, more buying potential, and a mix of video and audio. Therefore magazine publishers are increasingly looking for ways to offer their particular brand across a range of media – radio, television and downloads for mobile phones as well as websites. However, this means more than just putting a (paid for) magazine on to a (free) website. The online version must generate income either through additional advertising revenue or through retail sales of goods and services aimed at the magazine's particular niche reader. The *Nuts* website claims over 600,000 'unique users' per month. This means that the publishers need to ensure that the websites produce sufficient income to compensate for the drop in sales of the magazines as well as trying to encourage visitors to the websites to purchase copies of the magazines.

One of the attractions of lifestyle magazines is that they are usually a secondary media (see p. 133) and require little effort or concentration to consume. The PPA provides details of how readers acquire and consume magazines at http://www.ppamarketing.net/cgi-bin/wms.pl/630. The magazines are designed to be 'browsed' through, with regular features signposted and articles and advertisements designed to attract the reader's attention. These magazines will possibly be kept until the next edition arrives and so may be left lying around at home for some time. The magazines will therefore be looked at several times by the same reader or glanced through by new readers. Readers may have different patterns of reading magazines; perhaps when they do not want to be disturbed and can go somewhere quiet, or perhaps in the morning over a cup of coffee.

The readership of a magazine, therefore, is important as well as its circulation. Magazines aimed particularly at one market may have a significant number of readers from another market, for example, Emap claims that 30 per cent of *FHM*'s readership is female. Another large 'cross-over' readership is men who read women's magazines. Sometimes this is done 'secretly', as often men are reluctant to admit that they enjoy reading some of the features of women's magazines or they may only admit to reading the problem pages. There may be an element of titillation and vicarious pleasure from gaining glimpses of other people's sex lives. Sometimes this reading may be more open, for example, letters from the opposite sex regularly appear in both men's and women's magazines and some women's magazines have included sections aimed specifically at male readers.

'The most fun a girl can have with her clothes on!': teenage magazines

Sugar is currently the most successful teenage girl's magazine (see http://www.abc.org.uk/cgi-bin/gen5?runprog=nav/abc&noc=y) and is owned by Hachette Filipacchi, which is a subsidiary of Hachette Filipacchi Medias, publisher of over 222 titles worldwide. In the UK the company also owns *Elle*, *Red*, *B*, *Inside Soap* and *All About Soap*.

Although the style of contemporary popular 'teen mags' may have moved away from the photo-stories of *Jackie* and *My Guy*, much of the content deals with similar issues, albeit in a more up-to-date manner. McRobbie (1983), writing about the ideology underpinning *Jackie*, noted that it socialised female adolescents into a 'feminine' culture:

> **[*Jackie*] sets up, defines and focuses exclusively on the personal, locating it as the sphere of prime importance to the teenage girl. It presents this as a totality – and by implication all else is of secondary interest to the 'modern girl'. Romance problems, fashion, beauty and pop mark out the limits of the girl's concern – other possibilities are ignored or dismissed.**

(McRobbie 1983: 743)

These magazines offer advice, entertainment, amusement and escapism and speak to their readers in a language that they understand. As McRobbie suggests, however, it is important to question the extent to which teenage readers accept or challenge this reading of these magazines. For example, a study by Key Note Ltd, a market research company, suggests that although readers are more influenced by these magazines than they are by their parents, yet television and friends play a more important part in promoting ideas about how to live.

ACTIVITY

Choose a magazine cover and undertake a semiotic analysis. You might wish to re-read the section on semiotics (p. 33) or look at the article 'Semiotic analysis of teenage magazine front covers' by Siân Davies, available at http://www.aber.ac.uk/media/Students/sid9901.html. You should consider:

■ the images used on the cover, facial expressions, clothing, age and style of the model
■ the colours, typeface and language used in the written text
■ the types of stories featured on the cover and how the reader is addressed.

What assumptions are made about the reader?

Figure 11.2

Key Note Ltd is a market research publisher providing consumer information throughout the UK. In 2007 they summed up the teenage magazine market in the following way:

" The teenage magazines market is under threat from a number of sources. As well as the fact that the teenage population is falling, the nature of teenagers, and the way in which they spend their leisure time, is also changing.

Ironically, the 'Kids Getting Older Younger' (KGOY) phenomenon, which refers to the growing sophistication of those in their early teenage and sub-teenage years, and which was partly responsible for the development of the teenage magazines market, is now one of the things that is threatening it. Rather than reading magazines created especially for their age group, young teenagers are turning to women's lifestyle glossies and celebrity magazines aimed at older readers.

Another problem is that young teenagers now have many more claims on their pocket money – for example: clothes, which have become cheaper generally and are now affordable for many individuals in their early teens; mobile telephones; and music downloads.

However, perhaps the biggest threat to the market comes from other forms of entertainment, notably the internet, but also television and radio. Teenagers are now able to access information about music, and the other things that interest them, almost instantly through the internet, television and mobile telephones, and traditional teenage magazines struggle to compete with this trend.

Most magazines within the sector have responded by creating their own online presence, and some have extended their brands into television and/or radio. However, circulation figures for the traditional magazines continue to decline.

A number of high-profile companies cut back their presence in the teenage magazines sector, and/or left it altogether, during 2006. Those that have left the market include the two biggest UK magazine companies, IPC

Media Ltd and Emap plc. At the same time, there have been new entrants to the market, including Panini UK Ltd and Hubert Burda Media. A further new entrant is expected in April 2007 with the introduction of Popworld Pulp from customer magazine publisher Brooklands Group.

Key Note's exclusive consumer research revealed that respondents were in no doubt about the degree of influence that teenage magazines have on their readers. However, they were also aware of the power of the internet, with nearly half agreeing that most teenage girls prefer to spend time on the internet rather than reading magazines, and almost two-thirds saying that this is the case for teenage boys. Nevertheless, approximately a third of the sample agreed that most teenage girls enjoy reading magazines as much as, or more than, using the internet. **"**

(http:www.keynote.co.uk)

Mizz, *Bliss* and *Sugar* are all targeting the same audience, namely readers in the 12 to 16 age range – those who aspire to the maturity that being 17 years old seems to offer. Advertising in these magazines reflects this profile, with an emphasis on health and beauty products, fashion and music but also quite a lot of confectionery. Articles include 'how to cope with your parents' and 'how to stop smoking' as well as fashion tips, star profiles, showbiz gossip and horoscopes, which are all presented on high-gloss, full-colour paper.

Most of the readers of *Mizz*, *Bliss* or *Sugar* are under the legal age of consent, and a major part of these magazines' attraction is their 'problem pages', where readers can not only 'speak for themselves' but also read about problems and issues that may feature in their own lives and that they may have difficulty in discussing with their peers or family. The mode of address is personal, friendly and intimate. It is this area of the magazine that is perhaps the most 'reassuring', saying to its readers 'you are not alone, others are having similar problems and fears'. Typical letters might read:

I am not yet 16 and my boyfriend is several years older than me. We have been together for a year and been having sex for several months. He has asked me to take part in a bondage session with him and his friends. I like having sex with him but the thought of being tied up scares me. What should I do?

Or:

> **Recently I was caught by my mum snogging with my boyfriend. Now she says that she doesn't like us being alone together, and that I'm acting like a slut. But I haven't any plans for sex and I don't understand why my mum doesn't trust me.**

These types of feature have been the focus of a 'moral panic' (see p. 136) over the last few years. There have been accusations that these magazines condone under-age sexual activity and seemingly endorse sexual promiscuity as well as offering a 'guide' to different sexual practices. There have been calls for magazine editors to curb such sexually explicit content, although the editors and publishers have argued that they offer 'responsible' advice that their readers may otherwise not receive. For example, *Sugar* has advice pages focusing on 'You and your life', 'You and your heart' and 'You and your body' as well as advice on where to buy condoms and adverts asking 'Should I let my friends control my sex life?'. A recent report (see http://www.ppa.co.uk/cgi-bin/go.pl/news/article.html?uid=11905) suggests that these types of magazines are a useful tool in teaching young people about responsible relationships.

McRobbie suggests that magazines such as *Sugar*, *Bliss* and *Mizz* can be seen to offer reassurance and guidance to adolescent readers who are still learning about themselves.

Figure 11.3 'Over to you', from contents page of *Sugar*

Figure 11.3 is taken from the contents page of *Sugar* and identifies some of the ways in which magazines like *Sugar* try to promote a more personal mode of address. They also represent opportunities for readers of magazines like *Sugar* to interact with the magazine and become more involved with the products and lifestyle which the magazine promotes. The Key Note Ltd research suggests that they are key elements in the success of teenage magazines like *Sugar*. Conduct some research that looks at teenage girls' magazines, especially:

- the use of websites, email and text messaging to encourage readers to become more involved and to provide the magazine's producers with more demographic information (for example, *Sugar* asks its readers to text in their date of birth, their postcode and the make and model of their phone; this gives the marketing department useful information when trying to sell advertising space)
- the use of 'covermounts' to provide extra 'value' to encourage readers to purchase, or stay loyal to, the magazine. What types of products are most frequently on offer? What assumptions do they make about the magazine's readership?
- What 'brand extensions' can you find (for example, the ways in which magazine titles are used to promote other activities such as pop concerts or exhibitions)?

'She's a woman with responsibility . . . and a hangover': women's lifestyle magazines

Like McRobbie, Ferguson (1983) analyses women's magazines and the extent to which they are concerned with the practices and beliefs of a 'cult of femininity'. According to Ferguson, these magazines not only reflect the role of women in society but they also offer guidance and socialisation into that lifestyle. Ferguson suggests that women's magazines attempt to 'promote a collective female social "reality", the world of women' (1983: 185). Top-selling magazines such as *Woman*, *Woman and Home*, *Bella* and *Glamour* offer both guidance and membership into this 'cult of femininity'. (See also section 'Ideology and gender', p. 107.)

> **This is a world founded on conformity to a set of shared meanings where a consciously cultivated female bond acts as the social cement of female solidarity. . . .**

> **Through the selective perception and interpretation of the wider world from the viewpoint of the 'woman's angle', the editors of these sacred oracles sustain a social 'reality' that is 'forever feminine'.** ”
>
> (Ferguson 1983: 186)

These magazines can be seen to offer a representation of the 'ideal' in terms of the self, home, family, career, relationships and lifestyle.

To gain some idea of how the 'world of women' is represented, it is useful to look through the contents pages of some of the magazines.

Glamour is the most successful of these magazines. Owned by Condé Nast, it has a circulation of around 590,000. According to its media pack, *Glamour* is for 'successful, independent, modern women who know how to have fun, how to dress and how to spend'. *Glamour* is aimed at 'successful ABC1C2 women aged between 18-34' and it claims that 32 per cent of its readership will have a degree or above. *Marie Claire* is owned by IPC, in turn owned by AOL/Time Warner and it has a circulation of approximately 380,000 per month. The magazine targets ABC1 women aged 18 to 35.

Red was launched in February 1998 and is owned by Hachette Filipacchi. It has a circulation of around 195,000 and is aimed at ABC1 women aged 30 or over. According to its media pack, a typical reader will be a working professional (possibly in PR or the media) with a high disposable income, aged between 28 and 38 (what it describes as 'middle youth'), be urban based and living in a long-term stable relationship. The typical reader's interests will be fashion, travel, entertainment, dining out, reading and yoga. She will be intelligent and articulate and read the *Evening Standard* and the *Guardian*. She will holiday in Florence, Bali or the Lake District and shop at Josephs, Whistles, Jigsaw and Kensington and Notting Hill designer boutiques. *Red*'s mission statement states that

> “ *Red* **is the first magazine to speak your language. We believe in middle youth. We believe in enjoying ourselves. We believe that style, passion, and humour should fuel all our interests – whether it's fashion, food, interiors, entertainment, travel or gardening.** ”

ACTIVITY

Compare the contents pages of a selection of women's lifestyle magazines such as *Glamour*, *Red* or *Woman and Home* or men's magazines such as *Nuts*, *FHM*, *Loaded* or *GQ*.

- Is there a similar set of accepted subjects?
- What do the topics in men's or women's magazines suggest about their readers' lifestyle and the readers' role and place in society?
- How do these topics relate to ideas about stereotyping and ideology?
- How far do you think it is possible for audiences to resist the ideological messages of media texts such as these?

Monitor the success of the titles mentioned in this section.

- Are they all still in production?
- How do their circulation figures compare to those of their competitors?
- To what extent do they succeed (or fail) in being 'different' from their competitors?

Re-read Chapter 3 on Genre and choose a genre of magazines, for example, teenage, women's or 'lads'. Analyse a selection and identify the extent to which they share a common iconography (see p. 64) and/or mode of address (see p. 134).

Ferguson (1983) suggests that new magazines are launched either to offer competition in an existing market or to try to identify a new 'niche' for women – a particular set of experiences, age or income not as yet targeted. This diversification explains why new magazines are constantly coming onto an already crowded and competitive market.

As overall the number of magazine buying women is not increasing, both new and established titles have to fight to build and maintain their position in the market. One of the main ways of doing this is to try to appear 'different' whilst simultaneously offering the same benefits as the competition.

Ferguson suggests that each women's magazine is targeted at a distinct group, such as teenagers, housewives, young single women, mothers, brides or slimmers. There are magazines that specialise in almost every stage of a woman's life, offering 'step-by-step' guides, tips for survival and of course products to purchase. Originally women's magazines focused on romance, marriage and household management.

It is interesting to try to apply Maslow's Hierarchy of Needs and the different categories of 'socio-economic values' discussed on p. 128 to the range of titles within particular genres. This helps to identify the way in which a publisher will target particular 'niches' not only in terms of age and income but also in terms of psychological needs, for example, security and routine, independence and excitement or status symbols and economic 'success'.

However, as much as these magazines may say 'Get out there and show the world you are someone in your own right', Ferguson suggests that they also say 'Remember you must achieve as a wife and mother too'.

Ultimately, lifestyle magazines must leave their readers with a positive feeling, otherwise they may not return and buy the next edition. The July 2000 edition of *Red* carried articles on the menopause and troubled relationships with mothers, but the final paragraph of the editorial read:

> **We haven't forgotten that it's summer, that the sun is shining and it's the season for feeling good. The rest of this issue is packed with sunshine, lighting up fashion (pure gold), homes (gorgeously shabby, in a very chic way), food (delicious salads), not to mention lighting you up too, with our power-packed nutrition feature 'Eat Yourself Happy'. We hope that you do just that. And, while you're at it, check out the 'Sun Beauty Special' pages for the lowdown on the best fake tans as well as the make-up to give you that authentic sun-kissed glow. Then there's all the latest news on health, fitness and feelgood treatments . . .**

This paragraph serves several functions. It reassures the reader that not all of the magazine is going to be 'serious' and 'depressing'. It helps to reinforce the sense of 'personal address' ('we', 'you') by the manner in which it is written and the accompanying photograph of the editor smiling. It uses colloquial language (sufficiently everyday to appear like speech, for example, 'while you're at it' and 'gorgeously shabby'). It advertises other features in this month's edition; in fact it manages to mention nearly all of the magazine's content.

Website Activity 11.2: Worksheet for analysing magazines.

Nuts: grab yours every week

According to IPC Media, *Nuts* is the number one selling men's lifestyle magazine in the UK, accounting for two out of every five men's lifestyle magazines purchased.

Figure 11.4

Codes and conventions

Looking at the cover (Figure 11.4), we can see why the magazine may be so popular; there are seven pictures of young topless women with the word 'topless!' in bright yellow and in a font size that is bigger than the title of the magazine.

Intertextuality (see p. 94) is often a key selling point, for example, there is a strong reference to the television reality show *Big Brother* with three direct references and the splash 'It's a reality TV boob spectacular!' (again notice the use of an '!').

When analysing lifestyle magazines like *Nuts*, you need to undertake a detailed analysis of what is shown on the cover. Consider, for example, why there is an '!' after the word 'topless'; would the impact of the word 'topless' be as strong without the '!'? Do you think many readers notice the '!'?

The photographs have the name of the 'girls' covering their breasts, each name also has a '!' after it and the photograph of Lucy James, bigger than the others, uses the words pert! and perky! to cover her breasts. Why do you think she is treated differently?

- Why do they need to cover the breasts when inside the magazine they are not covered?
- Why do you think they have used the word 'boob'? What other words could have been used instead?
- What are the connotations of the word 'boob' in comparison with other similar words? Are some words more acceptable than others; if so, why?

At the bottom of the cover is a strip of different images; a Ferrari, a photo of an alleged OAP mass murderer, a football quiz and two champion league footballer look-alikes. There are no topless girls here but specific references to other 'male' interests (football, fast cars, crime). Again we have several exclamation marks being used. Altogether there are about 20 uses of the exclamation mark on the front page alone. The use of the exclamation marks and the bright colours seem to give the impression that the front page is shouting out to the reader, perhaps trying to attract the attention of a browsing consumer at a newsagents and trying to stand out from all the other similar magazines competing for purchase. This sense of trying to attract the reader's attention is reinforced by the colours of the typeface and their backgrounds; the red of the title on a white background, the yellow of 'topless!' on a red background. There is also some kind of pretend tear in the front page as if a corner has been torn off. Why do you think the designers have done this?

It is useful to think about other similar lads' mags and the ways in which *Nuts* is both similar and different. Pictures of attractive women are a common feature on the cover of all these magazines plus pictures of various gadgets or 'boys' toys' such as fast cars, sporting or electrical equipment. To what extent do these magazines use a common language (boob, babe, etc.) and mode of address? What do you think are the connotations of the title *Nuts*? Why do you think this was chosen as the title?

The *Nuts* brand also appears in various other formats and again it would be useful to consider how these various formats present themselves. Is there a similarity in appearance, images, language and mode of address between them? If so, can you describe these common features?

ACTIVITY

When analysing the appeal of lifestyle magazines, it is useful to also look at their websites. For example, visit the *Nuts* website at http://www.nuts.co.uk/ and conduct a semiotic analysis of the content and design of the website. Consider, for example:

- The ways in which the website encourages readers to spend money.
- Why the website has several advertisements for cheap loans.
- In what ways do you think that videos of the 'Top 5 Helicopter Crashes' (http://www.nuts.co.uk/blog/) might be considered as entertaining?
- Access the weblogs at http://www.nuts.co.uk/boards/index.php and think about the ways in which readers interact with one another and with the magazine. What do you think is the attraction of this activity?
- To what extent do you think the magazine lives up to its description 'With an alluring combination of women, sports, cars, gadgets, boys' toys, and lashings of humour it is easy to see just why *Nuts* has become so popular.' (http://www.magsite.co.uk/store/magazine-offer-with-free-gift/nuts-magazine-nuts-for-men-nuts-about-women/prod_56.html)?
- In what ways do you think the website might encourage readers to purchase a hard copy of the magazine?

Representation

In terms of gender representations, the *Nuts* cover appears to be very unambiguous: women should be attractive, young and topless; five of the seven girls are blond, all seven are white. However, it may be that the images empower women, they are after all celebrities and on the cover of one of Britain's major magazines.

The three images of the men at the bottom of the page appear to be less celebrity-driven, one, the OAP mass murderer, is disfigured with red paint (presumably to signify the blood of his victims) and the other two photos are of relatively ordinary-looking men. All three men are white.

Nuts is described as a 'lads' mag', what do you think this means? Who or what is a lad? How does the magazine present this idea of a 'lad'? Do you think that these types of magazines present a negative image of (a) women, (b) men? If so in what ways?

We should also consider the type of lifestyle being promoted by *Nuts* magazine: do you think it is aspirational or fantasy or a mixture of both? Do you think these types of magazines are dangerous in that they both convey and reinforce quite crude stereotypes or are they just harmless entertainment not to be taken seriously? Does the answer to this last question depend on who you are? For example, a black person might feel excluded from the images associated with this kind of lifestyle and someone who is worried about their appearance or body size may view these magazines negatively.

Institution

If you access the IPC Media website, there is a lot of information regarding the company that publishes *Nuts*. They claim that 'IPC Media is the UK's leading consumer magazine publisher. Its portfolio reaches over 70 per cent of UK women and 50 per cent of UK men.' IPC Media is owned by Time Inc., the publishing division of Time Warner and 'the world's largest media organisation'. They have five publishing divisions: IPC Connect, IPC Inspire, IPC Ignite, IPC Southbank and IPC TX. Why do you think their divisions have these types of names? Where does *Nuts* fit?

IPC employs over 2,200 people, and according to the website, 'it's their creativity, innovation, talent and commitment that drives our market-leading position in UK consumer publishing'. In what ways do you think the cover of *Nuts* shows creativity, innovation, talent and commitment?

It is interesting to see that IPC Media calls its magazines 'brands' and it is worth thinking about what this means. Presumably they are selling much more than just a magazine. It is also interesting to look at the other magazines that IPC Media publish, some of which seem to be in direct competition with each other (for example, *Horse* and *Horse and Hound*, *Motor Boat & Yachting*, *Yachting World*, *Yachting Monthly*, *Motor Boat Monthly* and *Classic Boat* or *TV and Satellite Week*, *TV Easy*, *TV Times* and *What's on TV*). Why do you think one company publishes so many magazines that are in competition with each other? Do you think it increases consumer choice?

Research indicates that men aged between 18 and 34 (they have plenty of disposable income and are one of the most desirable demographics for advertisers) tend not to watch a lot of television, preferring to spend their leisure time socialising in pubs or bars. This has meant that increasingly magazines like *Nuts* are moving into 'lads' television' and radio that attempts to replicate the laddish atmosphere of bars and clubs as well as continuing the successful *Nuts* formula of fast cars and scantily dressed young women.

ACTIVITY

FHM has its own television station, *Heat* has its own radio station and *Nuts* has launched its own digital television channel.

- Why do you think that brands like *Nuts* and *Heat* are moving away from just being magazines?
- Think about a radio station based on the *Nuts* brand: what sort of music would it play?
- What types of presenters would it have?
- What kind of products would be advertised on the station?

You can access more information about the *Nuts* television channel at http://www.ipcmedia.com/press/article.php?id=131539. Note the mention of 'developing a whole suite of new revenue streams.' There is also an article from the *Guardian* newspaper about the possible attraction of a television version of *Nuts* available at http://blogs.guardian.co.uk/organgrinder/2007/07/will_lads_mag_tv_drive_you_nut.html published before the channel started broadcasting. It now has about 1.6 million viewers and there is another article from the *Observer* commenting on

the success of the channel once it was up and running (see http://media.
guardian.co.uk/broadcast/story/0,,2200498,00.html).

Audience

Lifestyle magazines appear to share with their readers the problems and issues
of other similar people who also read the magazine. *Nuts*, for example, includes
a 'Readers' Facts, Tips and Tricks' on its 'Pub Ammo' page that appears to offer
a shared camaraderie between the producers and the readers in the magazine's
'laddish' attitudes and activities. As well as providing entertainment and escapism,
male lifestyle magazines appear to offer guidance and instruction on how to live
a particular lifestyle. Through both their articles and their advertisements, the
magazines offer aspiration in a variety of different spheres, such as relationships,
careers, material possessions or fashion and looks.

Some commentators suggest that magazines such as *FHM* and *Nuts* seem to
offer specific groups of people (predominantly heterosexual men between 18 and
30 years old) 'commodified' guidance on how to express a particular type of
masculinity, often requiring the purchase of a wide range of consumer goods from
grooming products and fashion items to holidays, gadgets and other electronic
equipment. Other commentators, such as Whelehan (2000), see magazines such
as *Loaded* as participating in a misogynistic backlash against 'new' definitions
of male sexuality that have evolved as a result of feminist critiques, the advent of
the 'new man' and increased male gay iconography. David Gauntlett, on the other
hand, is more positive about the role of men's lifestyle magazines. Writing on the
website associated with his book *Media, Gender and Identity* (2000), Gauntlett
says that

> **In the analysis of men's magazines . . . we found a lot of signs that the magazines were about men finding a place for themselves in the modern world. These lifestyle publications were perpetually concerned with how to treat women, have a good relationship, and live an enjoyable life. Rather than being a return to essentialism – i.e. the idea of a traditional 'real' man, as biology and destiny 'intended' – . . . men's magazines have an almost obsessive relationship with the socially constructed nature of manhood. Gaps in a person's attempt to generate a masculine image are a source of humour in these magazines, because those breaches reveal what we all know – but some choose to hide – that masculinity is a socially constructed performance anyway. The continuous flow of lifestyle, health, relationship and sex advice, and the repetitive curiosity about what the featured females look for in a partner, point to a clear view that the performance of masculinity can and should be practised and perfected. This may not appear ideal – it sounds as if men's magazines are geared to turning out a stream of identical men. But the masculinity put forward by the biggest-seller, *FHM*, we saw to be fundamentally caring, generous and good-humoured, even though the sarcastic humour sometimes threatened to smother this. Individual quirks are tolerated, and in any case we saw from the reader responses that the audience disregards messages that seem inappropriate or irrelevant or offensive.**

(http://theoryhead.com)

In what ways do you think *Nuts* conform to Gauntlett's idea that these types of magazines are 'fundamentally caring, generous and good-humoured'? To what extent do you think *Nuts* offers a return to 'the idea of a traditional "real" man, as biology and destiny "intended"'? To what extent do you think the magazine conforms to the four ways in which the PPA suggests magazines interact with their readers (see http://www.ppamarketing.net/cgi-bin/go.pl/scaleable/index.html)?

Go to http://www.davidrowan.com/2004/10/interview-phil-hilton-nuts-magazine.html where there is an interview with the then editor of *Nuts*, Phil Hilton. In the interview he says: 'If men wish to look at attractive, partially clothed women, it doesn't mean . . . that they want to take away the female vote'. The magazine, he insists, would never exploit women. 'Most guys are reasonable blokes with partners they respect and a very modern attitude to women,' he says. Based on your research and analysis of the *Nuts* magazine and website, answer the following:

- To what extent do you agree with this statement?
- How do you think a female reader would view the magazine?

There is more discussion available on the role and value of men's and women's lifestyle magazines on the Gauntlett website, for example, 'Are magazines for young men likely to reinforce stereotypical, "macho" and sexist attitudes in their readers?' by Lucy Brown, available at http://www.theory.org.uk/mensmags.htm.

Figure 11.5 Fanny Cradock

'Vol-au-vents like Fanny's': lifestyle television

One of the reasons for the rise in lifestyle television programmes is the increased leisure time and affluence that many people in the UK now enjoy. For example, buying and decorating property both in the UK and abroad, cookery, gardening, health and beauty and holidays as well as fashion are key industries in our increasingly consumerist society and important sources of income for companies. This growth in leisure and lifestyle is reflected in the range and popularity of lifestyle television channels and programmes that are now available. The BBC has a website (http://www.bbc.co.uk/lifestyle/) that includes sections devoted to food, health, gardening, parenting and consumers. The sites supplement the television programmes offering message boards, newsletters and other additional information such as recipes etc. that can be downloaded to mobile phones.

Website Activity 11.3: The 'grey market'.

Again it is useful to consider what these programmes offer viewers both in terms of direct guidance and information on how to successfully live a certain lifestyle and in terms of meeting those psychological needs identified by Maslow (p. 128).

Originally lifestyle programmes were limited to a few select areas such as cookery and gardening. One of the earliest 'celebrity chefs' was Fanny Cradock (Figure 11.5). She tried to introduce a sense of glamour into her meals, her target audience being mainly middle-class housewives who wanted to impress their husband's boss (for more information, see http://www.icons.org.uk/theicons/collection/mrs-beeton/features/tv-chefs-finished).

Today, however, programmes are much more aspirational and, increasingly, competitive. In cookery terms this means programmes like *The Restaurant*, *Come Dine with Me* or *Hell's Kitchen*, where members of the public or celebrities have to compete against each other. These can be seen as hybrid genres: part reality TV, part cookery, part celebrity show.

There is a sense in which television programmes are constantly trying to reinvent ways of presenting the same ideas in slightly different combinations. *The Restaurant*, for example, is supposed to be a cookery programme but takes much of its style and iconography from *The Apprentice*.

Cookery shows are now an integral part of a celebrity chef's brand image so that, for example, Jamie Oliver is not only on television and performing live but he also advertises products from Sainsbury's as well as having his own range of cookware. It is interesting to consider to what extent Jamie Oliver's own personality and lifestyle are part of his attraction for consumers. The way in which his early television shows were edited, the use of jump-cuts and unusual camera angles coupled with his motor bike and 'laddish' approach helped to create an impression that he is an 'ordinary person' like you and me, and that if he can produce quick and easy delicious meals, then so can we – especially if we buy the Jamie Oliver recipes, the Jamie Oliver produce, the Jamie Oliver knives and pans etc. We too can live the Jamie Oliver lifestyle. It is also undeniable that Jamie Oliver has used his fame to campaign for better school dinners (*Jamie's School Dinners*) and to help unemployed youngsters (*Fifteen*).

ACTIVITY

Choose a television celebrity chef such as Rick Stein, Nigella Lawson, Jamie Oliver or Anthony Worrall-Thompson and research the way in which they are selling both a brand (themselves) and also a lifestyle, whether it be fantasy, aspirational or competitive. Consider the products they endorse or that carry their name, the settings that are used to promote their recipes and food, and what messages these send about how we are supposed to create and consume food.

You might start by undertaking a web search to see what products and activities their names are directly associated with. You can then research other television cookery programmes and/or magazines to see how often they appear as 'guest' chefs, telling us where they go to have their favourite breakfast, for holidays or to buy ingredients. To what extent do you think that these testimonials are genuine?

Access their home websites (such as http://www.nigella.com/index.asp) to examine how the chefs interact with their audience whilst at the same time selling themselves and their products. The Nigella Lawson website, for example, has many photographs of Nigella: why do you think this is? How does it aid the selling of her products? Also go to 'Your page' on the Nigella Lawson website and read through the comments posted. To what extent are they about practical cookery information and to what extent are they about trying to seek comfort and reassurance from a particular lifestyle?

How does a cookery show like *The Hairy Bikers* fit into this model?

You could also undertake a semiotic analysis of a cookery programme such as *Nigella Express* or *Jamie at Home* and note the way in which the food is presented in relation to other lifestyle factors such as the presenters themselves, the way they dress, their body language and the space in which the cooking takes place. (It was revealed recently that the kitchen used in the television recording for *Nigella Express* is in fact a mock-up kitchen on an industrial estate on the edge of London rather than Nigella's own family kitchen. Does this affect the 'message' of the programme, what it is trying to present? Does it matter?)

Consider the way in which the presenters handle and refer to the ingredients they are cooking with. To what extent is this an important part of the show and of the chef's own personality?

continued

Consider how viewers might interact with these shows. Are these shows educational, entertainment, or both? Try to analyse the ways in which these shows offer viewers some kind of 'uses and gratifications' and/or can be related to Maslow's Hierarchy of Needs.

It would be useful to compare different shows/different chefs and so you might like to compare your results with someone who has analysed a different celebrity chef.

Conclusion

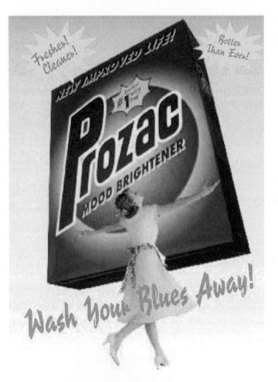

Figure 11.6

ACTIVITY

Figure 11.6 is a spoof advert from the anti-advertising campaigners Adbusters (http://adbusters.org/spoofads/misc/prozac/). There is also another Adbusters spoof advert (Figure 7.12) in Chapter 7 on audiences.

Choose an advert from a magazine, radio or television and create your own anti-advert that somehow subverts the message of the original advert. You can then test out your anti-advert on a group of people to see how successful (or otherwise) you have been.

OR

Go the the Adbusters website http://adbusters.org/the_magazine/73/Advertising_is_Brain_Damage.html and read the blog 'Advertising is Brain Damage' as well as the comments that the article generated. Try to sum up the key points of the various arguments and present your findings to your peers perhaps via a website, a poster or a short audio presentation. You should think about where you stand in the debate about the harmfulness of advertising and include your own views as a conclusion.

Lifestyle magazines and television programmes are primarily consumer-based products that aim to make a profit by 'selling' particular types of audience to advertisers. They are literally offering their readers a 'lifestyle' – in other words, a model on which to base their lives at this particular moment and the goods necessary to accommodate it. To do this successfully, the magazines and television programmes need to be able to make their readers and viewers identify with the lifestyle on offer but at the same time offer them slightly more than they may already have. They therefore offer both guidance and aspiration: 'You, too, can be like this if only you do this/buy that'.

The way this works for successful magazines is to have a clear sense of the target audience and to adopt an appropriate mode of address. Phil Hilton of *Nuts* explains: 'if you work in a building society, and you've had a pretty dismal day, you can open the magazine and see all these topless girls on a yacht. And you think, "I'd love to be on that yacht, I'll get back to the accounts later." That's what it's all about' (http://www.davidrowan.com/2004/10/interview-phil-hilton-nuts-magazine.html).

Website Activity 11.4: 'Pitching' a new magazine.

further reading

Ferguson, M. (1983) *Forever Feminine: Women's Magazines and the Cult of Femininity*, Heinemann.

Gauntlett, D. (2002) *Media, Gender and Identity*, Routledge.

McRobbie, A. (1994) 'More! New sexualities in girls' and women's magazines' in Curran, J., Morley, D. and Walkerdine, V. (eds) *Cultural Studies and Communications*, Arnold.

Nixon, S. (1996) *Hard Looks (Masculinities, Spectatorship and Contemporary Consumption)*, St. Martin's Press.

Stokes, J. (1999) 'Use it or lose it: sex, sexuality and sexual health in magazines for girls' in Stokes, J. and Reading, A. (eds) *The Media in Britain: Current Debates and Developments*, Macmillan.

12 NEWS PRODUCTION

In this chapter we:

- consider the nature of news and its sources
- look at the role of news in the output of television, radio and print media, and the competition that exists between these media forms
- consider issues of representation in the news and examine what powers exist to control and regulate news output
- look at how technology influences news output and examine the future of current news output in light of new media technologies.

Providing news has always been an important service provided by the media. From the first days of newspapers to the present day 24-hour digital rolling news channels, the media have exploited technological innovation to disseminate news information to mass audiences. News is an important media commodity as it satisfies people's need for surveillance or their desire for information about the world in which they live. Indeed, it can be argued that an important function of news is to help us make sense of a world which has become increasingly confusing, not least because of the amount of information that is available to us.

News is often described as a commodity. Like any other commodity, there is a market equation between supply and demand in which newspaper, radio, television and new media technology supply news to satisfy the demands of the audience. Also, as with any other commodity produced for a mass market, news is produced through what can be recognised as an industrial process or production line. This process takes 'events' that occur in the world, and sometimes beyond, and turns these into familiar and digestible packages of information for us, the audience, to consume. It is this process that is the focus of much of what follows in this chapter.

The reliance of the news production industries on technology is a significant one. Until recently it has limited opportunities for the production of news for a mass market to those people and organisations able to afford the expensive plant and equipment necessary for the process. In consequence, news has been in the control of a relatively small number of wealthy and powerful individuals. Furthermore, advances in technology have made the news-gathering process wider-reaching, so that news can be obtained and relayed almost instantly from remote and often inhospitable corners of the world. Satellite and digital technologies mean that events from places we may never have heard of can be delivered to our living rooms within hours of their happening. Marshall McLuhan, the media commentator, famously described this electronic reduction of the size of the world as a 'global village' (see Chapter 7 on audiences).

ACTIVITY

Consider your own news consumption:

- How do you get your news?
- Do you make an effort to keep up to date with the news every day?
- If so, what kind of news do you keep up to date with?
- Are there any types of news you do not want to hear?
- What is the main media platform through which you get your news?
- Why do you choose to receive news in this way?
- How far does the type of news you are interested in determine the platform from which you obtain it?

News is available to audiences across a range of media forms and platforms. News in the form of print media is primarily produced in newspapers, although there are a number of magazines that focus on current affairs coverage which is closely allied to news. The British press traditionally produced national newspapers in two basic formats: tabloid and broadsheet. These labels were also used to differentiate between newspapers that are serious and concerned with coverage of important national and international news (broadsheet) and those that are more frivolous and at times scandalous in their coverage of more trivial stories (tabloids). The distinction no longer holds water because many of the serious broadsheets have recently changed the formats of their newspapers away from the traditional broadsheet to compact or even tabloid editions. The *Guardian* switched from broadsheet format to Berliner in September 2005. This format with a page size of 470 mm × 315 mm is slightly larger than the tabloid format used by the *Sun* and the *Mirror*. Despite the change in formats, many press commentators like to differentiate upmarket titles like the *Guardian*, aimed at the ABC1 demographic (for an explanation of ABC1 demographics see Chapter 7 on audiences, p. 126) from the popular end of the national newspaper spectrum represented by titles like the *Sun*. The terms 'quality' and 'popular' are sometimes used in place of 'broadsheet' and 'tabloid'. The *Daily Mail*, which is tabloid in shape, likes to call itself 'compact' in order to avoid the negative connotations associated with the term 'tabloid'.

Television news is available as regular bulletins on all of the terrestrial television channels and continues to play an important role in the scheduling of programmes, especially in the evening. In addition, three of the major networks all have dedicated rolling news channels operating round the clock, providing a constant supply of national and international news. Viewers need access to digital technology to receive these channels. They can also keep up to date through the teletext news services providing 24-hour news.

ACTIVITY

It is sometimes argued that television news consumption is gendered in that it is largely males who are interested in news. Hence the role of the early evening news in attracting a male audience to hook them into the evening schedules.

■ Do you think the idea of a television news being primarily of interest to men is true today?
■ Are there other platforms transmitting news that are favoured by a female audience?

Radio is another source of news. Most radio stations, national and local, provide regular news bulletins. In addition Radio 5 Live provides a service similar to the rolling news channels on digital television. Radio news is particularly useful to people who are on the move as they can access it via their car radio.

New media technology has also provided audiences with new sources of news. The web provides such a service both through websites such as the *BBC News* and *Yahoo* as well as the websites of national and local newspapers, such as *Guardian Unlimited*. More recently, innovations in technology have enabled people to gain access to news information through their mobile phones, either via web access or subscription to news services providing specific news, such as sports or financial news, to their handset.

Like magazines (see also Chapter 11 on lifestyle magazines and television) the relationship between the print edition and the online edition of national newspapers provides an interesting study. Many newspapers such as the *Sun* have become concerned that if the online edition replicates too closely the print edition, this is likely to reduce sales and ultimately threaten the production of the newspaper if sales of the print edition are insufficient to sustain it. This process is called cannibalisation and a survey by News International reported in the *Media Guardian* (15

Figure 12.1 Radio news is useful to those on the move

November 2004) suggested that 93,000 readers could potentially stop buying the paper. In consequence, there is a pressure to make the online edition less complete than the print edition, so that it acts more as a teaser to tempt readers to buy the newspaper itself. The *Guardian* offers web users the opportunity to subscribe on a monthly basis to enable them to download the full print edition of the newspaper for use online. Certainly this latter option means that subscribers can gain access to the *Guardian* anywhere in the world that has internet access.

You may find it useful to undertake a comparison of a newspaper website with a print edition of the same title. Notice, for example, how the web edition allows for opportunities to incorporate moving images in its coverage, just like television, in a way that a print edition obviously cannot. Audience feedback and participation are also much more immediate via the web. Whereas a print edition can only reflect readers' responses by printing letters for example in the next day's edition, web-based versions allow immediate feedback at the end of the story. Readers are actively encouraged in most national online editions to join in the discussion of stories, in the form both of serious news and of sport and celebrity gossip. Online editions are also able to take advantage of new technology to develop stories and features much further. Many journalists use the online editions to produce blogs or podcasts, which allows a more informal engagement with the reader than can be achieved in a print edition. Look at RSS feeds that are available through online editions. These are designed to alert readers to new and updated stories as they become available.

Such news alerts also offer opportunities for the audience to choose the type of news that they want to receive. Alerts about a favourite sports team or rock band can be obtained via subscription, thus customising news consumption to ensure that fans have the latest information. Similarly, news groups bring together virtual communities of interest groups wishing to exchange information about any topic from postmodernism to motorsport. News groups also allow participation in the news process to the extent that the audience is potentially directly involved in posting news, thus reversing the familiar one-way process. We tackled in the Introduction the increasing use of 'user-generated content' (see p. 6).

Blogs and podcasts are not limited to professional journalists offering background or personal views of news stories. They can equally be personal accounts of events or sometimes diaries in which people give out information about their daily lives and share their views with the world. Bloggers, as they are called, often take pride in keeping their sites up to date. They are also able to circumvent many of the restrictions or controls that governments are likely to impose on the mass media. So in war situations or times of repression, as in Burma in 2007, bloggers can become a key source of information about what is going on in a country. Blog sites are generally interactive, which means that debates about issues can also be generated in a similar way to newsgroups. Of course, surrounding blogs is the issue of credibility. Audiences will not always be able to verify the truth of what they see on such sites. Some would argue that this is equally true of what they see on the television or read in the newspapers.

ACTIVITY

Do you or your peers blog or read other people's blogs? Undertake a survey to see how popular blogs are, which types are most popular, and what it is that they offer.

It is interesting to note how technological advance in one form can impact on another. One impact of the web as a source of news and information is the way in which television screens are now used. It is common on a news bulletin to have information in the form of words and graphics running at the same time as the bulletin itself. The ticker-tape and information boxes complement the information from the studio to provide the audience with almost instant updates of events taking place.

Sky Sports News, for example, requires viewers to follow a complex information narrative as it offers on screen a 'traditional' news bulletin complemented by ticker-tape information along the bottom of the screen and information in the form of football league tables in a block on the right.

One important aspect of news is that it must be up to date. Technology increases the speed with which news can be brought to us. Before the days of television, moving images of the news were available through such productions as Pathé news, which was a round-up of the week's news shown at the cinema before the main feature. This need to be up to the minute with news is called contemporaneity. It implies that any news that breaks is featured in the next edition of the news media. With a daily newspaper this means the following day if the news breaks before the newspaper is printed (usually in the early hours of the morning). With a radio or television news service, breaking news can be announced almost as it happens. Traditionally within the news media there has always been intense competition to be first with the news. Hence the use of a caption that says 'breaking news'.

Figure 12.2 News is now available on your phone, online, or on TV

Given this proliferation of available news sources, it is hardly surprising that there has been a decline in the consumption of news through the more traditional sources of newspapers and television.

Use the following web links to find up-to-date figures for newspaper circulation:
http://www.nrs.co.uk; http://www.abc.org.uk.

As you can see, there is a general trend for circulation figures for most national newspaper titles to fall, presumably as readers turn to other sources for news and information. As we have seen, New Media sources of news also permit readers to set their own news agenda, for example, by choosing precisely the type of news they wish to consume, be it celebrity gossip, sport or international news. This move away from standardised texts to more differentiated texts means that the audience for news, as with many other media products, is much more segmented and much less homogeneous, allowing it to choose the messages it wishes to receive from the many sources available. For many media commentators this is a significant shift as it has an impact on the important relationship between the sender and receiver of messages in the form of news.

One impact on newspapers of 24-hour rolling news channels is that they are less inclined to compete for speed of delivery of news, but instead have refocused much of their content. In consequence, national newspapers tend now to contain far more in terms of human interests stories, celebrity gossip and background features than they did previously. Such material is often referred to as infotainment.

So where does news come from? The media, most especially Hollywood, have created the myth of the raincoated hack pounding the streets in search of a good story. If such an image were ever true, it has long disappeared. Today's journalist is part of a slick industrial process as much concerned with cost effectiveness as investigative journalism. News is sometimes unexpected but most of the time news is carefully planned in advance, allowing the journalist ample opportunity to ensure that everything is in place and that coverage is as smooth as possible.

Regardless of how it is presented by different news media, most of the news that you read, see or hear is entirely predictable. At the centre of any newsroom, be it television, newspaper or radio, is the diary. The diary lists all the major events taking place on each day that are likely to be worthy of coverage. These will include court cases, for example, major trials at the Old Bailey, parliamentary debates and royal visits. Coverage of such events by journalists can obviously be planned well in advance. Other sources of news are those managed by organisations, including the government, who want to get particular information across to the public. For example, the government may wish to tell the country about a new crime-fighting or road safety initiative. There are a number of ways in which organisations can bring things to the attention of the media:

1 **Press releases**: A press release is a written statement circulated to the news media, providing information in a readily digested form for journalists to use. Often a press release may simply be re-written in the style of the newspaper, for example, and thus it becomes a news story. More likely a press release will alert reporters to a potential story by arousing their interest. For example, a publicity event might be staged which will provide an opportunity for a good press photograph or television news footage. A celebrity presenting a Lotto winner is a good example.
2 **Press briefings**: Press briefings can be either formal or informal. They are a device much favoured by governments to pass information to the news media either on or off the record. 'Off the record' means that the information is unofficial and the journalist is not expected to divulge where the information came from. When phrases such as 'sources close to the Foreign Office' are used, this is usually a sign of an unofficial, off-the-record briefing. With governments, this is part of the 'Lobby System' by which certain privileged journalists receive information about government thinking and plans. The system has been criticised for limiting information to a small clique of journalists trusted by the government. Press briefings are also used by other large organisations, such as companies, wishing to get information published in a way that it is favourable to them. Richard Keeble (2005: 57) suggests there is a view that 'the lobby system is bound into a culture of secrecy pervading all branches of government and into which journalists are too often sucked.'
3 **News conferences**: These are a favourite device of the police in their crime-fighting endeavours. News conferences are often called when a major crime is suspected, for example, when it is feared that a child may have been abducted. News conferences are likely to be attended by journalists working across a range of media forms, but their sense of drama, often with distraught and weeping relatives, brings a strong sense of drama to television news bulletins.

4 **Public relations**: The need for a positive media profile is recognised not only by commercial organisations' public bodies, but also by individuals, usually celebrities, who need to keep themselves in the public eye. One of the most famous publicists is Max Clifford, famous both for representing the interests of celebrities and for selling stories from people intent on making money by destroying the reputations of celebrities. Public relations consultants not only send out press releases and other materials to try to obtain positive coverage, they also arrange parties and other entertainments to which the press are invited. These are particularly used when a new product is being launched.
5 **Publicity stunts**: Given the visual nature of the news, organising news 'events' with a strong visual appeal is a surefire way to make headlines. The Fathers4Justice group are particularly adept at stealing headlines through outrageous publicity stunts which provide strong photo opportunities and news footage.

Clearly journalists are under a lot of pressure to report the message that the influential people and organisations want them to.

ACTIVITY

Track and document the media coverage of a celebrity over a period of three to four weeks. Consider how much publicity they receive is positive and how much is negative. What indications are there of the extent to which the celebrity has sought to influence the type of coverage they have received?

Newsroom roles

News gathering is a complex and often expensive business. The newsroom is the centre of this news-gathering operation. This is the base from which journalists work and where many will return to prepare their stories. One of the impacts of new technologies has been to turn the newsroom into what is known as a multi-platform news hub. Journalists who traditionally worked on platforms such as print media, now contribute to the editorial content across different platforms. The Telegraph group, publishers of the *Daily Telegraph* and the *Sunday Telegraph*, for example, has its editorial offices in London's Victoria. From here journalists and production staff produce both of these titles as well as the Telegraph's website and a range of other digital publishing services such as interviews, newscasts and alerts on a 24-hour basis. (See http://www.telegraph.co.uk/money/main.jhtml?xml=/money/2006/09/05/cnhub05.xml.)

The focal point of a typical newsroom is the news desk, occupied by a news editor. The news editor's job is to decide what stories will be covered and to allocate the job of covering each story to a particular journalist. Usually an experienced journalist, the news editor will have a good sense of what is newsworthy so that he or she can decide not only what stories will be covered but also the extent of the coverage, in terms of time allocated in a news broadcast or space in a newspaper. This late function is called copy-tasting and involves looking at incoming stories from staff reporters and freelance agencies to decide if they need greater coverage.

The newsroom is a professional working environment and as with all professions, journalists have their own professional practices and codes of conduct. Much of this conduct is enshrined in the codes of practice laid down by bodies that oversee and regulate the news media (see section on 'Press regulation', p. 280). However, it is interesting to note that there are also professional issues which guided the selection and presentation of news. What becomes news is remarkably consistent across the news media. If you consider the lead stories in the press and on the radio and television, there is often considerable consensus as to what constitutes the most significant news event of the day. Journalists claim to have a 'nose for a story', suggesting that they have an instinctive ability to determine what is important in terms of the news agenda and what is not. Academic studies on the selection of news suggest that there are also other factors at play. A much-quoted study by Galtung and Ruge (1973) offers a series of categories that have an influence on whether an event is newsworthy or not. Such factors as unexpectedness and reference to elite people, they claimed, play an important role in determining the prominence given to a news story. A more recent survey in which Tony Harcup (2001) revisits Galtung and Ruge's ideas, by considering a thousand page lead stories in three national newspapers, suggests an alternative list.

1 **The power elite**: stories concerning powerful individuals, organisations or institutions.
2 **Celebrity**: stories concerning people who are already famous.
3 **Entertainment**: stories concerning sex, show business, human interest, animals, an unfolding drama, or offering opportunities for humorous treatment, entertaining photographs or witty headlines.
4 **Surprise**: stories that have an element of surprise and/or contrast.
5 **Bad news**: stories with particularly negative overtones, such as conflict or tragedy.
6 **Good news**: stories with particularly positive overtones, such as rescues and cures.
7 **Magnitude**: stories that are perceived as sufficiently significant either in the numbers of people involved or in the potential impact.
8 **Relevance**: stories about issues, groups and nations perceived to be relevant to the audience.
9 **Follow-ups**: stories about subjects already in the news.
10 **Newspaper agenda**: stories which set or fit the news organisation's own agenda.

(Harcup, 2001)

One factor that you may have discovered to be important is that of convenience. Most news-gathering operations have their headquarters in London. This makes sense as the capital contains many important and newsworthy national institutions such as Parliament and government offices. This can, however, lead to a London bias in news reporting, with journalists reluctant to leave the capital unless forced to do so. In consequence, important news stories that do not take place in the capital may be overlooked by the national news media. Of course, this principle can be extended further to argue that one key feature of news coverage is ethnocentricity. Events that take place close to home, or that involve people from the United Kingdom, will receive more prominent coverage than events that take place in distant and remote parts of the world. In consequence, the death of a single person in this country or even a British person killed abroad, will be deemed more newsworthy than a natural disaster, such as an earthquake or flood, which kills large numbers in a far-off developing country. Cultural distance is also significant in the coverage of stories; culturally events in Australia are 'closer to home' than say those in an East European country like Bulgaria.

One way in which the news agenda is influenced is through the type of news available. Not all days are likely to provide an equal amount of news. When Parliament is sitting and business and financial institutions are open, there is likely to be a significant amount of news emanating from them. The weekend, however, is often a quiet time for this type of news and Monday's edition of most national newspapers often betrays this. It is also one reason that Sunday newspapers have a different feel to their daily cousins with far more investigative and speculative stories. The summer months when many people are on holiday and government all but closes down is often called 'the silly season' in journalistic circles, as this is a time for silly inconsequential stories used to fill space.

Of course, the idea that the news agenda is set by these news professionals has important implications. It can be argued that staff who work in the news media are recruited from quite a limited and elite background. Similarly, there is a pressure on those working in the news media to conform to the norms and professional working practices prevalent in the industry. Those who do not conform are likely to find opportunities for career progression strictly limited, if they exist at all. Consequently, audiences receive quite a restricted view of the world as interpreted and presented through the news media, one that reflects the interests of the powerful at the expense of the powerless. This is further compounded by ownership patterns. Other than the BBC, which is a public corporation, all news media are commercial interests usually owned by powerful corporations or powerful men like the Barclay Brothers, owners of the *Daily Telegraph*.

Governments put aside quite significant sums in their budgets to spend on publicising different campaigns and initiatives they have begun. Much of this government spending falls into the category of public information and has included the drink/drive campaigns and information about the new children's tax credits.

However, it is the unofficial government advertising and marketing that cause the most concern. In Britain there has been a Ministry of Information since the First World War. Especially during the Second World War, the Ministry of Information was responsible for both public information (for example, about food rationing) and also more general promotional activities (such as J.B. Priestley's talks on BBC radio) that were aimed at raising morale. It was, however, during the Margaret Thatcher years in the 1980s that the distinction between public and party interests became blurred. The government spent large sums of money advertising privatisation campaigns (such as the Gas Board's 'Tell Sid'), which many commentators felt were advertisements for Thatcherism as much as they were telling the public about share-buying opportunities. Bernard Ingham, Margaret Thatcher's press secretary, eventually became head of the government's Information Service.

Another important consideration is the rise of 'spin' particularly from the government and other political parties, where there is cynical manipulation of news agendas to secure positive coverage of current events.

When Labour came to power in 1997, a Strategic Communications Unit was established under the leadership of Alastair Campbell, an ex-journalist. Both Alastair Campbell and Peter Mandelson have gained reputations as 'spin doctors', people who try to control the flow of information between politicians and the media and, in particular, the way in which the government is presented within the media. To 'spin' a story means to highlight its positive aspects at the expense of those that might potentially be harmful or critical. This is done by using a variety of means such as off-the-record briefings, or 'leaking' stories, to favoured journalists and excluding those journalists who are critical of Labour policies and leaders. Spin doctors such as Alastair Campbell will often insist on being present at, or approving beforehand, any interviews that take place between journalists and politicians. They will also write speeches for politicians ensuring that there is a suitable 'soundbite'.

Part of the role of the spin doctor is to try to control the news agenda and this can include trying to suppress stories that are unfavourable to the government. Alastair Campbell, like Bernard Ingham before him, gained a fierce reputation as someone who would stand up to journalists and was described by many journalists as 'intimidating'. Alastair Campbell was particularly forthright in his criticism of the BBC's coverage of the war in Iraq in 2003, particularly the BBC's allegations that the government, and Alastair Campbell in particular, had 'sexed up' an intelligence report to justify going to war.

Figure 12.3 Alastair Campbell, former spin doctor for 10 Downing Street

The increasing numbers and power of spin doctors reflect the growing importance of promotion and presentation in politics, whereby political parties and their representatives are marketed in the same way that a soap powder or other product would be. Style, presentation and image become central to a type of 'designer' politics, which in America means that, instead of discussing policy, politicians spend millions of dollars running television campaigns that are no different in style and intention to other television advertisements for soft drinks, motor cars or deodorants. Some commentators suggest that this is part of a 'promotional' culture in which a growing proportion of daily life is seen to be constructed around the marketing, advertising and lifestyle discourses of consumer society. In addition, there is also the issue of news stories that are often simply ignored because they do not fit into the ideological position prevailing in the newsroom.

Of course, the setting of a news agenda by these professionals carries with it the danger that the audience's perceptions of the world become skewed by the way in which news is covered and the focus given to specific topics. The focus on crime, for example, the abduction of children, can create an atmosphere which exaggerates such dangers out of all proportion and leads people to become overprotective. At an extreme this becomes a moral panic (see p. 109), a term used to describe the hysterical reaction that news coverage can create within society.

Coverage of stories relating to asylum seekers and paedophiles has led to an over-reaction by creating tensions within our society. This is often because their behaviour is seen as deviant and therefore threatening to our society. The news media certainly seem to consider that they have a key function in watching over social values and protecting our society from such deviant behaviour.

A perennial example is to be found in media concern over the social issue of the use of illegal drugs, especially by young people. Writing in 1973, Jock Young coined the term 'consensualist' to describe the model of society held by the mass media and implicit in their reporting of both deviant and normal behaviour (Cohen and Young 1973). He argued that we live in a society where people have little direct experience of individuals with behaviour different from their own values and conventions. We rely, therefore, on the media to tell us about the 'social worlds'. In explaining the term 'consensualist', Young reveals the ideology behind media coverage of so-called deviant behaviour:

> **Its constitution is simplicity itself: namely, that the vast majority of people in society share a common definition of reality – agree as to what activities are praiseworthy and what are condemnable. That this consensus is functional to an organic system which they envisage as society. That behaviour outside this reality is a product of irrationality or sickness, that it is in itself meaningless activity which leads nowhere and is, most importantly, behaviour which has direct and unpleasant consequences for the small minority who are impelled to act this way. The model carries with it a notion of merited rewards and just punishments. It argues for the equitable nature of the *status quo* and draws the parameters of happiness and experience. Specifically, it defines material rewards as the payment for hard work, sexual pleasure as the concomitant of supporting the nuclear family, and religious or mystical experience as not an alternative interpretation of reality but as an activity acceptable only in a disenchanted form which solemnizes (their word) the family and bulwarks the *status quo*. The illicit drug taker is, I want to suggest, the deviant *par excellence*. For his culture disdains work and revels in hedonism, his sexual relations are reputedly licentious and promiscuous, and the psychedelics promise a re-enchantment of the world – a subversive take on reality.**

(Young 1973: 127)

This concern of the media, particularly the popular press, can, of course, lead to a great deal of emphasis being placed on negative or bad news. One criticism levelled at the news media is that they focus on the negative at the expense of more positive news stories showing the benevolent side of people and society. Certainly events that are disruptive of the norm are more likely to find their way into the public eye than positive stories. Strikes, civil disobedience or even bad weather feature strongly in the news agenda, not least because they have a negative and disruptive impact on people's lives. The way they are presented also lends itself to a greater sense of drama, especially where direct conflict is involved, for example, where protesters are confronting the forces of law and order and threatening disruption.

In many ways the debate around news values lies at the core of a debate about the role of the news media in our society. At the heart of this debate is the question whether the media reflect issues, concerns and trends within our society or whether they in fact create these. Clearly there is no simple answer to this question. In his book *Sociology of Journalism* (1998), Brian McNair points out that journalism is a disseminator of values as well as facts. Generally there will be some element of truth in stories covered by the news media, but the focus of attention on a particular issue may easily snowball, so that relatively minor incidents which might normally be ignored will receive prominent coverage. You might like to explore this idea by looking at some of the stories which cover celebrities, where a minor incident in their lives becomes the focus for a major story.

What is clear is that the news media play an important ideological role in interpreting the world for us in such a way as to shape our social attitudes and beliefs.

Martin Bell, the former BBC war correspondent, provides an interesting insight into how the news media affect individual lives through a harrowing tale of a journalist in Sarajevo during the war in Bosnia:

> This business I am in is not just physically dangerous, but morally dangerous too, and anyone contemplating a career in it could do worse than to ponder the following anecdote, which I hope is apocryphal, but believe is not. It is about a journalist who wished to write a profile of a sniper on a front line in Sarajevo. It doesn't matter on which side the sniper operated, for both sides have them and each side fears the others as much as it values its own. The sniper was peering out from between two bricks in his forward defences. 'What do you see?' asked the journalist.
>
> 'I see two people walking in the street. Which of them do you want me to shoot?'

It was at this point that the journalist realized too late that he was in absolutely the wrong place at the wrong time, and engaged on a story that was fatally flawed and that he should not even have considered. He urged the sniper to shoot neither of them, fabricated some excuse and turned to leave.

As he did so, he heard two shots of rapid fire from a position very close to him. 'That was a pity,' said the sniper. 'You could have saved one of their lives.'

(Bell 1995: 173)

Another perspective on news agendas is offered by Edward Herman and Noam Chomsky (1994) in their book *Manufacturing Consent* (see also Chapter 8, p. 168). They adopt what is known as the 'political economy' approach to the analysis of the output of the news media. Their argument is that the need to make profits and maintain stable business figures is an important dimension in how news media set their agendas. The influence of advertisers is clearly one important factor. If news media report stories that upset their advertisers, this important source of revenue is likely to be withdrawn. Similarly, news media must take care not to upset their major sources of news, which in many cases is the government itself. If they do so, it is likely that they may be marginalised by these news sources that have the power to shut out unfavourable news outlets. As a consequence, they will be unable to compete in reporting important stories and so lose readers and, therefore, profits.

Herman and Chomsky are writing primarily about news reporting in the United States, but their argument can be applied equally in this country. The Lobby System, by which news reporters are briefed about government policy, relies heavily on journalists maintaining the favour of their government sources. Negative reporting of government business can lead to lobby correspondents being frozen out from this major source of political stories. Of course, such a proposal runs counter to the widely held belief in Western democracies of the news media as guardians of our liberties. As Herman and Chomsky point out:

the democratic postulate is that the media are independent and committed to discovering and reporting the truth, and that they do not merely reflect the world as powerful groups wish it to be perceived. Leaders of the media claim that their news choices rest on unbiased professional and objective criteria, and they have support for this contention in the intellectual community. If, however, the powerful are able to fix the premises of

discourse, to decide what the general populace is allowed to see, hear, and think about, and to 'manage' public opinion by regular propaganda campaigns, the standard view of how the system works is at serious odds with reality. 🥟

(Herman and Chomsky 1994: xi)

Construction of a news story

The concept of narrative is an important one in looking at how news stories are put together. Whatever the media form, news stories tend to share the same construction. The often used description 'stories' is important here. Just as a fictional narrative unfolds to us information a little at a time, so too with the narrative construction of a news story.

Narrative is a means of revealing information in such a way as to both keep the audience interested and help their understanding of what is going on. In consequence, it requires the narrator to pass over the information in a series of chunks that will build together to form a coherent narrative. Each news story is an example of a shorter narrative inside a larger narrative, i.e. a news bulletin or a newspaper. You may have notice how similar in construction are the products that form part of each of these genres. Indeed, it is also possible to identify important similarities across these media forms. Whatever newspaper or website you open, you will always have a good idea where to find specific information. For example, sport often occupies the back of the paper while business news is somewhere around the middle. Similarly, television and radio news bulletins will locate these items in the middle and towards the end of the bulletin. You may be aware from your work on both genre and narrative that some degree of predictability and familiarity is reassuring for an audience, so knowing where to find things produces a comfortable feel.

Where news narratives tend to differ from fictional narratives is that while the latter work generally in terms of a linear or temporal narrative, news stories work in order of significance. This can be seen in the way in which agendas are set to prioritise stories into a hierarchical order within a bulletin or on different pages of a newspaper. One criticism of television news presentation is that it succumbs to adopting fictional narrative codes by using storytelling devices to maintain the interest of audiences. Indeed, it has been suggested that television news has adopted some of the conventions of soap opera with its interaction of familiar characters and serial storylines.

ACTIVITY

Can you find evidence in some recent news bulletins of the tendency of news broadcasts to adopt fictional narrative codes? Is it, do you think, more prevalent on one channel or another? Do you think other platforms such as online news sources and newspapers utilise similar devices?

Another useful activity is to look at the way in which a website prioritises stories in a similar way to both a radio or television news bulletin and a newspaper. Look, for example, at the way in which the *Sun Online* uses its homepage to offer a hierarchy of stories determined by size, the illustration and, above all, the position relative to the top of the page. Notice, how on scrolling down, other sections such as sport and showbiz have their own hierarchies. Navigation of the site also echoes that of the print edition with the sidebar menu inviting the browser to turn to pages of specific interest (see http://www.thesun.co.uk/sol/homepage/).

If you consider a number of news stories on a range of topics, it is likely you will find that journalists often present them from a human interest angle. This means that people will be at the centre of the story. Clearly many stories are about people and their lives, but often political and economic stories, potentially quite dry and uninteresting, are couched in terms of how they affect people. For example, when the Chancellor makes a budget speech, it is often reported through how it will impact on the lives of 'typical' people, such as families or pensioners. This is one reason why quotes or quotations are an important aspect of news stories. Quotes give a story the human touch by emphasising the importance of the people in the story. Quotes also add authenticity to a story, which is one reason why press releases will often contain at least one. They may vary in format: from expert opinion (for example, a hospital consultant talking about a flu epidemic), to that of the person in the street often in the form of a 'vox pop' where a radio or tele- vision reporter has interviewed people to get their views on a news topic or issue.

When a big story breaks, it is often in the interests of the news media to keep the story going in some way. This is partly because they will have invested time and money in getting key personnel on site to cover the story and need to recover their investment by having a supply of 'follow-up' stories. For example, after a great tragedy, such as a bombing or a natural disaster, correspondents are required to file follow-up reports from the location giving details of how the event has influenced people's lives.

ACTIVITY

Look at a story as presented on television, online and in a newspaper. Analyse how the story has been assembled. What similarities are there in the presentation of the story between the three media forms?

Television news presentation

Research by Gunter et al. (1994) showed that 70 per cent of the public get their information about world news through television and about 20 per cent through newspapers, whilst 40 per cent of the public said that they get their local news through newspapers compared to about 35 per cent through television. News bulletins are an important part of television output. The main terrestrial broadcasters construct their prime-time schedules around the early evening and the main evening news bulletins. Whenever a channel suggests changing the timing of a news bulletin, there is often a lot of angry debate in the country as to the desirability of doing so. Such an important role puts a lot of pressure on news to be entertaining as well as informative in order to prevent audiences turning over to other channels. This pressure has been increased by the arrival of rolling news channels such as Sky News and BBC News 24, which provide a round-the-clock news service that viewers can tune into at any time. This pressure is further compounded by newer channels such as Five and BBC3, introducing slick and fast-paced news bulletins aimed at the youth market who are assumed to be uninterested in news and to have short attention spans.

ACTIVITY

How far do you think it is true that young people have short attention spans and take little interest in the news? As well as giving your own personal response, carry out a survey among a range of people in and around your age group to find out what their attitude is to news.

The presenters themselves are a key part of the look of a news bulletin. Presenters are generally highly presentable, photogenic people. They tend to be good-looking, well-groomed and well-presented. They speak with cultured and authoritative accents which suggest they have been well educated. Indeed, it has been suggested that it is their appearance rather than their journalistic skills that qualifies them for the job. It is certainly noteworthy that many presenters become celebrities in their own right and many use their fame to develop careers outside of news-reading.

Figure 12.4 Zeinab Badawi – BBC World News

What is your attitude to newsreaders appearing on programmes other than the news? Consider, for example, newsreaders who take part in such programmes as *Celebrity Come Dancing* or who host quiz shows.

The quality of presenters is to appeal to the audience while at the same time bringing a level of authority to the news bulletin. Similarly, the studio itself is carefully constructed to create a specific impression on the audience. Newsrooms are busy places and the news studio echoes this quality. Often the studio features the actual newsroom in the background with journalists busy preparing stories for broadcast. This provides a sense of urgency about the process – the news-gathering operation is just next door to the studio – but also demonstrates that the process is in some way 'real', because it is happening now. News is being gathered as the bulletin goes on air. If a story breaks, then we are bound to hear about it because the newsroom is just next door. Although the presentation may be studio-based, it is firmly rooted in the real world. This sense of the 'real world' is further reinforced by the way in which reports are seen on location. A piece to camera, where a reporter directly addresses the audience from the scene, again reinforces the authenticity of the report. News studios are usually quite clinical in appearance, stainless steel surfaces and suffused lighting with muted colours suggest a sterile place remote from the outside world, thus conveying the impression of objectivity and detachment. This helps create the idea that news from this studio is a product that the audience can trust.

The way in which the news is presented to us has an important bearing on the possible readings that we can take from it. News on television is intended to be in some way objective and unbiased, not least by presenting the facts in a neutral and disinterested fashion. However, such factors as facial expressions, demeanour and body language of the presenters work in subtle ways to limit the different interpretations that the bulletin is capable of. A raised eyebrow, or the recent penchant for standing up to deliver certain items, contribute to the way in which we the viewer are likely to interpret the events reported to us. Certainly the presentational style adopted by many newsreaders makes it fairly clear when our disapproval is sought, for example, in the reporting of 'terror attacks'.

Of course, it can be argued that it is impossible for news to be truly objective and unbiased. The very process of selecting, editing and presenting is bound to carry with it some degree of interpretation on the part of the people who process the news. Rarely do facts speak for themselves. One of the mainsprings of narrative is conflict and news stories are no exception. A 'good' news story will inevitably involve some degree of conflict, from all-out war to a dispute between neighbours or two football managers. It is, however, incumbent on the television news channels to represent both sides of the argument in such conflicts. This is one of the fundamental principles of public service broadcasting, enshrined, for example, in the BBC Charter. This is obviously important in political debates when both the government and opposition viewpoints need to be represented. Objective and balanced reporting, however, should extend into other areas of news coverage. Industrial disputes, for example, should be covered in such a way as to represent both cases put forward by the workers as well as their employers. Interestingly, studies by the Glasgow University Media Group back in the 1970s suggested that reporting of such events as strikes was rarely objective and always favoured the employers' side.

ACTIVITY

Working with some of your peers, each of you should write a report of an event such as the stabbing of a peer and compare your results. To what extent do your reports agree? Disagree? How do you account for any differences?

One problem with the issue of objectivity is that it assumes there are just two sides to an argument or that an issue can be reduced to a conflict between two parties. Often the complexities of a news item will mean that there is a whole range of opinion that might be taken into account if reporting is to be truly objective. Given the constraints of time in news bulletins this is clearly not possible. Certainly a complex issue like Western attitudes to Islamic fundamentalism cannot be adequately represented within the confines of a news story in a television news bulletin without some simplification and reduction of the issues involved.

As Mark Peace points out, one important aspect of news presentation that has a bearing on how an audience is likely to interpret news is the positioning of the camera:

> **The fact that the viewer is positioned behind the camera has a great deal of influence on the presentation of reality by broadcasters. It means that we assume the point of view of the camera, so if it is positioned looking, for example, from a factory towards a picket line, we can, at least literally, see only the perspective of the employers. This means that, photographically, the news will always favour a particular group, side, or perspective at any one point.**

(Mark Peace, 'The construction of reality in television news', 1998)

Figure 12.5

Perhaps the important issue that underpins the problem here is that of ideology. News texts are inevitably presented from an ideological viewpoint. They therefore reflect the dominant belief system that is part of our culture.

ACTIVITY

Consider some stories that have been reported on the news recently.

■ How far do you think the news teams have managed to provide an object report of the events?
■ How far do you think their reports are biased in favour of one particular viewpoint?
■ Do you think it would be possible to be more objective within the confines of a news bulletin?

One important quality of news is that it is nearly always serious. It is also generally bad. Negative events are much more likely to make news headlines than positive ones. The nature of news then is bound to influence the way in which it is presented to us. News is also an important part of the ritual of everyday life. Turning on breakfast television, reading a newspaper on the way to work, tuning in the car radio to a news bulletin, or switching on the early evening news as soon as we get home, are all ways in which the ritual of daily news is reinforced.

It follows therefore that the presentational style of news is such that its gravity and role in our daily lives are accentuated. Let us consider the way in which television news is presented to us and analyse some of the qualities that constitute a typical bulletin and give it this sense of gravity and importance.

■ **Music**: The opening music to a news bulletin has an important interpellative quality. This means that it acts rather like an old-fashioned town crier shouting and ringing a bell in order to gather an audience to listen to what he has to say. As such it must be instantly recognisable. It has a certain pomp about it which signals at the very opening of the bulletin that an important programme is about to start so the audience should gather round and listen. (Listen to the opening music for bulletins for all the major channels and news channels. What do they have in common?)
■ **Studio**: News studios differ from news programme to news programme but all share many distinctive qualities. In the clean, sterile, self-contained studio with subdued colours and clean surfaces, there is always evidence of modern communications technology, such as laptops and plasma-screen monitors. Here is a place where important business is carried out in a neutral and dis-passionate way. In some we see the news-gathering operation going on in the

background to remind us of the resources being used to bring us our news bulletin. The BBC news studio was in fact for several year a virtual studio, basically a plain room with a computer-generated set to create the illusion of a fully equipped studio.

■ **The presenter(s)**: News presenters are always dressed quite formally to reflect the importance of their role. For male presenters this invariably means they are clean-shaven and wear a suit and tie. They often sit behind quite a large desk which has the effect of giving them a sense of authority. They always address the audience directly, reading from an autocue on the camera to ensure they hold us in their gaze. People who look you directly in the eye while speaking are generally held to be telling the truth. In fact the presenters are about integrity and sincerity. We can trust them because they are authority figures speaking directly to us. The accusation has been made that presenters are chosen for their appearance rather than their journalistic skills. This phenomenon has been called 'Ken and Barbie news', suggesting that newsreaders are chosen for their doll-like attractiveness. Certainly it is interesting to look at the way in which magazine style and regional news programmes often use this type of husband and wife team to bring a degree of informality which distinguishes such programmes from the more serious national news bulletins.

As Casey *et al*. (2002: 147) point out: 'The ambience of television news, then, is one of formality, sincerity and neutrality, bolstering the ideological claim that television news is essentially truthful.'

ACTIVITY

What other features of news presentation contribute to the way in which audiences are encouraged to receive it? You might like to consider what has been called the increasing informalisation of news presentation, in which presenters appear as friendly and approachable people.

Interestingly, one impact of digital technology has been to proliferate the number of channels available to audiences and in consequence to increase the competition between channels in providing news. Given the pressure from news providers in other media forms, there is an extreme pressure on both new and existing channels to make their bulletins attractive and entertaining. Some of the newer channels such as BBC3 are also intent on reaching the youth market, which is traditionally resistant to the serious business of watching news bulletins. This has led to the introduction of presentational strategies which have 'livened' up news presentation. Perhaps a turning point was when Kirsty Young on Channel Five sat on her desk rather than behind it, thus introducing a level of informality not previously associated with news presentation. Similar strategies are now to be found in ITN news bulletins, where presenters stand up and move about the studio in a carefully choreographed news presentation.

It is not only in its presentation that television news has battled hard to maintain its share of the audience. The content of television news has often been focused towards lighter, celebrity-based items seemingly at the expense of hard news coverage. This has led to the accusation of tabloidisation of the television news, where the news agenda has shifted to the trivial and the scandalous at the expense of hard and significant news stories and reflects more the agenda set by the tabloid press than the more serious broadsheets. The real concern about this is that television news is seen as the prime means by which people get information about the world. If serious stories about political, social and economic issues are to be replaced by trivial diversionary stories, then ultimately the basis of a democratic society is threatened as people become ill-informed and apathetic about these issues.

Case study

THE *DAILY MAIL*

Figure 12.6

continued

The *Daily Mail* is a well-known media product: some would call it a national institution. It has a circulation of around 2.4 million copies each day and it is common to see people reading a copy on the bus, train or tube on their way to work in the morning.

The *Daily Mail* is a highly influential media product. It does little to disguise its political and cultural allegiances, which are support for a right-of-centre Tory party, and its concern to represent the interests of 'Middle England', the conservative, property-owning middle classes.

The *Daily Mail* is an example of a national newspaper, which means that it circulates throughout the country rather than to one specific geographical area, as do some local or regional papers. The news it covers will therefore be of interest and concern to people across the United Kingdom. In terms of its format, the *Daily Mail* is also an example of a tabloid newspaper, although it prefers to call itself 'compact'.

Click on the link http://www.nmauk.co.uk/nma/do/live/cribsheetdailymail for a breakdown of the *Daily Mail* readership which shows a significant number in the AB social groups and a much smaller percentage of the readership being manual workers. The *Daily Mail* can be seen, then, as a quality mid-market title with a readership similar to that of many of the quality titles.

It has been suggested that if current circulation trends continue, the *Daily Mail* will become the country's most popular newspaper by the end of the decade. Much of the popularity of the newspaper is put down to the editor, Paul Dacre, who took control in 1992. The editor of a newspaper is obviously an important and powerful figure. The *Daily Mail* stance in representing the values of Middle England can be seen, however, to make this man even more of a powerful figure, especially at a time when traditional right-wing politics represented by the Conservative Party are in disarray. Indeed, it has been argued that Dacre's *Daily Mail* represents the real opposition to the New Labour government; certainly there is evidence to suggest that senior Labour politicians do attempt to avoid antagonising the newspaper unnecessarily.

The editor is usually the most powerful person in a newspaper's hierarchy, although in some cases it is argued that an editor may be a mere puppet doing the bidding of the proprietor, a view commonly expressed about Rupert Murdoch's News International titles. With power, however, comes responsibility, and it is nearly always the editor who is held responsible when things do go wrong. Editors in extreme cases can be sent to prison if their newspapers transgress the law.

Newspapers such as the *Daily Mail* are usually organised into departments responsible for such things as advertising, production and distribution. The news content is the responsibility of the editorial department under the direct control of the editor. The editorial department will consist of smaller sections with specific responsibilities, such as the features department. The main news-gathering operation is controlled by the news editor from the news desk. S/he is responsible for deciding which stories need to be covered and assigning tasks to individual journalists. Many of these tasks will be diary jobs, known about well in advance.

Where possible, stories will be covered by full-time journalists, known as staff reporters. However, where this is not possible, because a story is too remote from the nearest staff reporter, a newspaper such as the *Daily Mail* will use agency copy from a large news agency such as Reuters or the Press Association. It may also buy in a story from a local freelance journalist or 'stringer', who will be paid 'lineage', which is a fee for each line of copy that is used in the newspaper. Similarly, photographs will be provided variously by staff photographers, agencies and freelancers.

The design and layout of a newspaper are the responsibility of the sub-editors, or 'subs'. Working under the direction of a chief sub, the subs will check a reporter's copy for accuracy, both of fact and of grammar, before providing a headline and laying out the page, using an on-screen page-make-up programme.

The editor has the major, and final, say over which stories are included and how prominently each is displayed. The front-page lead is clearly the most prominent story, with inside pages carrying less-important stories.

Press regulation

As we have seen in Chapter 8 on Media Institutions, all media organisations are subject to some degree of regulation. Newspapers are, however, a special case. The 'freedom of the press' has been for many years a rallying cry in support of democracy and this concept has done a lot to preserve the newspaper industry from many of the regulatory controls imposed on television and radio. It would be a brave government that tried to impose further restrictions on the press. (See p. 172 for further info on the PCC.)

The regulation that does exist can be categorised into legal and self-regulatory controls. An example of a legal control is the law of libel. If a newspaper publishes a story, found subsequently to be untrue, that is defamatory because it lowers someone in the estimation of right-thinking members of society, then it has committed libel. The person who has been defamed has redress through the courts and is entitled to damages if the court finds in his or her favour. The main defence against libel is that the story as published is in fact true.

The problem with the libel laws as they stand is that because the loser in the case is likely to have to pay the costs of both sides, usually only the very rich can afford to take the risk of starting a court battle with a newspaper. One rich person who took on the *Daily Mail* and won was Nicole Kidman. In July 2003 she received 'substantial damages' after claiming in court that a *Daily Mail* article accusing her of adultery with Jude Law was untrue. She argued that the false accusations had caused her 'considerable embarrassment and distress'. The *Daily Mail* agreed to apologise and pay court costs.

Ownership

As mentioned in Chapter 8 on Media Institutions, many well-known media texts are produced by larger organisations or groups, often with international interests. The *Daily Mail* is no exception. It is part of a larger group called Associated Newspapers, which is in turn part of a larger group called the Daily Mail and General Trust Ltd, or DMGT.

Associated Newspapers publishes several well-known national titles in addition to the *Daily Mail*:

- **Mail on Sunday**: The *Daily Mail*'s sister paper, published on Sundays with a circulation very similar to that of the Daily Mail
- **Metro**: A free sheet distributed in London, Birmingham, Newcastle, Leeds, Sheffield, Manchester, Glasgow and Edinburgh by readers picking up copies at rail and bus stations, giving it a daily circulation in the region of 800,000
- **Loot**: A classified advertising paper with editions published in several major cities
- **Evening Standard**: Currently London's only evening newspaper, although Richard Desmond has plans to launch a free evening rival provocatively called the *London Evening Mail*.

Each of the above titles has an accompanying website. The relationship between a newspaper and its website is often a complex one. A newspaper publisher will not want to give away free via the web what it currently expects readers to pay for. Websites in consequence tend to be scaled-down versions of editions of newspapers, often with ancillary features geared towards supporting advertisers. An interesting example is the *Evening Standard*'s website, 'This is London' (http://www.thisislondon.co.uk). In addition to offering a news service, the site provides key lifestyle and cultural information about the capital. Many of the facilities, such as restaurants and cinemas, are regular advertisers in the print publication.

One of the reasons why newspapers have invested so heavily in new media technology is to ensure that they are future-proof against some of the rapid changes taking place in media technology. There is a distinct possibility that newspapers will one day be delivered electronically rather than as hard copy. Websites represent one way by which this might be done. This desire to ensure survival in the competitive media market also means that newspaper groups often seek to diversify into other media and into other media-related activities.

Typically DMGT has diversified its interests over a number of years. In addition to Associated Newspapers, it also controls Northcliffe Newspapers, which publishes 106 regional newspaper titles across the UK. DMGT Radio has commercial radio interests both in this country and in Australia, where it controls more than 30 stations. The Daily Mail Group also controls the Teletext service, which provides information via Channels ITV, Four and Five. Overseas interests include newspaper titles that have been acquired in Spain, Greece and Ireland. The group, which has a turnover of nearly £2 billion a year, also controls DMG Media, an exhibitions business, and the DMG Information business services division.

According to its website:

> **The success of many of the Group's businesses is inextricably linked with understanding and engaging with the communities that they serve, and this allows them to identify needs and to campaign effectively on the issues relevant to their customer base. This principle is as relevant to the *Daily Mail*, serving the whole of the United Kingdom, as to the *North Devon Journal Herald*, serving the population of Barnstaple in Devon, and to 6KG, one of our two radio stations serving the remote mining town of Kalgoorlie in Western Australia.**

(http://dmgt.answerbank.co.uk/pages/client0/annual_report/csr.htm)

As you will see, such an ownership profile is typical of many modern media organisations in that it has both diversified into different media forms and looked to extend its interest multinationally.

References and further reading

Allan, S. (2004) *News Culture*, 2nd edn, Open University Press.
—— (2006) *Online News*, Open University Press.
Bell, M. (1995) *In Harm's Way*, Penguin.

Casey, N. *et al.* (2002) *Television Studies: The Key Concepts*, Routledge.

Cohen, S. and Young, J. (1973) *The Manufacture of News*, Sage.

Evans, H. (1972) *Newsman's English*, Heinemann.

Harcup, T. and O'Neill, D. (2001) 'What is news? Galtung and Ruge revisited' in Rayner, P., Wall, P. and Kruger, S. (2003) *Media Studies: The Essential Resource*, Routledge.

Hartley, J. (1982) *Understanding News*, Routledge.

Herman, H.S. and Chomsky, N. (1994) *Manufacturing Consent: The Political Economy Model of the Mass Media*, Vintage.

Keeble, R. (2005) *The Newspapers Handbook*, 4th edn, Routledge.

McNair, B. (1994) *News and Journalism in the UK: A Textbook*, Routledge.

Wilcock, J. (2001) *The Tabloid Press: A Teacher's Guide*, Auteur.

Website

http://www.aber.ac.uk/media/sections/news.html

part **3**

CREATING MEDIA

13 PRODUCTION

In this chapter we look at:

- the principles of practical production
- production planning and research
- responding to a brief
- post-production and evaluation.

Figure 13.1

and to agreed budgets. There is also a degree of technological determinism at play in shaping the type of media product that we get to consume. This means that media products are as they are because they have been shaped by the technology that has created them. For example, most magazines look very similar in design and layout. This can be attributed to such factors as the software used to create the layout and the technology used to print the magazine. A printing press is generally geared up to create specific formats and not others.

Another important governing factor that shapes the nature of a media product is the perceived needs of the audience. Success in mass-media terms is determined by the size of the audience for a product. Circulation figures, box office and audience ratings are important measures of success. Creating a product that is likely to appeal to the audience is of paramount concern when a producer sets out on the production process.

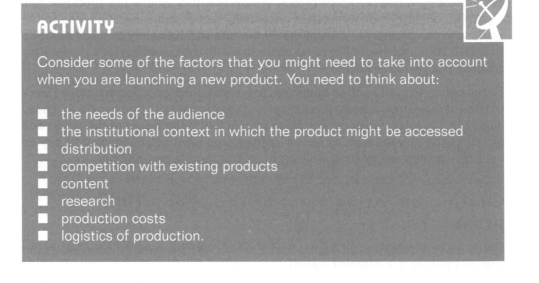

ACTIVITY

Consider some of the factors that you might need to take into account when you are launching a new product. You need to think about:

- the needs of the audience
- the institutional context in which the product might be accessed
- distribution
- competition with existing products
- content
- research
- production costs
- logistics of production.

Rather than having a free hand to 'be creative', most people who make media products do so under considerable constraints. Indeed, many would probably much prefer to direct their own independent movie rather than working on the next series of *Big Brother*. Sadly, few get the opportunity to work with such artistic freedom.

Creating media – MEST2

So how does all this fit into MEST2 practical production? One important aspect of your study of the media is to know why texts are the way they are. You need to be able to understand and analyse the factors that have determined the final form of a media product: why a television programme is the way it is; or what has determined the content and design of the front page of a newspaper. One way of learning about some of the factors at play is by actually having a go at producing your own media product. This is what MEST2 asks you to do.

Of course, you are not being asked to work to professional standards in creating your product. What you are expected to do is to emulate professional practices. You will need to set for yourself very similar ground rules to the ones that you might be expected to follow if your were creating your product for a mass audience. The process will help you to understand both the practice of professional media production and how this practice determines the final outcome. In this way your theoretical understanding will be informed by the actual process of creating your own media product – hence the symbiotic relationship. Making a product will enlighten you about the theory: the theory will enlighten you about the production process.

So how does this pan out in practice? The best place to start is by looking at what the specification asks you to do:

> **Candidates will offer for assessment two productions chosen from two of the three media platforms in their chosen brief, plus an evaluation of both production pieces with reference to the third media platform.**

Before we take a detailed look at how to go about the process of completing your production work for MEST2, it is a good idea to try to tease out some broad principles about how to create a media product. We will then link these to the precise requirements of the specification.

Clearly, the scope of this book does not allow a detailed exploration of all the possible forms and formats you may engage with in undertaking production work. What we have done therefore is to look at some of the broad principles of the process that are common to most formats. We will then look in detail by means of case studies at two specific production activities: video production and print. You can, however, use the website to get support on other production skills that you may need to acquire for this unit.

Getting started

So where to begin with a media production? There are six principal steps, outlined below.

1 **Look carefully at other available products that are similar to what you want to make.** This may seem pretty obvious but it is very easy to embark on a task that amounts to re-inventing the wheel. Learning from what other people have already done is an important first step to media production. Indeed, the AQA specification explicitly requires you to link your production

Notice the careful attention to detail in ensuring that everything is in the right place at the right time. This planning is called 'logistics' and means that you try to organise your production in order to make the most effective and efficient use of available resources. A good way to think about this is in terms of a budget for a production. Most media professionals work within tight budgetary con-straints. In the real world of media production, you would have to pay for the hire of your equipment, including time spent using a computer for editing or page layout, together with any technical expertise you bring, for example, a designer or editor. Logistically it makes sense therefore to get maximum use of these resources by preparing in advance to use them. Planning means that if you have arranged for equipment and technical support to be ready at a location, then all the other things you need should be there at the same time, including lunch for everyone if it is to be a full day's work.

5 **Planning also involves doing a good deal of research and writing in advance of going into production**. The precise nature of this will differ according to the format you are working with. For example, a fictional work will need careful scripting, whereas a more factual piece will need a degree of 'scripting' (e.g in relation to the questions you might ask a potential inter-viewee or actuality you need to record). Both will need research, both primary and secondary in most cases. You will need to check out the suitability of locations, for example, by visiting them beforehand and perhaps taking test photographs. People who might feature in your product will need to be checked out to see that they are suitable and will 'perform' in a way that is appropriate. Documentaries, while pretending to stumble upon people and getting them in front of the camera or microphone, are often extensively researched by assis-tants before a crew turns up to record them. A journalist will usually do a good deal of background research into a topic before going out to interview someone with knowledge of it. Any research or preparatory work that you undertake is almost bound to have a significant impact on both the quality of what you produce and the efficiency with which you undertake the production process.

6 **Organisation is also central to the process of production**. If you have carried out your planning and research effectively, you are well on your way to getting organised. If you are working in a group with other people, decid-ing and agreeing where responsibilities lie needs to be addressed at the very beginning of the process. You need to find a means of doing this that is accept-able to all members of the group. However you decide to work, it is important that all members of the group stick to what has been agreed and that everyone completes their allotted task properly and punctually. You might also wish to decide on a contingency plan in case something goes wrong. For example, a group member may be off sick or even leave the course. Who will take over their roles?

Useful guidance on preparing a video shoot for distribution is available on YouTube: http://www.youtube.com/t/studio_article_11.

A closer look at the AQA specification

Let us consider now the AQA specification and the demands that it makes on you for Unit 2 Creating Media. One requirement is that you must link your production work into the topic that you have studied in Unit 1, Investigating Media. The specification explains that you are expected to pursue your own media interests within a framework of media concepts, contexts and issues. This means that you are expected to link the work you do for production to the learning you have undertaken in Unit 1. In a nutshell, your production work should link closely to the theory that you have learned.

In practical terms you are being asked to create two productions. These must be chosen from two of the three media platforms: broadcasting, e-media or print. You are being asked to demonstrate that you have planning, technical and creative skills as well as a knowledge of the relevant codes and conventions. Again you are being asked to link closely practical production with your theoretical understanding of how media products are constructed. It should be becoming quite clear by now that to get a good mark in this unit you will have to demonstrate that you have made the vital connections between production work and your understanding of media theory.

The specification indicates that you should approach this as a three-stage process:

- pre-production work
- production work
- evaluation.

Let us consider each of these in turn. Pre-production requires you to explore three areas, very similar to those we have identified in the section above:

1 research into existing media products in the appropriate media formats to your own production tasks, e.g. film trailers of a similar genre to the one you intend to make
2 audience targeting and research
3 planning.

Production itself requires you to create two products. These must be linked and utilise two different media platforms. So a film poster and a film trailer are linked in that they both publicise a film, but one uses a broadcast medium, the other print. Alternatively you might look at the way in which film is promoted through e-media and substitute that platform, say for print.

The specification places emphasis on the quality of the productions that you create. It points out that there are a lot of marks for this unit and the quality of your final product should reflect this. The products should be fully realised. This means that they are expected to be completed using appropriate technology and not simply consist of pre-production drafts or scripts. The marking scheme requires you to demonstrate both creativity and 'clear technical proficiency' if you are going to get a top grade. You need, therefore to have good ideas and the technical skill to turn these into a quality production.

You are also expected to use 'substantially' your own words and images in making your products. It is not acceptable, therefore, to download images from the web or lift copy from another source. Taking your own photographs, filming your own sequences and writing copy and voice-overs are essential if you are going to do well in this unit.

The specification indicates that no more than 20 per cent of each production can consist of found material.

The specification points out that it is a valuable experience for you to engage in the full production process rather than lifting material from elsewhere. Certainly the experience of organising the logistics of shooting a film sequence, or more simply organising the *mise-en-scène* for a photograph, should offer you valuable insights into the way in which professionals make media products.

One big decision that you will need to make before you set out on your production is whether you are going to work independently or as part of a group. If you do work in a group (and for video production it is probably best that you do, given the complexity of the tasks and the roles to be filled), then a maximum size is four. Group work is only for the production work itself. 'The majority' of the preliminary pre-production work should be your own individual work.

The specification suggests that group work be limited to 'time-based media', for example, video production, and asks your teacher to monitor 'each candidate's contribution' and to mark it accordingly. That means that the more effort you contribute to the group, the better your mark. For the lazy who enjoy the spectacle of others doing work, the reverse is unfortunately equally true.

You will also be required to respond to a brief that has been set for you. It is important to understand the significance of what is meant by 'working to a brief'. The idea of a brief is that it sets out as precisely as possible what it is you are expected to do. It gives you a task to complete and sets both guidelines and boundaries you need to observe in undertaking the task. The reason for a brief is to ensure that all candidates taking the exam will be required to do the same thing. Of course, the outcome from candidate to candidate is likely to be very different, just as the responses that individual candidates offer in response to the same exam question will differ.

It is important that you consider carefully the brief that you have been set and that you stay within its boundaries. One important boundary is an indication of the scope or extent of the products you are expected to produce. For example, you might be asked to create two television advertisements each lasting 30 seconds. Alternatively, a print production might ask for three magazine advertise-ments, while an e-media production might require a production limited to three web pages. You should observe these parameters carefully; producing more or less than you are asked for is bound to adversely affect your mark.

CREATING MEDIA

Evaluation commentary

The practical production means very little unless it is accompanied by a commentary. This is where you have the opportunity to write a commentary, usually about 1,000 words, explaining the rationale behind the product, how you went about producing it, and how you would evaluate the finished product.

Everybody who works on a production team will have to produce their own commentary. It is your chance to articulate how your product illuminates your understanding of the key concepts of the Media Studies syllabus that you are following. As a guide, it's probably a very good idea to divide your piece of writing into three distinct parts: intention, process and outcome.

1 **Intention**: This section is very similar to the idea of a brief. You should explain what it is that you have set out to do and the ideas behind it. Explain why you have chosen the particular product and the subject material of that particular product, as well as suggesting the target audience that you are aiming for and how you intend to attract them. When doing this you should also explain the research that you have undertaken whilst planning your production. Refer to real media texts that you have studied. Show how your production will be linked to them in some way – either in terms of form or ideas. You should also refer to the key concepts of the course and it is here that you should reveal your engagement with those very key concepts and how your practical production puts that engagement into concrete form. Thus if you have decided to create a short horror-film trailer, then this is where you have the opportunity to discuss the media language found in such texts and also any issues of representation that you might decide to tackle. Media theory into media practice!

2 **Process**: In this section you should explain the actual technical process of getting your media product made. There is a danger here of going into far too much detail. With this in mind, you should watch the word count very carefully. What is *not* needed is a day-by-day, blow-by-blow account of the minutiae of the production process. But you do need to explain the reasons why the product has turned out the way it has – what decisions were made and the rationale behind them. It is also an opportunity to discuss any technical and other problems you encountered and how you overcame them. There will have been technical hitches. Explain how and why they occurred and how you dealt with them. Do not dwell on how one particular character kept on letting you down because this often ends up sounding like sour grapes. As your teachers and lecturers should be monitoring your production at all times, it is likely that they will already know who is doing what and, more importantly, who is doing very little.

3 **Outcome**: In this part of the commentary you should do to your production what you have been doing to other media products since you started the course. In other words, you should try, as objectively as possible, to evaluate the effectiveness of your product in terms of its use of the chosen media, its subject matter and its suggested target audience. Try to be as honest as you can. Do

not be overcritical, but at the same time try not to be too bland. Marks are not given for the following phrases: 'and I really enjoyed making it', 'I don't think it could be improved on' or 'all in all I think it's pretty good'.

It is important that you refer to the key concepts and show how they have illuminated your understanding of the production process and how, too, you have attempted to show your understanding of them in the final product. Where the specification asks that the production is linked in some way to areas studied in other modules, you must make those links obvious in your evaluation.

In all three parts of the rationale it is important to avoid description and concentrate on showing how you have got to grips with media concepts through the practical process. In other words, you need to be as critical and analytical of your own production as you have been with every other media product you have studied over the course. It is also an opportunity for you to reflect on your own learning and the relevance of what you think you have learnt in the past.

It will not be a perfect production – although it may well be very close to perfection – but the important thing is that the production will be assessed as positively as possible. With this in mind, anyone looking at the production and rationale should respond to a healthy dose of self-criticism in a flexible and encouraging way.

Finally, do not simply leave this part of the process to the last minute. It is a piece of work that has to be shaped and considered in exactly the same way as the product itself and can earn you a substantial rise in your marks. Keep to the word length, type the essay, spell-check what you have written and, again, ensure that it is well presented and relevant to the production that you have submitted.

Case study
FILM AND BROADCAST FICTION

The AQA specification offers a number of examples of production tasks you might be expected to undertake. We will look in detail at one for this topic area and consider how you might best go about responding to the task.

Here is the information from the specification:

Broadcast

Create a 2 minute trailer for a new '15' rated hybrid genre film and with a budget of roughly £30 million partly supplied by lottery funding.

Print

Write two features/reviews on the release of a new hybrid genre film, rated '15' and with a budget of roughly £30 million partly supplied by lottery funding. You should aim to produce an A4 page for each piece including images and text. The pieces should be specific to a named publication such as a newspaper, lifestyle magazine or specialist film magazine.

E-media

Create three web pages for the official site for a new hybrid genre film, rated '15' and with a budget of roughly £30 million partly supplied by lottery funding.

(p. 3 of AQA specification)

Bearing in mind that you are expected to approach your production by using two media platforms, it makes sense to decide which two of three is going to be best for you. Of course, that may already be pre-determined for you by factors outside of your control. For the purposes of the case study, we will consider how you might response if you choose the broadcasting and print options as your platforms, although you will see that you might easily substitute e-media for either.

The first thing you should do is to look carefully at the brief. You will notice that the film that you are being asked to consider is common to all three platforms. This means that you have a useful starting point by developing some ideas about the film in question. Notice you have been given a series of parameters that define the nature of the film:

- It is a hybrid genre
- It has a budget of £30 million
- It is 15 rated
- It is part lottery funded, therefore presumably British.

This information should signal to you a number of key areas that you need to research before you begin to think about the production tasks that lie ahead. Let us take each of the bulletin points in turn to consider what sort of research you will need to do.

Genre: Go back and have a look at Chapter 3 on Genre, most specifically the section on hybridity. You will see that a hybrid is a film that has been put together using one or more genres so that it exhibits the features of all of them. Find a good contemporary example of a hybrid genre and do some

Figure 13.3 Genre: *Shaun of the Dead*

research into how and why genres have been combined in this way. This is likely to entail you looking at films themselves, trailers for film and researching such sources as the Internet Movie Database (http://www.imdb.com). Further reading, as indicated at the end of Chapter 3, will also help your understanding of the nature of hybrids.

Figure 13.4

Budget: The budget for a film is significant in giving you some idea of the type of film you are considering and the kind of production values that it might have. A Hollywood blockbuster can have a budget of over $200 million. A typical home-made British offering is likely to have a much more modest budget by comparison. You should begin to get a sense of how the size of the budget can influence both the ambition behind a film and the final product. Certainly £30 million is unlikely to attract any big named Hollywood stars, such as Julia Roberts, who can easily earn £20 million for a film, unless they want to do it for love or the film's artistic value. In British terms a budget of £30 million is quite a lavish one. Many successful British films, such as *Shaun of the Dead*, have been made for less than £4 million. A good source of information about film budgets is the UK Film Council's website (http://ukfilmcouncil.org.uk/filmmaking/funding/features).

Figure 13.5

Lottery funding: The UK Film Council website is also a good source of information about lottery funding for films. You will see that funding via the lottery is anything but lavish. Even an expensive venture is lucky to receive £1.5 million from the lottery fund, as in the case of *Becoming Jane*, released in 2007 and based on the life of Jane Austen. You can also read up about the conditions that a production company has to meet in order to attract lottery funding. You might like to consider why the National Lottery should choose to help fund film projects and whether certain film projects might be more worthy of support from the fund than others. Consider, for example, the grant of £1 million to the less than universally acclaimed film, *Sex Lives of the Potato Men* (see http://news.bbc.co.uk/1/hi/england/3509931. stm).

The fact that a film is 15 rated clearly means that its appeal is to adults rather than to younger people. The 15 rating also implies that the content of the film will be for a mature audience. Check on the BBFC website for information about why a film will receive a 15 certificate. Here is a guide as to what might constitute the content of a 15 film: http://www.bbfc.co.uk/classification/c_15.php.

You will see from some fairly basic research into the brief you have been set that there are a number of complex issues to explore in relation to the broadcast aspect of your production work. This research might usefully form the basis for your initial research into existing media products. However, this research needs to be linked closely to the two productions that you are going to undertake.

Let us first consider film trailers. It is sometimes suggested that many film trailers are significantly better than the films themselves. What film trailers do is to recreate a film in miniature so as to market it to a potential audience. Trailers are generally shown at the cinema to promote a film that is about to be released. They are also used on DVDs to promote the film as a DVD release; by television channels, such as Sky Movies, to promote films they are going to transmit; and, increasingly importantly, on the web. These different contexts might require a production company to produce different versions of the trailer as one trailer might not be appropriate in all circumstances. You might like to bear this in mind when you are researching trailers. Here is a useful article on film trailers: http://film.guardian.co.uk/features/featurepages/0,4120,1449360,00.html.

The preliminary research you undertook should have given you a reasonably clear idea about the type of film that you are looking at. Your next job is to find some good recent examples and try to watch both the film and the trailer. A search of your DVD rental shop and satellite and cable listings is a good starting point. Once you have found some good examples of trailers, you need to subject them to detailed analysis. The first chapters in the book should help you here.

ACTIVITY

Start by looking at the trailer for *Sugarhouse*: http://www. sugarhouselane.com/flash/#/. The film did not get much press. Consider why this might be, and why the trailer did not seem to attract audiences.

For your broadcast production you are being asked to produce the trailer for the film. It is probably best to assume that the trailer will be the same classification as the film itself, although that may not always be the case. Some trailers are at a lower level of classification so that they can be shown to wider audiences.

Having completed your research into the production areas, you are now ready to get to grips with the production work itself. The specification requires you to create productions in two different platforms. Based on our research, these platforms will be broadcasting and print, although it would be a fairly simple task to swap either for e-media. Before you can get started, you need to make some decisions about the film you are going to promote. Both the trailer and the print article will rely on your promoting a film that fits the brief you have been set. So you need to sketch in some background detail for your film such as:

- a title
- a genre (hybrid)
- a plot
- characters
- actors
- director
- location.

In addition you need to have in mind a target audience for the film you are creating. You are advised to re-read the section on audience and demographics on p. 126.

You must also bear in mind that you need to make realistic decisions about what is possible in light of the demands on production resources later on. It is no good setting key scenes of your film in a location that you cannot either get access to or replicate. Similarly, films that rely entirely on school corridors for their location win very few BAFTAs.

Let's assume you have come up with a practical idea. You should now be ready to start production. An important logistical point to remember is that although you are working on two separate productions, you need to bear both in mind as you are working. For example, if you are setting up a scene to shoot for your trailer, take some stills for use in your print feature at the same time. Alternatively, make sure that you have the technology to grab frames from the video footage you have shot to use as stills illustrations for your print feature.

You will need to start by scripting your trailer. It may seem unusual to do this, given that trailers are generally cut from the film itself. However, in this case you are being asked to work on the trailer in order to give you a rather more manageable task than scripting a feature film. From your research into trailers you will know you have to achieve certain objectives:

- generate interest in the film
- show off the stars of the film
- show the film to its best advantage
- create excitement
- tell people what the film is about, e.g. the genre
- not give too much of the plot away
- showcase some of the best bits of the film
- give details about the production team.

It is a good idea to bear these in mind in the form of a checklist. This will help keep your focus on what it is you are doing and what you are trying to achieve. The theory you have learned about narrative should also help you in creating your trailer. If you look back to page 58, you will realise that the enigma code is an important element in the creation of narratives. It engages the audience by presenting them with enigmas than can only be resolved by watching the whole film. So your trailer must raise the interest and expectations of the audience. Similarly, you will need to create engaging characters who will drive your narrative. In a trailer there is less time to develop these characters so you will need to represent them through their words and actions within the 2-minute timeframe.

Website Activity: Read the step-by-step guide to shooting a film trailer in the Production Area on our website.

It is often said that editing can make a bad film seem quite good. This is nowhere more evident than in creating a trailer. When you come to edit your trailer, you need to combine a number of different elements into a coherent whole. How you go about this is critical to the impact your trailer will have. You need to look at how you can combine the footage you have shot with both music and voice-over to create the best effect. You will also have to generate and add captions and titles where these are needed. Look back at the way in which the trailer for *Sugarhouse* used intertitles to help the narrative flow. This can be a demanding task and you would do well to look carefully at a number of trailers to see how this is done by professionals.

Let us look now at the print production you have been asked to undertake. The first task you have is to narrow down from the vast array of materials in newsagents those that you want to focus on. You are required to produce two reviews/features for a named publication 'such as a newspaper, lifestyle magazine or specialist film magazine'. Clearly there is some research to be done by exploring these possible contexts for your work.

You might also think about the purpose and function of print materials that link to film. Coverage of cinema and film topics is quite extensive, with several specialist film publications as well as more general coverage in newspapers and lifestyle magazines. A good starting point is to look at the extent of the material available and to consider how it is presented to appeal to different audiences. You might also consider what specific need to fulfil in terms of these audiences. Put simply, why do people want to read about cinema and film? One reason is to find trustworthy information about which films are worth seeing. There are, however, other aspects that are likely to have an appeal to do with the star system, celebrity and fandom. One gratification is about being 'in the know' by having information that other people do not know yet. Research into the different contexts in which film is covered in the print media needs to consider these kinds of issues.

Similarly, print media usually combines word and image. A film review will often be accompanied by a still from the film or a photograph of one of the stars. You should explore as part of your research how different publications link words and images and whether one is more important in some publications than others. This should lead you to a consideration of how pages are laid out and some of the typographical and graphic devices used in creating an attractive and effective page layout.

You will also need to look carefully at the copy that has been written for the review or feature. There are a number of conventions that are established for writing critical reviews. These may vary between publications but are likely to be consistent within an individual publication. For example, most reviews will give you the title of the film, the classification and often the reviewer's rating of the film. Specialist magazines are likely to offer more detail about the film, such as the names of the stars and the director.

The specification asks you to produce two reviews/features which will fit on to an A4 page. It is probably best to see this as one page (slightly reduced) of a magazine or half a page of a tabloid-sized newspaper. You need to think about the ratio of word to image that you are likely to use. An image much smaller than 25 per cent of the total page is unlikely to appeal to the reader. You are likely to need a headline and possibly a by-line, or picture by-line, an example of which is shown in Figure 13.6. The article contains roughly 1,000 words. This should give you some indication of how much copy you can fit on to the page.

Website Activity: Look at the guidelines to laying out a magazine or newspaper article in the Production Area on our website.

Writing on evaluation

The specification makes it clear what is expected from you in the evaluation, which is in itself worth 25 per cent of the total marks available for this unit. There is a limit of 1,500 words and you are expected to word-process the evaluation and give the word count. You are expected to produce a combined evaluation for both productions but your evaluation must be your own individual work. Here is what the specification tells you to do:

> **The evaluation should engage with the intentions of the pieces in terms of the candidate's research, but the body of the text should consist of an analysis of how the productions themselves work in the light of their specific target audiences, research, media concepts and contexts.**

Given the weighting of marks for this part of the process, it is clearly worth taking seriously. A good evaluation can lift the mark of mediocre productions. Conversely, many a solid production folder will be let down by a weak evaluation. What are the ingredients of a good evaluation? Here are some guidelines:

Figure 13.6

- It reflects back on the original purpose of your production. This will include not just the original intention but also the context in which it will be produced and the target audience.
- It will assess the degree of success achieved in fulfilling these intentions, the appropriateness to the context and meeting the needs of the target audience.
- It will make critical connections back to the initial research into the topic area and seek to explain how theory and practice have mutually informed each other. It will do this by showing a grasp of both concepts and relevant theoretical perspectives.

You are also asked to consider in your evaluation how your ideas might be applied to a third media platform. In the example we have looked at above, there is an obvious opportunity to write about both the production company's website and the websites of the magazines and newspapers. You might like to consider how these sites relate to the film itself and the print productions you have considered.

One way in which you might look at an evaluation of your productions is to consider the strengths and weaknesses. Be careful though not to err too far towards either side by praising what you have done too highly and being blind to its flaws or by embarking on some deprecating put-down of anything you might have achieved. It will be a very good production that does not lend itself to some sort of improvement and a very poor one that is wholly without merit. Try to offer an objective appraisal of what you have achieved while keeping an eye out for how it could be better.

Don't forget that you need to make your evaluation sound authoritative. You need to sound as though you are someone who knows about Media Studies and the concepts and theories that underpin this discipline. One way to do this is to make sure that you adopt the appropriate terminology of the discipline. Employ the vocabulary you have learned in dealing with the theoretical side of Media Studies as well as the production terminology that comes from your practical work. When you have completed your evaluation, check the spelling and grammar to ensure that these are as accurate as possible.

14 PLANNING/ ORGANISING YOUR STUDIES

In this chapter we consider:

- how to look at media products
- how to plan and get the best from your own media consumption
- using textbooks
- using the internet
- other sources of information.

One of the key aspects of studying the media is that there are no 'simple answers'; often there is no obvious 'correct' answer at all. The skills that you are developing are the skills of analysis, interpretation and the capacity to argue a particular position regarding some aspects of the media. If, for example, we take the debate about the effects of advertising (see p. 139), it becomes clear very quickly that there is no one answer but that it is a matter of looking at various points of view, various pieces of evidence and opinion, and then coming to your own conclusion, which you can justify. Quite often you will end up raising more questions than you started out with, but a sign of success can be knowing what questions to ask.

This means that studying the media can be both exciting and empowering for you but that at times it can also be quite frustrating and difficult to grasp.

One of the keys to success for a Media Studies student is to develop a wide knowledge of the media 'out there'. Most of us have a few favourite websites, radio stations, television channels, newspapers or magazines that we consume regularly. Most of us are reluctant to change or to try something different; rather we develop a routine or habit in our media consumption. However, as a media student you should take risks, try different types of newspapers, magazines, websites, radio stations or television programmes. You might be pleasantly surprised and discover something new that you like and it will help you understand the range and variety of media products that are available to us all. Having a wide knowledge of media products will also help you to use your own examples instead of relying on those given to you in this book or by teachers. Independent thinking and the ability to transfer concepts and apply them to different examples is a characteristic of the successful Media Studies student.

How to look at media products

The world is full of media products waiting to be studied. For the student of the media, this provides easy access to a wide range of texts for consideration. For most people the media exist simply as a source of information and entertainment. For the media student, however, they are also a source on which to base serious academic study. It is important, therefore, that you bear this in mind whenever you are considering a media text.

By the end of your course, it is very likely you will say: 'I can never look at a media product in quite the same way again.' So what is the fundamental shift that you need to undergo to change from being a media consumer to a media student? The first step you have to take is to start thinking more deeply about the media you consume. When you go to a restaurant and eat a meal, you will likely think that it was good or it was bad: 'I enjoyed eating that' or 'That tasted awful'. A chef having an evening out eating the same meal may well have a similar response. However, because the chef understands the process of cooking and serving food, s/he will probably be thinking about the raw ingredients that were used, the cooking process, the way the food is presented, and even how much profit the restaurant is making on the dish.

Similarly, a media student should look beyond a superficial response to a media product in terms of pleasure and enjoyment, and be prepared to consider a broad range of issues and concepts relating not only to the text itself but also to its production and consumption. Media consumption becomes a much broader consideration of how different people consume a media product, how it is constructed, and the conditions under which it was produced.

The hard bit is to identify the difference between enjoying a media text and applying the skills you have learnt to look at the text in a more considered or academic way. In this chapter we hope to consider ways in which you might start to do this.

How to plan and get the best from your own media consumption

Studying the media is an important skill that you, the would-be student, need to develop. Some academic disciplines define reasonably clearly how you should study. You may need to refer to books on the subject, or perhaps undertake practical or research work. In some cases it may even involve watching a DVD or a television programme. For the media student, however, surfing the web, watching television, going to the cinema, reading a magazine, or even looking at the billboard at the side of the road can all claim to be part of any study of the media.

Media Studies is an academic discipline with its own language and terminology and its own conceptual understanding. To be a good media student you need to develop a set of skills that will enable you not only to look at the media and its texts with a critical and discriminating eye, but also to grasp the principles of academic study that consider how media products are produced and consumed. For example, although we usually associate the word 'text' with something that is printed or written, in Media Studies the term is used to refer to all media products. This can include television programmes and/or adverts, photographs, films either on DVD or in the cinema, newspaper articles (or the newspapers themselves), radio programmes and/or jingles, billboards, computer games or websites. The term 'text' is mostly associated with one particular method of studying the media, semiotics, which is the study of signs and sign systems (see p. 33).

Figure 14.1 Different types of 'texts'

Many of the important skills you need to develop in order to study media will be very similar to the skills you need for other academic disciplines. A wide variety of self-help guides are available to help you develop these broader study skills. Some suggestions are given at the end of this chapter in the 'Further Reading' section. Consequently our focus here will be on identifying some of the basic skills you need for media and other subjects.

The ability to make notes from a range of sources, such as lectures, class discussion, websites and reference books, is a key skill for every student. Similarly, your ability to make sense of your notes from these sources over a period of time can mean the difference between success and failure.

The key to effective note-taking is to be conscientious and to stick to an organisational method that works. For many students, this means not only taking an initial set of notes, but also revisiting these notes while they are fresh and expanding or developing them in such a way that they will make sense later. Many students find that the most efficient method of doing this is to transfer handwritten notes on to a computer at the earliest opportunity. If no computer is available, then writing them up in long hand into a logical and clear format is the next best thing.

Broadcast Fiction

**Case study – Heroes**

Episode 1: **_Genesis (pilot episode)_**
Transmitted: **_25th July BBC 2_**
Characters in the episode: **_Peter Petrelli (nurse); Nathan Petrelli (politician); Isaac Mendez (artist); Claire Bennet (cheerleader); Hiro Nakamura (businessman); Niki Sanders (internet stripper); and Mohinder Suresh (professor)._**

Out of the 7 characters above:

- **_5 are men; 2 are women_**
- **_5 are American; 1 is Japanese; 1 is Indian_**
- **_Both women are Caucasian with blonde hair_**
- **_All American men are Caucasian with dark hair_**

Stereotypes used: **_the pretty, blonde cheerleader; the artist junkie_**
Non-stereotypical roles: male nurse

Comments: **_The pilot sets up the main characters and the world in which they live – a world we are supposed to recognise as our own. Is this a true representation of American demographics? Why are there only 2 non-American characters? Are these token characters? What does the choice of using so many Caucasian American characters tell us about the expected audience of the show?_**

Figure 14.2 Rewriting your notes clearly by hand or on computer will make it easier to use them at a later date

ACTIVITY

Choose a topic you have covered recently, either in Media Studies or another subject. Now look through your notes and see how easy it is to retrieve information on the topic. What has the result told you about your level of organisation?

Organisation is a skill closely linked to note-taking. The most accurate and detailed set of notes imaginable will be quite worthless if you cannot retrieve them for use when you want them.

Whatever system of storage you have, be it a computer or simple A4 binder, you need to develop a method of filing and organising your notes in such a way that you can confidently gain access to them whenever you need to. If you are able to store information on a computer hard disk, do not forget to make a back-up copy on a removable disk or a memory stick, especially if you are not the only person to use the computer.

The need for organisation, however, goes far beyond simply filing your notes for easy retrieval. Probably the single most effective way to improve your ability to study lies in organising your time, or 'time management' as it is often called. The simple act of drawing up a timetable or a daily action plan can help you optimise the use of your time. This can be especially important to a media student; time spent on recreational activities and time spent on study can sometimes become blurred. A visit to the cinema, for example, might well be considered a pleasurable social activity as well as a feature of your study of the media. It is up to you to try to make sure you get the best of both worlds.

Website Activity: There is a blank timetable in the Test Yourself area on our website that you can fill in online and print out.

Now let us get back to some of those specific study skills and good habits that are so essential to the media student. As you gain an understanding of some of the underlying principles of Media Studies, through using this book for example, you will begin to realise that there are a number of key concepts that can be applied to media. For example, look at the three main areas into which this book is divided:

- key concepts
- investigating media
- creating media.

These three headings can be used to provide you with a framework for looking at any media text you encounter. For example, when you are considering a media text, you may want to ask yourself:

- How is it constructed?
- How is it consumed?
- Where was it created?

If you can get into the habit of applying these questions to media texts you encounter, you will be making an important step towards looking at them in a Media Studies context.

It is also important to ensure that you have some method of making a note of your responses to and thoughts about media texts that you find particularly interesting. Many media students find it useful to keep a diary or log in which they note their thoughts and media consumption on a daily or weekly basis. Such information can be very useful later in your course when, for example, you may be looking for ideas for coursework or production, or perhaps some texts to illustrate an essay you are writing.

Figure 14.3 You may find it helpful to keep a diary of your media consumption – remember to note the channel and time as you may need these later

It is a good idea to be considering ways you can preserve some of the key texts that you come across. You will probably want to keep copies of important texts that you can use as examples in essays, such as copies of television programmes, newspaper or magazine articles, websites and radio programmes. You are also likely to come across quite a lot of material in the media about the media itself, such as a documentary about the launch of a new magazine, a newspaper article about a new television programme, or a radio programme discussing the ethics of the press. All of these are potentially valuable sources of information and ideas that can be used in your media work. So keep a look-out for them and ensure that you either record them or save particular articles in a scrapbook.

One way in which you can make yourself a better media student is to select your own texts when you are illustrating a particular point in an essay or piece of coursework. Far too many students limit their examples to those discussed in class. Inevitably that leads to a whole class of students writing essays that are very similar to one another. If you can show you have understood a concept or principle by providing an example from a text that you yourself have chosen, this is likely to be rewarded much more highly than the work of the student who has relied on the teacher's example. Indeed, if the example you choose is an appropriate contemporary text, you will have demonstrated clearly your own up-to-date engagement with a study of the media.

It should now be clear just how important it is to plan your media consumption. Of course, there will be recurring texts you need to look at, for example, the *Media Guardian* every Monday or a monthly film magazine such as *Empire*. Remember that these are available online (http://media.guardian.co.uk/ and http://www.empireonline.com/) or should be available in libraries, so you do not have the expense of buying them regularly and you can also look at archives or back copies.

Keeping up to date with key issues and debates in the media is an important aspect of your study and looking in such places as the media sections in the broadsheet newspapers is a particularly good way of doing this.

Getting hold of a good listings magazine that has details of the week's television and radio programmes is an effective way of identifying useful programmes that are likely to help you with your study. Don't forget to look in some places you might not normally consider. Radio 3, Radio 4 and some of the local radio stations have quite a lot of speech-based output, some of which you may well find interesting, stimulating and probably quite accessible, once you have given it a try.

Using textbooks

Even though we live in an age of electronic information, books are still an important source for the media student and using a textbook is an important skill that needs to be developed. The first challenge is to find the right book. You will need to consider both the content of the book and the level at which it is pitched.

Figure 14.4

A lot of Media Studies books are aimed at students who are well ahead of A Level and are used to a much more sophisticated level of language and concepts than people at your stage of study. Unless you are prepared to spend hours wrestling with the ideas and looking up unfamiliar words, these books will not be very helpful. Also there is a wide range of media books across a variety of different media topics. Finding the best one for your needs is bound to be tricky. Here are some tips to help you select the right book at the right level:

- Check the jacket or cover copy. If you are browsing in a library or bookshop, read it to see if the book covers the topics you are looking for.
- Check the contents page to see if it covers the right ground. You may also find information about the level the book is aimed at. Ideally you want a book that is geared to the needs of a reader looking for an introduction to the topic. You can check this further by reading half a page of the text inside the book to see how easy or difficult you find it.
- Check the name of the writer(s). This may also be a hint about the usefulness of the book. Is this a writer whose name you have heard mentioned in other books or in class, perhaps?

Once you have found the right book, the next step is to learn how to get the best from it. It is always a good idea to read the introduction to any textbook. This should signal the approach the writer is going to take and what s/he intends to cover.

It is unlikely that you will have the time to read a whole book, so you need to learn how to select the sections that are especially relevant for what you are doing. One device that may help here is the index. This will outline for you all the references to a particular topic. Where these are fairly detailed, you will find they span several pages (for example, 68–73), so that is always a good place to start looking. Note also that most textbooks give a chapter summary at the beginning of every chapter, outlining what is covered. It is a good idea, therefore, to check each chapter in turn to see if it is likely to contain any relevant material. To help you with this, look at the section headings within each chapter as a way of navigating your way to the information you are looking for.

The next stage is to make some notes. Some students like to photocopy useful sections of books. If you do this, you need to check with your school or college that you are not infringing copyright laws. Whilst photocopying can be a useful tool, it is often much better to make some notes from the book you are using. The reason is that the process of transferring information in this way helps to reinforce your learning – not least because you need to read and understand the original before you can write down your own version, but also because it is important to learn the skill of summarising other people's ideas in your own words; taking notes will help you to perfect this skill. On a very few occasions you will want to lift direct quotations from a book. When you do so, remember to put them in inverted commas; in this way you will not forget to attribute the ideas to their original source.

Write down all the publication details of any book you use. Every time you use a book, make a note of:

- author
- title
- publisher
- date of publication
- ISBN (international standard book number).

It is also a good idea to make a note of the page numbers from which your notes have been taken. If you are using a reader or collection of essays by different people, you also need to write down the name of the individual contributor whose work you are using.

An important reason why you need to make a note of the source of your information is that when you come to use it in an essay or a piece of coursework, you have to attribute it. That means that you should not try to claim that it is an original idea of your own but should acknowledge the source from which it comes. Otherwise you can be accused of plagiarism, which means taking and using other people's ideas without properly acknowledging them.

The bibliography

A bibliography is where you list all the information sources that you have used in your research. You should provide all the details necessary for someone else to be able to trace and look up the original data. For books and articles from magazines, you should use the Harvard system, listing the author, date, title and publisher. Many books also give the place of publication. If you look at the further reading sections of this book, you will see how the Harvard system is set out. It is useful to keep a record of the details of any books or articles that you look at as you go along because it is sometimes difficult later on to remember where a particular piece of data came from.

The rules for referencing non-print-based material are a little less clear. Again it is important to provide enough information for the original data to be traced. For data from websites, you should include the URL and the date you accessed it to allow for any subsequent modifications. If you use video or television programmes, you should, where possible, provide details of.

- director (if appropriate)
- title of the film or programme
- broadcasting channel
- series title
- date of broadcast.

Using the world wide web

We live in an information-rich society. Indeed, many people see a new division within society between those who have access to information and those who do not: 'the digital divide'. In general, students belong to the former category, especially when they have access to the web and possess the skills and knowledge necessary to retrieve information from it. However, the privilege of such access has its downside. So much information is now available through the average student's computer that it is very easy to suffer from an overload of information and data. It is important to learn how to be selective in gaining access to and retrieving information. Equally important is how to make the most effective use of the information you have obtained.

Despite some potential drawbacks, the web has become a real boon to students, allowing instant access to information 24 hours a day. For the student who has taken the trouble to learn how to use it effectively, it is a valuable shortcut to rich sources of information. Compare this to the situation just a few years ago, when a student often had to wait several weeks for a library to transport a book across the country or even across the world.

For the media student, the web offers some unique advantages as well as disadvantages. The chief advantage is the way it provides swift access to contemporary information. A problem with much of the information in a textbook is that it may become out of date. In a subject such as Media Studies, important issues like patterns of consumption or audience figures can change rapidly as new media products are launched and gain popularity. The web is an especially useful way of keeping up to date with important data. For example, a site such as http://www.abc.org.uk offers details of up-to-date circulation figures for a wide range of magazines.

Similarly, most of the bodies who are responsible for the regulation of the media industries (the Press Complaints Commission, or Ofcom, for example) all have useful websites (http://www.pcc.org.uk/ and http://www.ofcom.org.uk/). Not only do these offer background information about codes of practice and complaints procedures, but they also provide details of recent cases on which they have adjudicated.

One disadvantage of the web is that it can increase the risk of plagiarism, either because you lose track of where information has come from or you are tempted to copy parts of other people's work in the hope of not being discovered. Increasingly, schools, colleges and examination boards are using software such as turnitin (http://turnitin.com/static/index.html) which instantly identifies papers containing unoriginal material. The penalties for plagiarism can be severe.

If you are using a computer that does not belong to you, make sure you have a means of saving your work. It is a good idea to reserve one folder for keeping a list of bookmarked sites that you have found especially useful. If you download information for future reference, keep a detailed note of the contents so you can find it again without having to search through each of your folders in turn.

Just as many textbooks available to you are pitched at a range of different levels, so it is with websites. Many sites that deal with media-related issues are aimed at a general audience. This is especially true of many of the cinema-related sites, such as the Internet Movie Database (http://www.imdb.com). Other sites are directed towards students with quite a sophisticated level of understanding. Just as you will have found it necessary to dip into a textbook to see if it is useful or not, so it is with a website. Wikipedia is a site popular with many students and although it may be useful as a source of general information, it is not suitable as an academic source.

One difficulty that the web is likely to present to you is probably also its chief attraction. Using hypertext links allows you to move quickly from one site to another in search of related information. The danger is that, unless you adopt a very disciplined approach to your use of the Net, you can end up skipping from site to site until you lose all sense of what it was you were originally seeking. You will get the best from your session exploring the web if you can avoid getting sidetracked and keep to a focused exploration of the topic you are concerned with. One way to do this is to set yourself a time limit; staring at a computer screen in a tired frame of mind is not conducive to getting the best from the internet.

Finally, although the web is about freedom of speech and ideas, it is still necessary to acknowledge any information you intend to use in your own work. So remember to make a note of all the details, including the URL or address, just as you would when using a textbook.

Warning: As well as information that you are likely to find useful, there is also an awful lot of irrelevant material on the internet. One thing you must learn quickly is how to discriminate. In many cases it is only experience that can teach you this, so you must learn to be cautious in the early stages and keep an open mind about the value of the information a site is offering. One useful test is to ask yourself if you have come across this information source elsewhere. Another is to consider how long the site has been in existence. A site such as that of the BBC or *The Times* would clearly have credibility on both counts and could be considered a source of reliable information.

ACTIVITY

A contact from overseas is doing some research into British media and the bodies that regulate them. Find three website addresses for regulatory bodies that might be useful and provide a brief description of what is available on each site. You might also like to 'rate' the usefulness of each site.

Other sources of information

There are a number of other ways in which information can be obtained by the Media Studies student. These tend to involve primary sources of information, which means getting information first hand, direct from someone who knows. In the Chapter 7 on Audiences, we saw how important information obtained from interviewing people can be, for example, to find out about audience consumption.

Another useful way of finding information is going on a visit, say, to a media organisation such as a local newspaper, or a museum that exhibits media issues, or going to hear someone speak at a conference or workshop. Similarly, your teacher may arrange for someone with a media interest to visit your class. Make sure that you prepare for such an event by making a list of some pertinent questions that you would like to ask. Make sure also that you jot down some detailed notes, including, for example, any useful information on follow-up opportunities.

Another way of obtaining primary information is to approach an organisation or individual directly for help. This is especially relevant when you are undertaking coursework and need some special information about an organisation or its products. Before you get in touch, think carefully about what you are doing:

- Make sure that the information you want is not already readily available elsewhere, in a magazine or on the web for example.
- Be very specific about what you want to know. Letters that begin 'I am doing a Media Studies project on advertising' rarely produce anything more than a very general response, if any response at all. Remember that some information is likely to be commercially sensitive, so a firm may not want it to fall into the hands of a competitor.
- Address your request to the right department or individual; the press office or public relations office is always a good place to start.
- Do not waste people's time. Media organisations are nearly always busy, so only ask for information if it is essential and there is no other way to find it. Be specific about what you want and why you want it.
- Consider enclosing a stamped addressed envelope so that it is easy to reply.

And finally . . .

We, the authors, believe that studying the media, although undoubtedly important, should also be fun.

Consuming media texts, whether on radio, television, in the cinema or via a computer, is often a highly social activity and can be entertaining; making your own media texts through websites, video, radio or newspaper production will hopefully be extremely creative and very satisfying; developing your own interests, reading what other scholars think about the media and their products, and carrying out your own research should be stimulating and satisfying.

Further Reading

Barrass, R. (1984) *Study!*, E & F.N. Spon.
Chambers, E. and Northedge, A. (1997) *The Arts Good Study Guide*, Open University Press.
Drew, S. and Bingham, R. (1997) *The Student Skills Guide*, Gower.
Fry, R. (1999) *The Great Big Book of How to Study*, Career Press.
Stokes, J. (2003) *How to Do Media and Cultural Studies*, Sage.

GLOSSARY

action code A narrative device by which a resolution is produced through action, for example a shoot-out.

actuality Recordings of images and sounds of events made on location as they actually happen for inclusion in news reports or documentaries.

ADSL (asymmetric digital subscriber line) A telephone network that turns an ordinary telephone copper wire into a high-speed connection for internet, broadcasting and video-on-demand services.

anchorage The fixing or limiting of a particular set of meanings to an image. One of the most common forms of anchorage is the caption underneath a photograph.

anti-narrative A text that seeks deliberately to disrupt narrative flow in order to achieve a particular effect, such as the repetition of images or the disruption of a chronological sequence of events.

blogosphere A term used to describe all blogs and the way they link to each other.

breaking news A news story, the details of which are unfolding as the story is being reported.

bricolage The way signs or artefacts are borrowed from different styles or genres to create something new.

broadsheet A large rectangular newspaper, such as the *Daily Telegraph* or *The Times*. Broadsheets are visually associated with serious journalism, reporting important events at home and abroad. They are targeted at an upmarket, professional readership.

catharsis A purging of the emotions through pity and terror, leaving an audience less likely to behave horribly because they have experienced the results vicariously.

cliffhanger A narrative engima that is introduced at the end of an episode and resolved in the episode that follows.

closed questions These demand a very limited answer, often just yes or no.

codes Rules or conventions by which signs are put together to create meaning.

connotation The meaning of a sign that is arrived at through the cultural experiences a reader brings to it.

content analysis A method of collecting, collating and analysing large amounts of information about the content of media products, such as television advertisements, in order to draw conclusions about such issues as the representation of gender roles.

convergence The coming together of different communication technologies such as the telephone, the computer and the television.

denotation What an image actually shows and what is immediately apparent, rather than opposed to the assumptions an individual reader may make about it.

dissolve Film term for the transition between two images whereby one 'dissolves' into the next.

docu-soap A hybrid genre in which elements of documentary and soap opera are combined to create a series about the lives of real people.

encoding A process by which the media construct messages.

end credits At the end of a film or television production, a detailed list of all the people who contributed to the production, from producers and directors to actors and technical, administrative and support crews.

enigma A narrative device that teases the audience by presenting a puzzle or riddle to be solved.

feature In newspapers this is generally an article that concerns itself with a topical issue while not having any hard news content.

film noir A cinematic style of crime thriller that flourished in the 1940s and 1950s in Hollywood, famous for its low-key lighting.

genre The term used for the classification of media texts into groups with similar characteristics.

hard news News that is important and is happening at the time it is reported. A rescue attempt on a cross-Channel ferry, the death of an important national figure or a rise in mortgage interest rates could all be classified as hard news.

hegemony The concept used by the Marxist critic Antonio Gramsci to describe how people are influenced into accepting the dominance of a power elite who impose their will and worldview on the rest of the population. Gramsci argues that this elite is able to rule because the rest of the population allow it to do so. It can be argued, therefore, that the ideological role of the media is to persuade us that it is in our best interests to accept the dominance of this elite.

homage The imitation of a style in order to pay tribute to its aesthetic worth.

horizontal integration This involves the acquisition of competitors in the same section of the industry. It might be possible for one company to seek to control all of the market – a monopoly position – but most capitalist countries have laws to prevent this happening.

hybridisation The linking together of two genres to create a new one.

hypodermic needle theory A theory that suggests that the media 'inject' ideas into a passive audience, like giving a patient a drug.

hypothesis An assumption or question about something that the research will investigate and, it is hoped, either prove or disprove.

icon A sign that works by resemblance.

iconography Those particular signs that we associate with particular genres, such as physical attributes and dress of actors, the settings and 'tools of the trade' (for example cars, guns).

ideology A system of beliefs that determines how power relations are organised within a society.

independents Companies (usually relatively small ones) that maintain a status outside the normal big-business remit and therefore tend to focus on minority-interest products.

index A sign that works by a relationship to the object or concept it refers to; for example, smoke is an index of fire.

infotainment The combination, usually in news and current affairs programmes, of information and entertainment.

interpellation The process by which a media text summons an audience in much the same way as a town crier would ring a bell and shout to summon an audience for an important announcement.

intertextuality The way in which texts refer to other media texts that producers assume audiences will recognise.

linear narrative A plot that moves forward in a straight line without flashbacks or digressions.

media imperialism The idea that powerful and wealthy countries can exercise economic, cultural and social control over others through control of media industries.

media saturation A term used to describe the extent to which our experience of the world is dominated by the media, not only at an individual level but also nationally and globally.

mediation The process by which a media text represents an idea, issue or event to us. This is a useful word as it suggests the way in which things undergo change in the process of being acted upon by the media.

methodology The system or manner used to carry out research; the different ways in which 'data' can be captured.

mode of address The way in which a particular text will address or speak to its audience.

moral panic A mass response to a group, a person or an attitude that becomes defined as a threat to society.

multiplex A cinema that contains several screens under one roof, usually with one projection booth servicing all screens. The number of screens can vary; the new Warner Village in Birmingham contains thirty screens.

multi-tracking The process whereby different instruments and voices are recorded separately and then mixed together in a recording studio.

narrative The way in which a story is told in both fictional and non-fictional media texts.

narrowcasting The opposite of broadcasting. Where texts are aimed at very small, special-interest groups.

niche market A small target audience with specific interests, for example DIY, classic cars or royalty.

noddy A response by an interviewer that can be edited into a report in order to maintain continuity.

open questions Those that start with 'what', 'where', 'why', 'when', 'how' or 'who'. These encourage the interviewee to 'open up' and talk freely.

parallel action A narrative device in which two scenes are observed as happening at the same time by cutting between them.

parody The deliberate imitating of another text often to ridicule or make fun.

pastiche The limitation of style derived from another text or texts.

podcasts Audio files that people have recorded that can be downloaded from the web.

polysemic The way in which a text has a variety of meanings and the audience is an important component in determining those meanings.

postmodernism The social, political and cultural attitudes and images of the late twentieth and early twenty-first century.

primary media Where we pay close attention to the media text, for instance in the close reading of a magazine or newspaper, or in the cinema where we concentrate on the film in front of us.

process model This model considered the audience's interaction with the media as part of a linear process (sender–channel–message–receiver) in which the meaning of the message is thought to be 'fixed' by the producer.

PSB (public service broadcasting) Introduced in the UK in the 1920s by Lord Reith, later Director General of the BBC, with a remit to 'inform, educate and entertain'. The yearly licence fee was payable first to cover radio sets and then, after the Second World War, to include televisions, too. This form of financing meant that the service was not reliant on outside commercial backing and could therefore, in principle, remain unbiased. PSB is designed to ensure a balanced coverage of different types of programme.

qualitative research A type of research that attempts to explain or understand something and may necessitate much discussion and analysis of people's attitudes and behaviour. It usually involves working with small numbers of people or 'focus groups'.

quantitative research A type of research, usually based on numbers, statistics or tables, that attempts to 'measure' some kind of phenomenon and produce 'hard' data. It often involves working with large groups of people.

realism Representation by the media of situations or ideas in such a way that they seem real.

representation The process by which the media present to us the 'real world'.

secondary media Where the medium or text is there in the background and we are aware that it is there but are not concentrating on it.

semiotics The study of signs and sign systems.

sensationalism A term usually associated with the popular press, when events are written about in an exaggerated and disproportionate manner.

sign The sign consists of two components: the signifier and the signified. The signifier is a physical object, for example, a sound, printed word or advertisement. The signified is a mental concept or meaning conveyed by the signifier.

simulacra Simulations or copies that are replacing the 'real' artefacts.

situated culture A term used to describe how our 'situation' (daily routines and patterns, social relationships with family and peer groups) can influence our engagement with and interpretation of media texts.

soundbite A snappy and memorable quotation that can easily be assimilated into a broadcast news story (for example Tony Blair's 'Education, education, education').

spin doctor A person who tries to create a favourable slant to an item of news such as a potentially unpopular policy.

strings A series of messages in response to a posting on the web.

structuralism This approach argues that identifying underlying structures is all-important in undertaking analysis. In linguistics, for example, it can be argued that all languages have a similar underlying grammatical structure, which we are born with the capacity to learn. Similarly, certain social structures, such as the family unit, may be common to many cultures.

symbol A sign that represents an object or concept solely by the agreement of the people who use it.

syntagm A series of signs put together in a specific order.

tabloid A compact newspaper, half the size of a broadsheet, designed to appeal to a mass audience. Tabloids, particularly at the lower end of the market, are associated with sensationalising trivial events rather than with comprehensive coverage of national and international news.

tertiary media Where the medium is present but we are not at all aware of it. The most obvious examples are advertising hoardings or placards that we pass but do not register.

text In Media Studies this term is used to refer to all media products.

uses and gratifications theory The idea that media audiences make active use of what the media offer. The audience has a set of needs, which the media in one form or another meet.

utopian solution The fantasy element and escapism from daily routines and problems provided by entertainment genres.

vertical integration This involves the ownership of every stage of the production process (production + distribution + exhibition), thereby ensuring complete control of a media product.

voice-over An off-screen voice that provides a commentary.

weblogs/blogs A website to which people can contribute, often combining text, images, links and web pages.

wiki Computer software that allows users to create collaborative websites.

BIBLIOGRAPHY

Abercrombie, N. (1996) *Television and Society*, Polity Press.

Allan, S. (2004) *News Culture*, 2nd edn, Open University Press.

—— (2006) *Online News*, Open University Press.

Ang, I. (1985) *Watching Dallas: Soap Opera and the Melodramatic Imagination*, Methuen.

—— (1991) *Desperately Seeking the Audience*, Routledge.

Barker, M. and Petley, J. (eds) (2001) *Ill-Effects: The Media/Violence Debate*, Routledge.

Barnard, S. (2000) *Studying Radio*, Arnold.

Barrass, R. (1984) *Study!*, E & F.N. Spon.

Barthes, R. (1993) [1957] *Mythologies*, Vintage Classics.

Baudrillard, J. (1993) *Simulations*, trans. P. Foss, P. Patton and P. Beitchman, Semiotext(e).

Bell, M. (1995) *In Harm's Way*, Penguin.

Berger, J. (1972) *Ways of Seeing*, Penguin.

Blumler, J. and Katz, E. (eds) (1975) *The Uses of Mass Communications: Current Perspectives on Gratification Research*, Sage.

Bordwell, D. and Thompson, K. (2006) *Film Art: An Introduction*, 6th edn, McGraw-Hill.

Boyd, A. (2001) *Broadcast Journalism: Techniques of Radio and TV News*, 5th edn, Focal Press.

Branigan, E. (1992) *Narrative, Comprehension and Film*, Routledge.

Branston, G. and Stafford, R. (2006) *The Media Student's Book*, 4th edn, Routledge.

Casey, B., Casey, N., Calvert, B., French, L. and Lewis, J. (2002) *Television Studies: The Key Concepts*, Routledge.

Chambers, E. and Northedge, A. (1997) *The Arts Good Study Guide*, Open University Press.

Cohen, S. (2002) *Folk Devils and Moral Panics: The Creation of Mods and Rockers*, MacGibbon & Kee.

Cohen, S. and Young, J. (1973) *The Manufacture of News: Deviance, Social Problems and the Mass Media*, Constable.

Corner, J. (1996) *The Art of Record: A Critical Introduction to Documentary*, Manchester University Press.

Creeber, G. (ed.) (2004) *Fifty Key Television Programmes*, Arnold.

Crisell, A. (1994) *Understanding Radio*, Routledge.

—— (1997) *An Introductory History of British Broadcasting*, Routledge.

Curran, J. and Seaton, J. (1997) *Power Without Responsibility: The Press and Broadcasting in Britain*, Routledge.

Davies, S. (2002) 'A Semiotic Analysis of Teenage Magazine Covers' http://www.aber.ac.uk/media/Students/sid9901.html.

Dirks, T. (1996) 'Film Genres' http://www.filmsite.org/genres.html.

Drew, S. and Bingham, R. (1997) *The Student Skills Guide*, Gower.

Dyer, G. (1982) *Advertising as Communication*, Methuen.

Dyer, R. (1977) 'Entertainment and utopia', *Movie*, vol. 24.

Eco, U. (1981) *The Role of the Reader: Explorations in the Semiotics of Texts*, London: Hutchinson.

Evans, H. (1972) *Newsman's English*, Heinemann.

Ferguson, M. (1983) *Forever Feminine: Women's Magazines and the Cult of Femininity*, Heinemann.

Fiske, J. (1987) *Television Culture*, Methuen.

—— (1990) *Introduction to Communication Studies*, 2nd edn, Routledge.

Fiske, J. and Hartley, J. (1978) *Reading Television*, Methuen.

Franklin, B. (ed.) (2001) *British Television Policy: A Reader*, Routledge.

Fry, R. (1999) *The Great Big Book of How to Study*, Career Press.

Galtung, J. and Ruge, M. (1973) 'Structuring and selecting news' in Cohen, S. and Young, J. (eds) *The Manufacture of News: Deviance, Social Problems and the Mass Media*, Constable.

Gauntlett, D. (2002) *Media, Gender and Identity*, Routledge.

—— http://www.newmediastudies.com/intro2000.htm – long live new media studies.

—— (2004) *Web.Studies*, Routledge.

Geraghty, C. (1991) *Women and Soap-Opera*, Polity Press.

Gerbner, G. and Gross, L. (1976) 'Living with Television: The Violence Profile' *Journal of Communications* vol. 28, no. 3.

Glaessner, V. (1990) 'Gendered Fictions' in Goodwin, A. and Whannel, G. (eds) *Understanding Television*, Routledge.

Glasgow University Media Group (1985) *War and Peace News*, Open University Press.

Gunter, B., Sancho-Aldridge, J. and Winstone, P. (1994) *Television: The Public's View 1993*, Independent Television Commission Research Monographs series, John Libbey.

Gray, A. (1992) *Video Playtime*, Routledge.

Grierson, J. (1996) 'First principles of documentary', in Macdonald, K. and Cousins, M. (eds) *Imagining Reality: The Faber Book of Documentary*, Faber & Faber.

Halloran, J. (1970) *The Effects of Television*, Panther.

Harcup, T. and O'Neill, D. (2001) 'What is News? Galtung and Ruge Revisited' in Rayner, P., Wall, P. and Kruger, S. (2003) *Media Studies: The Essential Resource*, Routledge.

Hartley, J. (1982) *Understanding News*, Routledge.

Hebdige, D. (1988) *Hiding in the Light: On Images and Things*, Routledge.

Herman, E.S. and Chomsky, N. (1994) *Manufacturing Consent*, Vintage.

Hill, A. and Calcutt, I. (2001) 'Vampire Hunters: the scheduling and reception of *Buffy the Vampire Slayer* and *Angel* in the UK' in Rayner, P., Wall, P., and Kruger, S. (2003) *Media Studies: The Essential Resource*, Routledge.

Hobson, D. (1982) *Crossroads: The Drama of a Soap Opera*, Methuen.

Jameson, F. (1991) *Postmodernism, or The Cultural Logic of Late Capitalism*, I.B. Taurus.

Katz, E. and Lazarsfeld, P. (1955) *Personal Influence*, Glencoe IL, Free Press.

Keeble, R. (2005) *The Newspapers Handbook*, 4th edn, Routledge.

Klein, N. (2001) *No Logo*, Flamingo.

Livingstone, S. (1998) *Making Sense of Television*, Routledge.

Lyotard, J.-F. (1979) *The Postmodern Condition: A Report on Knowledge*, Manchester University Press.

McLuhan, M. (1964) *Understanding Media*, Routledge & Kegan Paul.

McLuhan, M. and Fiore, Q. (1997) [1967] *The Medium Is the Massage*, Wired Books.

McNair, B. (1994) *News and Journalism in the UK: A Textbook*, Routledge.

—— (1998) *The Sociology of Journalism*, Arnold.

McRobbie, A. (1983) 'Teenage Girls, *Jackie* and the ideology of adolescent femininity' in Waites, B. *et al.*, *Popular Culture: Past and Present*, Croom Helm.

—— (1994) '*More!* New sexualities in girls' and women's magazines' in Curran, J., Morley, D. and Walkerdine V. (eds) *Cultural Studies and Communications*, Arnold.

Media Guardian *2007 Media Directory*, Guardian Newspapers.

Meech, P. (1999) 'Advertising' in Stokes, J. and Reading, A. (eds) *The Media in Britain: Current Debates and Developments*, Macmillan.

Messenger Davis, M. (1989) *Television Is Good for Kids*, Hilary Shipman.

Miller, T. (ed.) (2002) *Television Studies*, BFI.

Mitchell, C. (2000) *Women and Radio*, Routledge.

Monaco, J. (1981) *How to Read a Film*, Oxford University Press.

Morley, D. (1980) *The Nationwide Audience*, BFI Publishing.

—— (1986) *Family Television*, Comedia.

—— (1995) *Feminism and Youth Culture – From* Jackie *to* Just Seventeen, 2nd edn, Macmillan.

Mulvey, L. (1975) 'Visual pleasure and narrative cinema', *Screen*, vol. 16, no. 3.

Neale, S. (ed.) (2002) *Genre and Contemporary Hollywood*, BFI.

Nelmes, J. (ed.) (2007) *An Introduction to Film Studies*, 4th edn, Routledge.

Nixon, S. (1996) *Hard Looks (Masculinities, Spectatorship and Contemporary Consumption)*, St. Martins Press.

O'Sullivan, T., Dutton, B. and Rayner, P. (2002) *Key Concepts in Communication and Cultural Studies*, 3rd edn, Routledge.

—— (2003) *Studying the Media: An Introduction*, 3rd edn, Arnold.

Orwell, G. (1998) *1984*, Penguin.

Packard, V. (1979) [1957] *The Hidden Persuaders*, Penguin.

Paget, D. (1998) *No Other Way to Tell It: Dramadoc/Docudrama on Television*, Manchester University Press.

Peace, M. (1998) 'The construction of reality in television news', http://www.aber.ac.uk/media/Students/mbp9701.html.

Perkins, T. (1979) 'Rethinking stereotypes' in Barratt, M., Corrigan, P., Kuhn, A. and Wolff, V. (eds) *Ideology and Cultural Production*, Croom Helm.

Petley, J. (1999) 'The Regulation of Media Content' in Stokes, J. and Reading, A. (eds) *The Media in Britain: Current Debates and Developments*, Macmillan.

Propp, V. (1968) *Morphology of the Folk Tale*, University of Texas Press.

Radway, J. (1984) *Reading the Romance: Women, Patriarchy and Popular Literature*, Verso.

Ryall, T. (2001) 'The notion of genre', *Screen* 11:2, 23–6.

Saussure, F. de (1983) [1916] *Course in General Linguistics*, Gerald Duckworth.

Stacey, J. (1994) *Star Gazing: Hollywood Cinema and Female Spectatorship*, Routledge.

Stokes, J. (1999) 'Use it or lose it: sex, sexuality and sexual health in magazines for girls' in Stokes, J. and Reading, A. (eds) *The Media in Britain: Current Debates and Developments*, Macmillan.

—— (2003) *How to Do Media and Cultural Studies*, Sage.

Stokes, J. and Reading, A. (eds) *The Media in Britain: Current Debates and Developments*, Macmillan.

Storey, J. (1993) *An Introductory Guide to Cultural Theory and Popular Culture*, Harvester Wheatsheaf.

Strinati, D. (2004) *An Introduction to Theories of Popular Culture*, 2nd edn, Routledge.

Taylor, L. and Willis, A. (1999) *Media Studies: Texts, Institutions and Audiences*, Blackwell.

Tilley, A. (1991) 'Narrative' in Lusted, D. (ed.) *The Media Studies Book: A Guide for Teachers*, Routledge.

Todorov, T. (1973) *The Fantastic: Towards a Structural Approach*, Case Western Reserve University Press.

Trowler, P. (1996) *Investigating Mass Media*, 2nd edn, Collins.

Tunstall, J. (1983) *The Media in Britain*, Constable.

Ward, P. (2005) *Documentary: The Margins of Reality*, Wallflower Press.

Watson, J. and Hill, A. (1996) *A Dictionary of Communication and Media Studies*, Arnold.

Whelehan, I. (2000) *Overloaded: Popular Culture and the Future of Feminism*, The Woman's Press.

Whitehorn, K. (2000) 'Same Old Story', *Guardian*, 1 December.

Wilcock, J. (2001) *The Tabloid Press: A Teacher's Guide*, Auteur.

—— (2000) *Documentaries*, Auteur.

Williams, K. (1997) *'Get Me a Murder a Day': A History of Mass Communication in Britain*, Arnold.

—— (2003) *Understanding Media Theory*, Arnold.

Williams, R. (1974) *Television: Technology and Cultural Form*, Routledge.

Williamson, J. (1978) *Decoding Advertisements: Ideology and Meaning in Advertisements*, Boyars.

Winship, J. (1987) *Inside Women's Magazines*, Pandora.

Winston, B. (1995) *Claiming the Real: The Documentary Film Revisited*, BFI Publishing.

Wright Mills, C. (2000) [1956] *The Power Elite*, Oxford University Press.

FIGURE ACKNOWLEDGEMENTS

The following were reproduced with kind permission. While very effort has been made to trace copyright holders and obtain permission, this has not always been possible in all cases. Any omissions brought to our attention will be remedied in future editions.

i   7 July 2005 – the bombing of the London underground
Licensed under a Creative Commons licence. Photo by Adam Stacey

ii   11 September 2001 – the Twin Towers burning
© Reuters/Sara K. Schwittek

v   Protesters in Burma
Licensed under a Creative Commons licence. Photo by Ogglog.

vi   *Manhunt 2* – a banned game
Courtesy of Rockstar Games

vii   Communicating in the modern world
Phone photo © Jenny Rollo

ix   *Borat: Cultural Learnings of America for Make Benefit Glorious Nation of Kazakhstan*.
© 20th Century Fox / The Kobal Collection

x   Digital Identity Mapping
Licensed under a Creative Commons licence

xi   Second Life avatar
Copyright 2007, Linden Research, Inc. All Rights Reserved

xii   Japanese pagoda
© Matthew Storry

1.1   Diesel 'Global Warming' advertising campaign – London
© Marcel Paris

1.3   Mobile menu
© Nokia 2007

1.4   Dolce & Gabbana advertisement
Used with permission of Dolce & Gabbana

1.5   Flowers outside Kensington Palace following the death of the People's Princess
www.dgphotos.co.uk. Used with permission

2.1 *Shaun the Sheep*
© 2007 Aardman Animations Ltd. All Rights reserved.

2.2 Monks protesting in Burma
© AFP/Getty Images

2.3 *Shaun of the Dead*
© Big Talk/WT 2 / The Kobal Collection/Upton, Oliver

2.4 *Citizen Kane* plot segmentation
Source: *Film Art: An Introduction*, D. Bordwell & K. Thompson (1993), courtesy of McGraw-Hill

2.5 *Bowling for Columbine*
© Alliance Atlantis/ Dog Eat Dog/ United Broadcasting / The Kobal Collection

2.6 Crank
© Lions Gate Films / The Kobal Collection

3.1 *Goodfellas*
© Warner Bros/ The Kobal Collection

3.2 *Meat Market 3*
Licensed under a Creative Commons licence. Photo by Joel Friesen

3.3 *Airline*
© ITV plc

3.4 *Dixon of Dock Green*
© BBC Picture Archive

3.5 *The Bill*
© Pearson Television Limited

4.1 The Eiffel Tower
© Matthew Storry

4.3 Shot/reverse shot – an interview for *60 Minutes*
© AFP/Getty Images

4.4 Pete Doherty
© Shaun Curry/AFP/Getty Images

4.5 David Beckham
© Photo by Jean Baptiste Lacroix/WireImage

4.6a Jordan/Katie Price & Peter Andre
© Photo by Mj Kim/Getty Images

4.6b Jordan/Katie Price & Peter Andre
© Photo by Mj Kim/Getty Images

4.7 *Little Britain*
© BBC Picture Archive

4.8 Muslim 'Bomb' nutter works on the trains – the *Sun*
© NI Syndication

4.9 Mido in fury over bomb slur – the *Sun*
© NI Syndication

5.1 *The Simpsons Movie*
© 20th Century Fox/The Kobal Collection/Groening, Matt

6.3 *Police, Camera, Action!*
© ITV

FIGURE ACKNOWLEDGEMENTS

INDEX

AS Communication and Culture: The Essential Introduction

Third edition

Peter Bennett and Jerry Slater

Praise for the second edition:

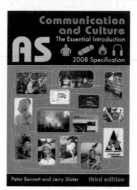

'A really helpful and student friendly text' – *Brenda Hamlet, Lecturer & Course Leader, Amersham & Wycombe College*

'A very useful student and teacher friendly book' – *N. S. Williams, Deputy Head of English, West Bridgford School*

'An extremely useful, accessible text for students new to communication studies' – *Gill Clayson, Assistant Head, Sandy Upper School*

'I have used it since it was published and feel reassured about its credibility with students. It is an excellent text for student self directed study and investigation' – *Alan Hackett, Head of Media and Communications, Campion School*

AS Communication and Culture: The Essential Introduction is fully revised for the new 2008 GCE Communication and Culture Advanced Subsidiary specification with full colour throughout, over 120 images, new case studies and examples. The authors introduce students step-by-step to the skills of reading communication texts and understanding the link between communication and culture, as well as taking students through the tasks expected of them to pass the AQA AS Communication and Culture exam. The book is supplemented with a website featuring additional activities and resources, quizzes and tests.

Areas covered include:

- ◼ an introduction to communication and culture
- ◼ cultural and communication codes
- ◼ semiotics, communication process and models
- ◼ the individual and contemporary culture
- ◼ cultural contexts and practices
- ◼ how to do the coursework
- ◼ how to do the exam
- ◼ examples from advertising, fashion, music, magazines, body language, film and more

AS Communication and Culture: The Essential Introduction clearly guides students through the course and gives them the tips they need to become proficient in understanding and analysing communication texts and everyday culture.

ISBN13: 978–0–415–45512–1 (pbk)

Available at all good bookshops
For ordering and further information please visit:
www.routledge.com

AS Film Studies: The Essential Introduction

Sarah Casey Benyahia, Freddie Gaffney, John White

AS Film Studies: The Essential Introduction gives students the confidence to tackle every part of the WJEC AS level Film Studies course. The authors, who have wide-ranging experience as teachers, examiners and authors, introduce students step by step, to the skills involved in the study of film. The second edition follows the new WJEC syllabus for 2008 teaching onwards and has a companion website with additional chapters and resources for students and teachers that can be found at http://routledge.tandf.co.uk/textbooks/9780415454339/. Individual chapters address the following key areas, amongst others:

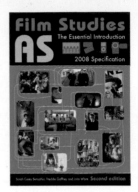

- British stars – Ewan McGregor
- Genre – Horror
- British Production – Working Title
- Social-Political Study – Living with Crime
- US Film – Westerns
- Film form
- Spectatorship
- The practical application of learning

Specifically designed to be user friendly, the second edition of *AS Film Studies: The Essential Introduction* has a new text design to make the book easy to follow, includes more than 100 colour photographs and is jam-packed with features such as:

- Case studies relevant to the 2008 specification
- Activities on films like *Little Miss Sunshine*, *Pirates of the Caribbean* and *The Descent*
- Key terms
- Example exam questions
- Suggestions for further reading and website resources

Matched to the new WJEC specification, *AS Film Studies: The Essential Introduction* covers everything students need to study as part of the course.

ISBN13: 978–0–415–45433–9 (pbk)

Available at all good bookshops
For ordering and further information please visit:
www.routledge.com